Franz Schubert

FRANZ SCHUBERT

from the drawing by L. Kupelwieser

Franz Schubert
THE MAN AND HIS CIRCLE

NEWMAN FLOWER

A New and Revised Edition
Twenty-eight Illustrations

CASSELL & COMPANY LIMITED
LONDON, TORONTO, MELBOURNE, SYDNEY
WELLINGTON

First edition, 1928
Second edition (revised), 1949

PRINTED IN LUXEMBOURG
BY IMPRIMERIE BOURG-BOURGER

28553

CONTENTS

LIST OF ILLUSTRATIONS

FOREWORD

*T*HIS book is the story of a man and his friends, and not a technical survey of his music

A man of great personality. A man of genius who earned in his whole life-time only the sum of £575 by his compositions. Throughout the world his work is performed every day; that was his gift to posterity. And he lived on £575 to make that gift.

The story of great musicians is replete with tragedy. But it is doubtful if Schubert realised the measure of his tragedy until the closing days. Hope eternal lived within him. His poverty was a continual plague which yet permitted him to live—somehow. He never starved. But he worked—even in his gay moods, and those moods were mostly his—beneath the brutal flail of a world which scarcely recognized his presence.

After long research and intimacy with Schubertian haunts in Vienna and elsewhere this book was published first in Schubert's centenary year, 1928. Since then I have been able to bring later information up to the present time. Some of the places in Vienna which were Schubert's, and with which I was familiar, were destroyed in the last War. But, happily, others have survived to carry their story—the living story—of one of Vienna's greatest sons.

In the research and preparation for this book I had the help many ardent Schubertians. In particular, Professor Otto Erich Deutsch, who is unquestionably the greatest Schubertian scholar of this age. Also to the late Mr. Van der Straeten, the great authority on music and musical instruments, I owe much for his researches in Vienna for the purpose of this book.

I am also indebted to Frau von Ravenstein of Karlsruhe, the daughter of Schubert's great friend, Moritz von Schwind, for information concerning her father's relations with the composer—that bond of friendship between the twain which I have endeavoured to outline in this book. Also she gave me permission to reproduce, for the first time, the portrait of Caroline Esterhazy which whom Schubert was so closely associated. Moreover, I had the rich Schubertian treasures of the Friends of Music at Vienna placed at my disposal. Mr. William C. Smith, late assistant Keeper of Printed Books at the British Museum made the excellent bibliography, which should be of great help to students.

The most fortunate thing in connection with the research for this book was access to the Luib correspondence. A few years after Schubert's death Luib wrote to the Composer's friends and relatives asking them to relate their recollections of the Composer.

Luib's intention was to be Schubert's first biographer. He gathered in these letters from Schubert's friends—a mass of correspondence. Then, before he could set pen to paper and begin his biography, he died.

Succeeding Lives of Schubert appeared, but did not touch on this correspondence. Kreissle knew nothing of Luib, nor did Grove. No Life of Schubert in English contains the Luib correspondence. Three German biographers—Dahms, Kobald and Stefan—have touched the fringe of it. But apparently these writers were not able to obtain access to the whole. Therefore it happens that the Luib correspondence appears in this volume for the first time, and is important because it reveals so closely the varying moods of Schubert.

Biographers of Schubert have drawn freely, as I have, from the diaries of Schubert's friend, Bauernfeld. But his " Alt Wien ", which contains even more intimate material about Schubert than his diaries has been largly overlooked. Therefore, I have been able to derive from " Alt Wien " some intimate information regarding the personality of Schubert.

I have endeavoured to give portraits of Schubert—this little man only 5 ft 1 in. in height—and those of his Circle based on research and the letters of those who knew the figures in what must be regarded as one of the most remarkable band of intellectuals of the years. So, too, I have endeavoured to outline the man who made £575 by his total composings, and still had courage to laugh at Life—it may be because he knew what he was leaving to Posterity. A man who would be very humble in the presence of clever people who were not acquainted with genius as he was. And when he met genius he was frightened and humble. Consider his letter to Goethe (p. 120). How low he bowed his knee!

And always remember what his friend Anton Holzapfel said of him :—

" He was a very little man. But he was a giant."

CHAPTER I

The Vienna of the Schuberts

(CIRCA 1797)

On January 31st, 1797, Vienna became possessed of a new citizen of presumptive unimportance. That the wife of Schoolmaster Schubert of the Lichtenthal district had brought another son into existence was a matter of no great moment. Even if some prophet abroad in the streets of the city had been able to foresee what the name of Franz Peter Schubert would ultimately mean to the world, or had proclaimed his reading of the child's destiny from the housetops, he could not have stirred Vienna with any interest in the new arrival. Nor could he have thwarted the ultimate tragedy of Franz Schubert, born into a city that cared for nothing save itself, its pleasures, its passions.

The Vienna of Schubert's birth-year, and the first years of his youth, was a place of indolence, ignorance and echoes. Its population of less than 400,000 stood servilely observant of the drum-beat of discipline served out by a brutal Government and a Court that crushed all private initiative. Life moved in the slow dread circles of fear. Whatever happened in high places became known to the people only by rumour. Wars were vaguely discussed in the coffee-houses. The Army departed somewhere, leaving a wake of rumours, and the life of the city, temporarily hindered and inconvenienced, fell again into its normal course of sloth.

To feed with men this Army that marched to all manner of strange countries at the expense of the tax-payer, every male citizen was compelled to put down his name—be he land-owner or grocer. A magistrate then decided at his pleasure which of these persons should be selected as cannonfodder. The unfortunate man so chosen was uprooted from his work, bustled into uniform, drilled in inadequate fashion, and, at an hour's warning, was pitched somewhere into a war. The mother or wife left behind was given

1

a trifling bounty as a sop for the inconvenience thus brought about, or was provided with work on the city walls or fortifications which in itself was considered to be sufficient recompense. If the family of the person so taken ever saw the missing one again it was a miracle, for the country had lost 1,150,000 men on the battlefield in fifteen years. Or should the wanderer ultimately return, by the grace of God, he became at once an inconvenience, since on his departure the family had rearranged itself, and forgotten the absentee. Nor did the family utter any open recrimination or rebuke against those who did these things. The Law ruled, and to its yoke one bowed with respect.

The few main streets radiating outwards from the Cathedral of St. Stefan were always in a filthy condition. Only the Graben was paved, and the sidewalks on the other streets were level with the road, so that house-owners were accustomed to make a ridge in front of their doors to keep the mud back, and put a plank across for people to walk over. Even the Kärntnerthor Gate—one of the most important in Vienna—had a large mud-pool in front of it which remained there for many years, even to as late as 1816.[1]

For the rest, Vienna was scored with narrow lanes running between rows of high buildings—lanes to which sunlight seldom penetrated. Malefactors of various degrees in crime shrank into the dark doorways of these lanes to accost those who emerged from the more obscure coffee-houses, and, if alarmed, ran away and disappeared down mysterious steps that led somewhere into the bowels of the city. The foot passenger, whether in road or lane, was not there to be respected. The cab-drivers urged decrepit vehicles through the narrow crowded thoroughfares, bawling and cracking their whips. If in their progress a pedestrian was struck they seldom stopped to inquire into the accident, the theory being that the road was made for vehicular traffic. The aristocracy drove with even greater speed through the streets, with one or two footmen carrying blazing torches by night, running panting beside the coach. And, as if in contrast, sedan-chair bearers, dressed in scarlet, waited on the ranks for possible customers. They were numbered and under the surveillance of the police. They were licensed to carry anyone or anything, save a sick person to a hospital or a dead body.[2] One hired a chair and haggled about the fare, to become a victim to extortion if no policeman happened to be near.

[1] Dr. Karl Wagner: From " Neuer Krakauer Schreibkalender."
[2] Johann Pezzl's " Beschreibung von Wien ". Franz Ziska.

In spite of the restrictions upon all liberty in private life, which cramped enterprise and made individual thought unnecessary and abortive, the streets were in striking contrast to such restraint. They were openly licentious. Things were done in them which could not be practised in private houses because of the existence of the *Naderer*.

The *Naderer* was not a trade union. It was not a secret society. It was a form of vagrant secret police. In the days of Franz Schubert's youth a man could be arrested, tried and sent to prison on the mere word of a fellow-citizen. Therefore to breathe a rumour about the Court or Government at the most select dinner-table in the best house in town was a matter of peril, because, very probably, all the servants, who, with such dignity and sense of humility, filled the glasses with Madeira and del Capro, were *Naderers*. These *Naderers* were recruited from the lower classes of commercial employees, servants and workmen, and even from prostitutes, who acted as police spies. At one time 10,000 of these people were banded together in Vienna. If a visitor entered Vienna and brought his own servants, hoping thus to escape the thrall of these traffickers of the dark, it was of no avail. In a fortnight every member of his suite had been enrolled among the *Naderers*.[1]

They wrapped Vienna in a cloak of suspicion and fear. Public matters ceased to be discussed at the dinner-table, and disappeared from discourse in the coffee-houses. The conversation as a result became licentious for want of a better theme. Literature and the Arts were at a discount; a clever literary man at a festive gathering was no better than a mounte bank, because the people had almost ceased to read. The Government had suppressed all circulating libraries. It censored very heavily the news in the papers or turned the angle of such news to its own convenient end. It suppressed foreign papers except those whose Viennese correspondents had written just what they had been bribed to write.

The average Viennese lived, therefore, in what was tantamount to an island city, cut off from all matters of international importance that might be happening, and purposely blindfolded to the life about him. Vienna thus became a city of brilliant disorder, its lights and glamour never grew dim. It was outwardly calm because of the fear of the official knout, but inwardly full of disruption and rot.

Where thought is thwarted and forbidden in a people mental disease must follow. At the beginning of the nineteenth century

[1] Charles Seafield: "Austria As It Is." Translated by Victor Klarwill.

there was no art in Vienna. The theatres were crowded with those who came to see and hear bad French operas. Those houses which put on the most French comedies, full of foul matter, badly translated, were patronized the most readily. One could buy the best stall for 2s. There was no reproof for any daring act or word; there was no law of common decency. The censor was either eccentric in his suppression or impotent in his jurisdiction over this public nuisance. " The loud laugh at the jokes of a favourite comic actor, and the encoring of some smutty vulgar songs was quite in the style of the shilling gentleman."[1]

Occasionally some sensations came to Vienna which turned a sex-ridden populace to a new adventure. A ventriloquist arrived in the city from Paris—a man who could cry on one side of his face and laugh on the other at the same time. The opera became deserted, the most decadent theatres played to a poor box office. Mobs tore and fought to gain entrance to the theatre where this magician grimaced. Women fainted at the sight; men fought their way to the stage to see if the fellow wore a mechanical mask. For a month this man created pandemonium, then suddenly departed as mysteriously as he had come.

The pendulum swung full circle. Now there emerged from northern Germany into Vienna the Reverend Herr Zacharias Werner, a mystic. He had been a dramatist and a writer of forceful opinions for the small circle of the thoughtful press. Then he became a convert to the Church of Rome, was ordained and developed into a revivalist preacher. He came to St. Stefan's. The little crowd outside the Cathedral which knelt there in prayer long hours into the night grew more and more considerable. Ultimately multitudes were pressing to the doors to hear from this man's lips the word of God, which the City seemed to have forgotten. The vast aisles of St. Stefan's were crowded to overflowing with princes, generals, ambassadors, dignitaries, merchants, citizens and even beggars. The priest's hollow-sounding voice, his pale face and ascetic appearance, his powerful eloquence and expressive gestures in the dim light of the Cathedral made a deep impression even upon those who failed to understand his words.[2]

The conversations at the dinner-tables of Vienna changed in tone. Licentiousness became partially obscured. A wave of religion set in, rose and fell again. The old scandals returned. Father

[1] Dr. Reeve's Journal, p. 20.
[2] Count de la Garde: " Pictures of Vienna."

Werner had departed, leaving in the secret places perhaps a few disciples loyal to a memory. He had been a glimmer of light in the dark. The kneeling crowd before St. Stefan's at dusk remained for awhile, then thinned away. The revivalist had left no deeper impression than that.

Vienna in those days lived section by section above itself. Separate houses were scarce and their rents expensive. The *élite* occupied select flats which had a main staircase, and at night the servants belonging to the various flats were jumbled together in the ground-floor entrance hall. In these flats entertaining continued in a never-ending round. Vienna was more awake by night than by day. Huge quantities of wine were consumed—del Capro, Rota (a red Spanish wine), and Madeira—and drunkenness was habitual at these regular orgies. The birds of the night sat playing *Ombre* for high stakes until the first light of morning disturbed them.

The poor existed in mean tenements piled one over the other. The main staircase was noisome with fruit-skins and stale refuse flung out of any doorway. No one removed these things. The mud of the streets was trodden into the staircase and retrodden by other feet. The revellers of the night fell into the main entrance and were rescued by some Samaritan at daybreak and helped to their tenement, or led off to the free baths for the poor, which were in wooden houses near the Tabor bridge.

Fires were frequent, and it was customary for the Emperor and his sons to turn out at once on an alarm and, mounted on horseback, superintend the salvage operations. The presence of royalty at every fire was due to an old law which ordained that the Emperor should watch over the people.[1] Indeed, until his Majesty arrived on the scene the work of rescue was not seriously begun. Any delay in the arrival of the Emperor therefore meant that a building might be destroyed, nay, a row of buildings, before the Imperial plans for salvage were disclosed.

The suppression of thought in Vienna evoked among all social grades a disrespect for one another. The poor man flung insults across the street to a count. For the latter, it was a case for silence not for retorts. The market-women scattered abuse to all and sundry like chaff from a flail. There were two women in particular who excelled in abuse, one called Barberl, who had a stand at the bridge before the Burgthor (the town gate to the castle) ; the other by the Roten Turm (Red Tower) was called Anna Katherl. No

[1] Dr. Reeve's Journal.

5

one passed their stands without being hailed by some greeting or derisive word. If a customer bought anything and paid an exorbitant price, he was acclaimed " Your Excellency." But if one dared to bargain, the avalanche would begin, a crowd gather, and the police approach, only to stand aside and laugh. There was only one possible end to the episode—flight.[1] The market-women always won.

Innumerable races dressed in their national costumes mixed in the streets, which, when crowded, wore the aspect of a carnival. There were Italians in plenty; Greeks and Turks in their thousands. The two latter nations had, by the treaty of Passarowitch, been given the right to settle in Vienna and ply what trade they liked without having to obtain the permission of any authority, and without paying any tax. Adventurers and malefactors availed themselves of this privilege. They made fortunes by falsifying bills of exchange, and they set up in a considerable way of business without any capital whatever.[2] Thereby they created commercial confusion and disruption everywhere, and then, full and bloated by their swindling, disappeared from the city that had yielded the harvest.

The noise in the streets was a babel. Germans, Italians and Croatians cried their wares in their several tongues. There were women with egg-baskets and flowers, Croatians with onions and cheese, and Italian salami vendors, simnel bakers, Slovaks selling rush covers, Tirolean carpet dealers, bird-catchers and sellers of mouse-traps all shouting the quality of their goods at the same time. There were broadsheet and ballad sellers with their blood-curdling stories, and the deep melancholy cry of ' an Aschen! an Aschen! ' of the dustmen, and the rattle of the *litte post,* the man who went down the streets collecting letters, for there were no letter-boxes.[3] A medley of raucous noise.

Those women who could afford it dressed in masculine overcoats made of heavy cloth, while the men walked abroad in the streets in winter wearing muffs. Such was the topsy-turvydom of fashion. And in the fashionable quarter one saw numbers of women sitting cross-legged on the ground and wearing jack-boots. These were the barbers who clipped and shaved the poodle dogs.

Only three days before Franz Schubert was born, Haydn had received the Royal approval of his national anthem. The Emperor

[1] Wenzel Kremer: "Memoirs of an old Lützower Jäger."
[2] Dr. Reeve's Journal.
[3] Dr. Karl Wagner: From "Neuer Krakauer Schreibkalender."

Franz had ascended the throne scarcely a year previously, and his armies were losing their battles. Ere Haydn's national anthem could be publicly sung, Napoleon at Rivoli defeated the Austrian general Alvinci, who, with tired troops, was hurrying to relieve General Wurmser now besieged and hard pressed in the fortress of Mantua. A month later Wurmser and his handful of starved men surrendered their swords.

The news, distorted but with its certain undercurrent of truth, came to Vienna. Napoleon himself would soon be knocking at the city gates, so they said. The city arose to a man to assist the troops in its defence. The University formed its own brigade, which, smartly garbed in grey trousers with green waistcoats and grey tail-coats faced with green, and three-cornered hats, marched to the Palace to receive its colours from the Emperor. The old amusements and the customary licentiousness were forgotten. The city talked only war, and, still more feverishly, the work on the fortifications went on.

Then the cloud of war, small as a man's hand, passed for a while beyond the horizon. But the fears of the city remained. Commerce and invention and science strove like small irrepressible plants trying to push up life in a place of sand. Vaccination was introduced into Vienna and laughed at. Senefelder invented lithography. A little later Mardersberger invented the sewing-machine, and inventions for the production of beet-sugar, boot-making and weaving came from the city in suppression. Posters advertising articles of commerce began to appear and signboards for shops were executed by famous painters. And lo! on the walls of the Roten Turm gate, an enterprising company had created a new mode of advertising which ultimately was to embrace the commercial life of the world—it had set up the first wooden advertising hoarding for the benefit of its customers![1]

Such was this city of ebb and flow, of suppression and unrest, when Franz Peter Schubert was born on that January morning in 1797.

[1] "Wiener Chronik," by R. V. G.

CHAPTER II

Schoolmaster Schubert and His Sons

(1800-1808)

*T*HE father of the composer was one of those outstanding figures which periodically occur and become pivotal in the life of a family. He had no abnormal gifts and no clamouring ambition. He worked unceasingly, and when he was not working he wrote long letters to his children, binding them one and all the closer to him by his personality and devotion. As a schoolmaster he was sound, and for four generations the Schuberts were schoolmasters.

This Franz Theodor Schubert, the destined parent of one of the greatest musicians of the centuries, had been born in 1763 at Neudorf near Altstadt in Moravia, and his father was a farmer and local magistrate. He was the fifth of the farmer's children. At the age of eighteen he elected to follow the profession of schoolmaster. After serving as a junior assistant for three years, he procured a copy of his birth certificate and joined his elder brother Karl, who for a number of years had been a teacher in the Leopoldstadt quarter in Vienna.[1]

For two years he worked with his brother at a pitiable wage, and in 1786, on the recommendation of Bishop Gall, was appointed by the Nether-Austrian County Government (Landesregierung), head teacher at an elementary school in the Lichtenthal district, at the Sporkenbüchel. At this period Lichtenthal was a suburb of Vienna outside the line of fortifications.

In spite of the stress of poverty the young schoolmaster married, and he married a cook named Elizabeth Vitz. He was twenty-two

---

[1] Leopoldstadt No. 408 (Brunngasse).

8

years of age when the event took place, and his wife was twenty-nine. Like her husband, she had come from Austrian Silesia, and her father was a master-locksmith.[1] Since the twain met in Vienna she was undoubtedly in service there as a cook at the time.

None would have foreseen in this mating the parentage of a genius. The schoolmaster, ardent in his task, was troubled continuously by poverty. The poor had little money to spare for education; and it was the poor he taught. He loved music. He played the violoncello, never well, but with the enthusiasm of the amateur to whom music is a delight. His wife, on the contrary, displayed no knowledge or love of the arts. She was quiet and extremely reserved, a woman much respected and God-fearing and a good mother.

Fourteen children were born of this marriage, but only five survived to maturity. The first son, Ignaz, appeared in 1784, a year after the marriage. Ten years elapsed and the children born during those years passed away in infancy, so that even their names are forgotten. In 1794 Ferdinand was born, and it was in his arms that his younger brother Franz, the composer, was to die in the fullness of time. In 1796 came Karl destined to become a painter of some renown, and a year later Franz the immortal. Four years more elapsed, then in 1801 the last child by this wife, Theresa, was born, and lived until 1878.

The schoolmastering at the Lichtenthal Seminary went on year by year in the same monotonous fashion. The life was soulless, it numbed the brain to outward things, it was terrible in its merciless discipline. But in spite of the buffeting of poverty the master did not lose his zeal. It was fortunate perhaps that Death had stalked so freely through that house where the Schuberts now lived (No. 54 Nussdorferstrasse),[2] for even with only a few children to maintain the schoolmaster was compelled to sell some of the stocks left to him by his father in order to pay his rent.

The year before Franz was born the schoolmaster made a bid for change. His school had prospered in numbers. But, as so many

---

[1] Her baptismal entry at Zuckmantel, dated October 10th, 1756, shows that she was the daugther of the master-locksmith Franz Vitz and his wife Marie Elizabeth, *née* Riedl of Bielau, and she was baptized by the vicar Franciskus Vitz, probably a relative.

[2] The house at the time of Franz Schubert's birth in 1797 bore the sign 'Zum Rothen Krebsen" (The Red Crayfish), and was owned by a man named Mathias Schmidthuber. In 1858 the number-plate of red marble was taken down to make room for the memorial tablet and was presented to the city of Vienna by the owner of the house, Rudolf Wittmann. The house was acquired a few years ago by the City and arranged as a permanent Schubert Museum.

of the children were taught for nothing, his work had increased without a corresponding addition to the family purse. He therefore wrote to the Government and applied for the post of headmaster at the school in the Leopoldstadt (in the Grosse Pfarrgasse) which had become vacant on the death of Principal Lueger. He had good claims and he urged them strongly. He pointed out that all other assistant teachers to whom the Lichtenthal School had been offered before him had refused the appointment on account of its dubious prospects. He declared that when he took over the school it had so decayed that, owing to its bad reputation, it did not possess a single pupil. It had taken him years to live down the evil repute which clung about the place. He explained, too, that in order to regain the confidence of the Lichtenthal people for the school he had been compelled to teach poor children gratuitously. He could not pay the rent, nor could he find the ninety-six florins required for furniture until he had sold his father's shares. Debts had overtaken him and swallowed him up; he had borrowed from money-lenders; and he was teaching for eight hours a day.

The school of ill-repute, which lacked even one pupil when Schoolmaster Schubert entered it, had 174 pupils at the time that he made his application for a transfer to the Leopoldstadt. But his financial position was such that, on account of the poverty of the pupils' parents, the necessity of keeping an assistant, and procuring the bare comforts of a home in which luxury was never known, he was compelled to give lessons at 1 florin, 30 kreutzer per month. He had had a family of eleven children; seven were dead, and the four living depended upon him for their maintenance.

With the evidence of his sound work at the Lichtenthal School behind him, Schubert had belief in his claim. Moreover, the application had the support of the superintendent of the Austrian schools, Provost Spendou, who gave him a brilliant testimonial, and always proved himself a staunch friend of the Schubert family. He helped Ignaz and Ferdinand by procuring for Ignaz a scholarship,[1] thereby relieving the strain on the father's slender resources. But all in vain: the Government authorities put him off for " another suitable occasion." He must proceed with his teaching, a stoic. The great men of education forgot ambition, declared the Government-Officials in refusing the application. They must be stoics. *Stoics,* the officials emphasized again. The intrigues of the departmental favourites were, as usual, successful.

[1] Professor Otto Erich Deutsch: " Schuberts Vater."

The struggle with penury in the Lichtenthal School went on. At the beginning of the year Franz was born; another life to maintain on a family exchequer already strained too far. Two months after the birth of the child that was to bring such lustre to his name, the schoolmaster—now thirty-four years of age—applied again for transfer. This time it was the vacancy at the parochial school of St. Augustin's on the Landstrasse that attracted his attention. He was refused. December came, and with it a vacancy at the ancient school of the Metropolitan Church of St. Stefan. His application for the post again brought refusal. There was no temper, no protesting letters. Education must forget ambition! He struggled on aware that preference was being given to others of less achievement, till, three years later, he begged very humbly in a letter that he should be given equal treatment with other schoolmasters in respect of the food tax.

It was now obvious to Schoolmaster Schubert that officialdom intended to do nothing for him. In their superior wisdom these people probably surmised that he was too good a man to lose from the Lichtenthal School. So long as he was content to remain there and administer sound education in return for little or no reward, officialdom felt that all was well. Therefore it was in the house in the Nussdorferstrasse that Franz spent the first three years of his life. It is a small and compact house in a row with a courtyard at the back, a winding wooden staircase, a stunted roof that intensifies its look of complete unimportance, and with five small windows let into that roof.

When Schoolmaster Schubert took over the Lichtenthal Parish School it was on the Sporkenbüchel (lordship, or manor, of Himmelpfort)[1] in the house " Zum Schwarzen Rössel " (now Säulengasse No. 3) referred to as Himmelpfortgrund No. 12, then 14, and finally 10, which then (1786) belonged to the builder Georg Löwensorger. At that time Schubert took lodgings for himself and his family in the house " Zum Rothen Krebs " (The Red Crayfish), Lichtenthal No. 42 (afterwards 72, and now Nussdorferstrasse No. 54), which was close by.

In 1801, May 27th, Schubert and his wife, conjointly, bought the house on the Sporkenbüchel, *then* No. 14 and owned by Elisabeth Mölzer, for the sum of 3,200 florins (according to the official entry in the communal ground-book of Vienna).[2] Thus it came about that

---

[1] Professor O. E. Deutsch: "Schuberts Vater."
[2] Professor O. E. Deutsch II, p. 1, No. 5.

11

one half of the house afterwards belonged to the four children of the schoolmaster's first marriage. In addition to the purchase money he also had to pay a ground-rent amounting to 45 kreutzers per annum, and five florins for rates.

He moved into the Säulengasse and began to build up his school afresh. He gave to it all the energy of a man who had discovered some new interest in life. Ultimately he had as many as three hundred pupils, but how he managed to crowd three hundred urchins into those small rooms—rooms ill-lit and with low-pitched ceilings— it is difficult to say.

Then he began to attract attention. The strength of his character, his refusal to be discouraged either by official neglect or by the pressure of poverty, brought its slow reward. He was made assessor of the Schoolmaster's Widows Association, and Domscolast Spendou, in whose honour Franz afterwards composed the Cantata, Op. 128, sent him his congratulations in cordial and encouraging words. A little later they made the schoolmaster fifth assessor of the Ministerial Bench, and in doing so proved that at last they had reached the measure of the man. It was announced that the appointment had been made " because he is not only a man of excellent moral character and absolute integrity, but also because, whereas he is bound to instruct only twenty poor children gratuitously in the school, he has voluntarily taken forty from various parishes; and because his excellent method of teaching is so generally known that his school is frequently attended also by pupils from more distant suburbs, so that they cannot find accommodation even in the several rooms of his house."[1]

Outside influences made the problem of living more difficult for Schoolmaster Schubert. In 1805 Napoleon reached Vienna after the battle of Austerlitz. The French Army marched into Vienna, each man with a loaf of bread and a piece of meat on his bayonet point. It was as if a plague of locusts had descended upon the place and eaten it up. The price of food rose to appalling heights. Children starved in the homes from which they feared to venture out. Butter rose to 3 florins a pound, eggs to 4 kreutzers a piece. All day long came the procession of French wounded through the

---

[1] Two years later (1805), the Archiepiscopal pastor of Lichtenthal, Mich. Merroth, wrote of Schoolmaster Schubert: " On account of his gentle character, lovable treatment of the children, peaceable conduct towards all people, a sober and orderly christian life, untiring fulfilment of his duties as a teacher, he gained not only the love and confidence of the young, but also of his own and other parish communities to such an extent that he has increased the number of his pupils from a few to over three hundred."

streets, hundreds of them with their ears cut off by the Russians. Talleyrand occupied the Emperor's apartments at the palace, and sat in his box at the theatre.

But worse was to come, and Schoolmaster Schubert's position began to be perilous. An order was posted by the French that Vienna must pay a fine of ten million gulden, and that every householder whose income exceeded one hundred gulden must pay a sum equal to half the rent of his house or shop, and the landlords half the amount of the annual taxes.

Money disappeared from the city; there was no money discoverable. Tradesmen received no payment for their goods, the higher classes no rents. A petition to Napoleon, now comfortably housed at Schönbrunn, to grant a stay of execution of the order, brought no reply. Couriers were sent to him asking for an advance of some money to enable the city to exist. They came back with empty hands. One man, mistrusting the paper money that had been rushed from the press and put in circulation, laid out all his savings, the equivalent of four thousand pounds, in wine as representing his capital. Scarcely had he done so than the French descended upon him and drank it. Vienna to its survivors became a place of terror, chaos and rape. But Schubert still contrived to keep his school open, even if the number of his pupils diminished.

If the school in the Säulengasse did not yield rich reward, it at least provided the master with a living when the French Army departed. Then he brought his eldest son, Ignaz, into the work of the school as his assistant, and such he remained for many years until death separated them. Ignaz had his father's temperament to a marked degree. In his youth he had been dull-witted and slow to learn. But knowledge when acquired remained in a retentive memory. He was phlegmatic and silent. He had no opinions and was dead to ambition. But in him was that same love of family life—life that must be true to orbit, true to discipline, to God—so characteristic of the father. The second son, Ferdinand, was also brought up to the profession of a schoolmaster, and it was the intention of Schoolmaster Schubert to train Franz for the same work. He could not see a future for any of his sons outside the profession by which he lived. Even when a little later Franz gave signs of possessing more than an average talent for music, the father ignored those signs. So he declared. And in the end the parent, true to his creed, had his way till experience taught him that neither God nor man would ever make a teacher out of Franz. He was too irresponsible.

13

But, in spite of his misguided views about his son's future, it was the Schoolmaster who taught Franz his notes, and it was Ignaz who carried on his musical education. Ignaz trained him to the violin. It was Ignaz, who, at a later date, had to acknowledge that the younger brother made such rapid progress with the instrument that the pupil outstripped the teacher, and left him so far behind that he could never hope to overtake him.

When Ignaz Schubert gave up the musical tuition of Franz, he was handed over to Michael Holzer, the local choirmaster. Holzer, according to Holzapfel, one of Franz Schubert's friends from his school-days, was a sound contrapuntist and very addicted to wine. But he recognized the genius in this boy; he was the first to recognize it. Franz, a little stubby fellow, had developed a voice of such beauty that his singing in the Lichtenthal church attracted attention. He played the violin so well that whenever an opportunity occurred he was made to play in the church.

Holzer, in spite of his drinking habits, gave young Schubert ceaseless attention. He was proud of him. Holzer's big heart, throbbing in a fatted body, yielded nothing to mediocrity. Wine did not disturb his judgment nor swerve his opinion. Drunk or sober he was supremely sound in musical discernment. At the pianoforte, the organ, or the violin the boy absorbed knowledge in miraculous fashion, and Holzer knew that he had in his hands a prodigy of infinite promise. The whole of this queer ungraceful piece of youth seemed to be soaked with music.

It cannot be conceived that Holzer, occupying a comparatively insignificant post but a shrewd judge of music, did not discuss with Schoolmaster Schubert the talent which he had discovered in his son. And yet the Schoolmaster did not swerve from his plan. The Schuberts must teach. This boy who scribbled bits of music on odd pieces of paper would, in the fullness of time, learn the *métier* of the Schuberts. The carefully ordered mind of the schoolmaster realized this fact.

Franz was too young to discuss the prospects of a living by music. If he had done so, doubtless the parent would have warned him that teaching yielded a living, and music a living death. This family that had lived on commonplace lines, without enterprise or adventure, that had faced each morning the mighty problem of making a living, could never be expected to understand a genius cast down, as it were by accident out of nowhere, into its midst. Generations of Schuberts had produced no genius, but only sober-living wage-earners.

14

To Schoolmaster Schubert music was a recreation, no more than that. One admired music in Vienna in 1808, but one did not attempt to live by it. To play an instrument was merely a decorative addition to the ordinary process of living. Only fools became professionals, and only one fool in a million made wealth.

The mind of the father worked like a ponderous machine—a machine that would never break down or fail in its mission. Safe—so absurdly safe. But Schoolmaster Schubert lived to bury a son famous throughout Europe. He grew to be proud of him in a distant manner of misunderstanding. He wrote him beautiful letters in his worst days, and he strove above all things to keep his mind fixed on God. Somehow God had established Himself as the fixed image behind his stoicism, but it was a God of no appeal. He never once went into ecstasies over the mighty works of Franz, possibly because Franz was nearly always a pauper.

He listened to Holzer, doubtless, dozens of times on the subject of Franz. He was just as unmoved by the merits of his son Karl, when he showed ability at his painting. Schoolmaster Schubert was still teaching poor children, and he received from twenty to forty florins in bank-drafts per child. At no time did he make more than four hundred florins in the year, while his assistants received one florin a month for their services, in addition to board and lodging.

The cleverness of Franz would one day solidify into the twenty to forty florins per quarter scale. That was the measure of School-master Schubert's visioning. But the solid station of his own life, and the brilliance of this freak of a son, enabled him to place him in that respectable seat of learning—the Imperial Convict, a preparatory school for the University in Vienna.

Without knowing what he did, Schoolmaster Schubert had pitched his son into the place that nurtured the love of music in him, and developed a genius.

CHAPTER III

At the Convict

(1808-1812)

FRANZ SCHUBERT was eleven years and eight months
old when he was sent as a pupil to the Imperial Convict.
It had been a Jesuit school until the Emperor Joseph II closed it for
no outward reason other than a fit of royal pique, following a feud
with certain Jesuit dignitaries. But his successor, the Emperor Franz,
was not concerned with the squabbles of Joseph. The school had
done good work, its name was honourable, some of the best citizens
of Vienna had been educated there. He resolved to reopen it. So
in 1802 the school reappeared in the same weather-beaten building,
but the Emperor placed it in charge of the Piarists, who worked
ceaselessly for education.

When Franz Schubert joined the Convict it contained not only
pupils of the Gymnasium (the Convict School), but also students
who attended the lectures at the University on the opposite side of
the road, generally with the exception of those intended for the
medical faculty. The majority of these youths were scholarship
holders, but others were accepted if they were in a position to
contribute towards the cost of their maintenance.

The Convict building still stands, unchanged since the days
when the boy, not yet twelve, first went up its steps and through
its forbidding door that might have been the entrance to a prison
house. There is no atmosphere of romance about the Convict—one
passes through that door into cold and draughty passages, stone-
flagged and gloomy. Narrow windows, placed high, let in a
suffused light, but the buildings at the back cluster so closely that
the sun has to struggle for admission. The rooms are built with the
same narrow tall windows. They would almost seem to have been

16

designed to prevent a wretched pupil, beaten and bullied, from making his escape from a penitentiary of misery. There is a sense of coldness, of discomfort in the rooms; an impress is left on the mind of antagonism and brutality from the very building itself.

The Convict was controlled by a Director, Dr. Lang. He was a man of discipline, who, if strict and given to birching, was liked by his pupils. He had no distinctive brilliance, yet lacked no qualities which the school required of him.

The tuition was general in character, but the Convict contained scholars who were compelled to take part in the performances at the Court Church, together with the boys of the Chapel Royal. The fact that pupils who sang or played well were obliged to take part in the church ceremonies does not mean that they were allowed to neglect other studies. In fact, when Schubert received a " 2 " in Mathematics in 1813, and the question arose whether he should receive a further scholarship for the Royal Chapel boys, the Emperor wrote in his own hand on October 21st, 1813, concerning Schubert and two other boys: " . . . inasmuch as singing and music are only of secondary importance, good manners and diligence in studies however of primary importance, and an irremissible duty in those who wish to enjoy the tenure of a scholarship . . . ."

The Court Capellmeister, Salieri—the friend of Beethoven—had been under the patronage of Gluck. Moreover, he had earned the enmity of Mozart, who declared that he had been poisoned by him. This Salieri, brilliant and more than a little pompous, but, nevertheless, kindly disposed towards his pupils, was the chief examiner in music at the Convict. He was quick to anger, and intense in his hatreds. His amanuensis, a man named Philip Korner, was singing-master at the Convict. Anton Holzapfel, a fellow-student of Schubert's, wrote of him: " He was a thin, dried-up figure with a long thin pig-tail, who often regaled us boys with a beating, and pulled our ears. But he was one of the best known figures of the musical world of Vienna at that time."[1]

It was these men who had Franz Schubert up before them for examination in music when on the morning of October 1st, 1808, he entered the Convict for the first time. He was dressed in a smock of light-blue whitish cloth, so conspicuous in colour that the boys laughed at him and called him the son of a miller. But the boy with a wonderful voice who had so often sung solos at the Lichtenthal Church proved at that examination the superior of those

---

[1] Anton Holzapfel in a letter to Luib.

who jeered, and he was promptly put into the uniform trimmed with gold braid which denoted that he was a chorister of the Imperial Chapel.[1]

He was a stumpy little figure wearing steel spectacles, so shy that he shunned his fellow-students, and for a long time kept almost entirely to himself.

It was his music that absorbed him. Almost as soon as he joined the Convict he was composing in secret, but those compositions were hidden and lost almost as soon as they were committed to paper. Salieri's tuition was of a superficial nature. He did little more than correct Schubert's exercises in part writing, and gave him certain instruction in the reading and playing of scores. Occasionally Salieri would seem to climb down from his throne, drive the awe from the minds of his pupils and treat them—Schubert among them—to ice-cream obtained from a lemonade hut on the Graben. At first Schubert was made to work through a tedious string of old Italian scores, then through the whole of Gluck's works, from which he often played to his friends.[2]

These friends in the process of time formed a little coterie and became closely attached to him. There was Josef von Spaun, tall and lean, a youth eight years older than Schubert, and a musician of considerable quality. For some time he was the leader of the Convict orchestra. He afterwards recorded how on one occasion he heard a fellow-student playing cleverly behind him, and looking round saw Schubert for the first time. So was born a friendship which remained unspoiled throughout Schubert's life. There was Anton Holzapfel and Albert Stadler, Johann Senn, who later became a poet of distinction, Josef Kenner, Franz Eckel and Leopold Ebner. Senn, it may be added, was eventually expelled from the Convict for setting free from the school prison a colleague who had been unjustly locked up there, and in 1813 Schubert's friend Rueskefer was expelled for participating in a revolt to ensure the liberation of an incarcerated pupil. It was to Spaun that Schubert first confessed that he had attempted to compose, and the big-hearted Spaun provided the poverty-stricken Franz with music paper during the Convict days when the boy had no money with which to buy such necessities.

Spaun had been born at Linz, and he was studying philosophy, history and mathematics when the family had to flee to Vienna to

[1] In the advertisement for a soprano boy for the Imperial Choir, it states that the boy must be in good health and must have got over small-pox.—Deutsch II, p. 3.
[2] Anton Holzapfel: Letter to Luib.

escape the invading French Army. He was then admitted to the Convict as a paying pupil through the intervention of a Government official, and his musical ability was such that he was soon made leader of the second violins. He relates how the orchestra came to be formed.

" When in the second year the Convictist and Music Director Stubenreiter left the Convict, the Convict Director (Principal) Lang appointed me, to my greatest astonishment, as Director of Music. As I was one of the weakest musicians I thought the Director was having a joke with me, but he said he meant it, and that he knew very well why he had appointed me—my zeal overcame many obstacles. The young people liked me; I considered their wishes in the choice of the pieces that were to be performed, and even the cleverest among the little virtuosos—who often had whims like the greatest—gave in to my remonstrances. I went without food in order to be able to buy music. I flattered the Court organist Ruschitzka (Ruziczka), and the violin director, a Polish theologian named Modscherovsky, who thereupon warmly embraced the cause, and in that manner a youthful orchestra came into being."[1]

One evening after they had played a symphony by Haydn, and an overture by Mehul particularly well, the Director invited Spaun to take breakfast with him the next morning and treated him to chocolate, a rare occurrence which in the Convict was looked upon as a cherished honour. Spaun had little money. His parents had returned to Linz, but remittances to the youth at school were few and far between. In the year that Schubert joined the Convict, Spaun had to walk from Vienna to Linz for his summer holiday, as he had spent the money that had been sent to him for his fare in order to buy two symphonies. Moreover, he could not resist the temptation to see the great actor Iffland, who was then appearing as a visitor at the theatre in Vienna.

Under Spaun the Convict orchestra made rapid headway, and, a few weeks before the youth Schubert appeared at the seminary, Spaun had been invited by the Archduke Rudolph to take his orchestra to the Schönbrunn palace to perform there. The youths were fetched in Court carriages, and when the Palace was reached they discovered that Beethoven was present. The master expressed a regret that they had not brought one of his symphonies to perform. It was suggested that one should be hastily obtained, but Beethoven jumped up quickly in protest. He declared that he could only stay

[1] Spaun: Memoirs.

19

a little while, and, in any case, was rather particular about listening to his own symphonies. Only Beethoven could have given expression to this slight.

When in the same year (1808) the Emperor Franz was married to the Archduchess Ludovika of Modena, Spaun was one of the deputation sent to the Palace to convey to the Emperor a message of congratulation from the Convict.

" The Empress received us in a friendly manner," Spaun says,[1] " but was somewhat shy. She was radiant in a cerise red dress with an overdress of white lace, and wore white roses in her hair, in youthful beauty and grace."

It was the enthusiasm of Spaun for his orchestra that caused the desire in Schubert to break into expression. Not that Schubert neglected his general instruction at this stage, although as music took the ascendancy he did become slothful through lack of interest in the curriculum. But he had been so well grounded by his father before entering the Convict that the lessons over which other boys toiled were acquired by his quick brain in a short space of time. He trained himself, moreover, to learn rapidly in order that he should have more time to devote to his music. Only in mathematics did he flounder in such hopeless fashion that the impossibility of ever making progress was apparent. He hated mathematics. It was because of his mathematical ignorance that eventually he had to leave the Convict. Other courses which he disliked were attacked with such zeal that he could keep his class-place and yet have more time than his fellows for leisure, which was usually spent alone. Then the boy seemed to withdraw into himself. The smiles and laughter which he gave to his friends disappeared. He became moody, as if held by the passage of his thoughts.

Schubert's school-mate Anton Holzapfel, left a little pen-picture of the boy in those years.

" When I came into closer touch with Schubert he was in the 4th grammar form, a short, sturdy boy with a friendly round face, and strongly-marked features. He was not a particular favourite of the clerical professors, yet he was no particular trouble to them by excessive liveliness. He proved that he possessed one of those quiet deep minds which made superficial pedagogues misjudge his silent nature as a sign of little talent. He was even then far in advance of his years mentally, as was proved by a poem written at that period which I kept for a long time but have since

[1] Spaun: Memoirs.

lost, and which was written in the style of Klopstock's Odes, hardly comprehended by us pupils, but which had for its theme God's omnipotence in the Universe. . . . Schubert had, as long as he was at the Convict, the tiresome task of looking after the music as well as the instruments of the orchestra, to see that they were properly strung, attend to the tallow-candle illuminations, give out the parts and place them on the music-stands, besides playing the violin."[1]

After the midday meal, said Kenner,[2] Stadler and Holzapfel would play pieces by Beethoven and Zumsteeg in their spare time, while Kenner formed the entire audience, for the music-practice room was not heated in winter and was therefore terribly cold. Occasionally Spaun came also, and after he left the Convict Schubert came in. Stadler played, Holzapfel sang, and now and again Schubert sat down at the pianoforte. Holzapfel speaks of Schubert at that time as a still imperfect pianist.

Schubert had been a pupil at the Convict exactly six months when once more the French armies rolled up at the gates of Vienna. A wave of patriotic ferment spread through the Convict, and, hearing of the approach of the enemy, a Students' Corps was hastily formed to assist in the defence of the city. The Convict youths were forbidden to join the Corps. An appeal to Dr. Lang met with a firm refusal. Patriotism was not an ideal for the young, he explained. This business with the French was serious, and he would not take responsibility to the parents for hare-brained adventuring. But his refusal was a challenge which the elder boys at the Convict immediately took up. They all escaped from the school, enlisted, and returned to the Convict wearing the red and white ribbons of recruits.

Principal Lang, aflame with anger at the escapade, was waiting for them at the steps of the Convict when they returned. He ordered them at once to their rooms, but he could not damp their spirits. Next morning the young rapscallions escaped again, marched out in a body and went into the city for drill. It was organized rebellion too dangerous to tolerate. Lang had become a puppet in his own school. The Archduke Rainer then took the matter in hand, and issued an order sending all the recruits back to the Convict. Once more they came into the clutches of Principal Lang, who imprisoned them in their rooms for days.[3] The military enthusiasm of the

[1] Anton Holzapfel: Letter to Luib.
[2] Jos. Kenner: Letter to Luib.
[3] Spaun: Memoirs.

Convict soldiers then became less fiery. Principals could be defied, but Archdukes were mightier than the law.

By the grace of God young Schubert was not destroyed by a French cannon-shot, which fell into the Convict. " On May 12th," says Spaun, " the bombardment began in the evening. It was a magnificent sight to see the fiery cannon-balls fly through the night sky, a sky lit up by many fires in the city. In front of our eyes a *Haubitze* (explosive bomb) fell in the University Square and exploded in one of the beautiful fountains. Suddenly a great report was heard from a bomb which fell on the Convict building; it passed through various stories and exploded in the room of the prefect Walch. Fortunately the prefects were not in their respective rooms on the various floors, otherwise all three would have been killed, which some young rogues seemed to regret, as it would have relieved them of their tormentors."

The French crowded into Vienna, and once again Napoleon installed himself at Schönbrunn. The iron key of the city had been specially gilded before it was placed in surrender in the conqueror's hands. He issued orders, brutal and devastating, to the Viennese. To impress his power on them he decided upon a public review of the Imperial Guard. The troops were paraded in the Square and the man of battles passed slowly down the line. Suddenly a Viennese youth named Staps, the son of a clergyman, sprang from the onlookers and rushed at him with a knife. Two of Napoleon's generals, Berthier and Rapp, flung themselves upon the youth and hurled him to the ground at the very moment when the blade was about to enter the Emperor's body.

Napoleon addressed the youth with great unconcern. " What harm," he said, " have I done you? "

" To me, personally, none," replied the young assassin. " But you are the oppressor of my country and the tyrant of the world, and to have put you to death would have been the highest glory of a man of honour." And he was led quietly away, put against a wall and shot, regretting only that his attempt had been abortive.

News of this event soon reached the Convict. It roused to fresh tumult the blood of those who had been imprisoned in their rooms and kept on but a scant allowance of food for obeying the natural impulse of patriotism. Principal Lang was now execrated by most of those who had hitherto held him in some degree of esteem. Negotiations for peace began with Napoleon, only to be long drawn out because the Emperor was busy quarrelling with the Pope. On the 17th of May he issued a decree declaring the sovereignty of the

FRANZ SCHUBERT AT 18

FRANZ SCHUBERT'S FATHER

STREET SCENE IN VIENNA
(engraved by A. Bogner after Schoeller)

THE HOUSE IN WHICH SCHUBERT WAS BORN

Pope to be absolutely at an end. He lingered in Vienna like a scab on the flesh of a people till October 16th, and then departed, leaving a waste of misery for a disordered city to cope with.

The marauder had gone and life at the Convict returned to its old habits. The concerts and orchestral performances which had ceased during the turmoil, because so many members were in durance vile, were restarted. The coterie which the boys had formed apart from the orchestra, for the practice of quartets and quintets and the singing of songs, began anew and was encouraged by Principal Lang.

The musical fervour of the Convict suffered not at all by Napoleonic interference, but in many respects life there had become more brutal. Bullying of the most rabid type was practised not only by the older students and prefects, but by the teachers. Director Lang, sitting in solitary state in his chamber, was either unaware of these things, or too dilatory to correct them. But in one instance at least he had to take action. Josef Spaun's younger brother, Max, a talented and retiring boy, received such brutal treatment from the teachers of religion that he asked Josef to be present at his examination, and he was. When he saw the brutality with which the teacher treated Max he ran out of the room. Twice did the wretched boy ask his brother to take him from the Convict to spare him further suffering, and Josef did so; but Max was always brought back again. At last Director Lang agreed that Max should live with his brother outside the Convict and only come up for examinations. The terror of those days lived with Max Spaun for the rest of his life, and in later years, when he held an important appointment in Vienna, he always avoided going across the University Square so that he might not see the hated walls of the Convict.[1]

Six months later—in May, 1810—Schubert composed the first work of his to be preserved. It is a Fantasia, a duet for the pianoforte, consisting of more than a dozen movements, each varying in character from the other. Schubert's biographers, Kreissle and Reissmann, erroneously speak of it as a " Death Fantasia " (*Leichen*, corpse), which arises from a misunderstanding of Ferdinand Schubert's statement that his brother's first compositions consisted of . . . *Hagar's Lament, Death Fantasia,* and a pianoforte duet Fantasia. *Leichen-phantasie* (*Death Fantasia*) is a setting of Schiller's poem; the existence of this composition was for a long time unknown.

---

[1] Spaun: Memoirs.

Schubert was now not only playing the violin in the Convict orchestra, and composing in the secrecy of such empty rooms as he could find, but was also a vocalist for several years in the Imperial Chapel and the Convict concerts, till the sweet voice of his youth broke and left him a weak tenor. He frequently sang at the concerts in aid of the Musicians' Widows Fund in Haydn's *The Return of Tobias, The Last Seven Words of the Saviour, The Seasons,* and *The Creation*; also in Eybler's *The Four Last Things* and Peter Winter's *Timotheus* or *The Power of Music*. On Sundays and holidays he joined the family in the Säulengasse school until in a fit of temper Schoolmaster Schubert forbade him the house because he was neglecting his ordinary studies for the practice of music. Twice was Schubert driven from home by his father, in spite of his love for his mother.[1] For a long time Franz was kept outside his family circle by this edict. So far as records go, they lead one to believe that he was actually kept out of his home until the death of his mother in 1812.

His penury became extreme; his musical enthusiasm as extreme as his penury. It was useless for him to appeal to the Schoolmaster, for the family purse was in jeopardy. In a torment of hunger in 1812 he wrote to his brother Ferdinand:

" I've been thinking for a long while about my position, and find that in most respects it is good; in others it could be improved upon. You know from experience that a roll or an apple, or more, can be enjoyed after an 8½ hours' fast with only a small supper to look forward to. This need has become so pressing that I must change it. The two groschen my father sends me are gone in a few days. If, therefore, I have to depend upon you I hope I may do so without feeling ashamed. (See Matt. ii. 4.) So I thought: How would it be if you were to advance me a couple of kreutzers monthly? You would never miss them, whilst I should shut myself up in my cell, and be quite happy. As the Apostle Matthew says: ' Let him that hath two coats give one to the poor. . . .' "

The physical suffering of Schubert at this stage cannot be exaggerated. He had no money. The food at the Convict was scant and poor. And two groschen a month from his father! Moreover, the money conditions in Vienna had reached an appalling condition. In 1811 the State went bankrupt, and the paper florin was reduced to a fifth of its value. He worked in cold rooms on an empty stomach. He moved into another cold room because it was silent,

---

[1] Dr. Eduard Hitschmann: "Franz Schuberts Schmerz und Liebe."

and wrote down bits of melody that were fresh in his brain. But if his body suffered, his mind refused to record that suffering. He was wildly happy. He lived for nothing but his composition.

Anton Stadler in a letter[1] written in later life describes Schubert's method of composing during the time he was at the Convict. " It was interesting to see him compose. Very rarely did he use the pianoforte. He often said that would interrupt the train of his thoughts. Quietly and little troubled by the talking and noise of his fellow-students—unavoidable at the Convict—he sat at his little table, a sheet of notepaper in front of him, and stooped closely over that and the text-book (he was very short-sighted), chewing the pen, sometimes playing (as if trying a passage) with his fingers on the table, and writing easily and fluently without many corrections, as if it had to be just so and not otherwise."

Another of his friends at the Convict, Franz Eckel[2] confirms the companionable attraction and at the same time the solitude of Schubert in those years.

" Schubert lived as a youth for the most part in an inner meditative life, which seldom expressed itself to the world except in music. Even to his own most intimate friends, among whom at the time were Anton Holzapfel and myself, who read and sang his first songs composed at the town Convict almost before the paper was dry, he was scant of words. He was almost entirely uncommunicative except about things which concerned the Divine Muse to which he dedicated his short but complete life, and whose favourite he was.

" An innate but tactful measure of seriousness and calm, friendliness and good nature, admitted neither of friendship nor enmity such as exists usually among boys and youths at educational institutes—the less so since Schubert, except in study and class time, spent almost all the hours granted for recreation in the music-room, mostly alone, and which Holzapfel and I only shared with him when he had created a song.

" Also during the common walks of the pupils (Zöglinge) he kept himself mostly apart, his head bent downwards, looking in front of him, his hands on his back, his fingers moving as if playing on the keys. Withdrawn into himself he walked as in deep meditation. I never saw him in a passion. He was always vivacious, although this was manifested more in facial expression than in

[1] Anton Stadler: Letter to Luib.
[2] Georg Franz Eckel, Member of the Medical Faculty: Letter to Luib.

words, which were usually few in number and revealed a deep fund of humour. I saw him laugh but seldom, but he often smiled, sometimes without reason, as if it were the reflex of the thoughts passing in his mind. Professors and colleagues praised him for his sober conduct which never led him into quarrels and never gave cause for them.

" Neither do I remember that Schubert ever received a disciplinary punishment. Everybody honoured him because he had already given manifestation of an extraordinary musical talent; although only a few were acquainted with his songs composed at the Convict. All knew him as the first soprano of the Imperial Chapel, first violinist and subconductor of the excellent Convict orchestra.

" To his moral rectitude and musical genius he also owed the very exceptional favour of the Directors, who exempted him from the strict rule whereby no one could leave the Convict alone. This was done in order that he might take lessons from Salieri in thorough-bass and composition."

These lessons were continued for four years. But from the beginning of 1811 he was composing steadily. At Christmas that year he produced *Der Vatermörder,* for pianoforte and voice, a work which reflects the conscience-stricken son who detects evil thoughts within himself. " Thou, holy Conscience, art—the last friend of Virtue," begins the final verse, and to some extent it explains the conflicting emotions which always existed in Schubert. During 1812 nine works of a brilliant nature, including an overture, two string quartets, a sonata, and a quartet overture came into existence. The year following he composed altogether twenty-one works of differing nature, including a cantata for his father's birthday on September 27th,[1] and his first symphony to celebrate Principal Lang's birthday on October 28th. He gave definite proof in this year of the genius hidden within him. He was composing songs at the Convict with greater felicity than Latin exercises.

One of the students at the Convict who remained there between the ages of twelve and eighteen was Benedict Randhartinger, the principal singer of the Imperial Choir, who possessed a fine tenor voice. He was probably the first to sing the *Erl-King.* He after-

[1] Regarding this Cantata Professor Otto Erich Deutsch says: " The object of this ' names-day celebration ' (*Namensfeier*) is uncertain; perhaps it is identical with the *Gratulationskantate* which Schubert is said to have written for his brother Ferdinand (according to the latter's statement) and which was intended probably for Ferdinand's superior, the director of the orphanage, Franz Michael Vierthaler."

wards wrote:[1] " The uniform which Schubert and I wore for a long time at the Convict consisted of an old-fashioned, low, three-cornered hat, white neck-cloth, open-breasted, dark-brown coat with a little gold epaulette on the left shoulder, bright polished buttons, a long old-fashioned waistcoat right over the stomach, knee-breeches with buckles, and shoes with buckles, but no sword."

Albert Stadler, the friend of Franz till his death, gives another glimpse of Schubert at the Convict. Stadler entered the Convict when Schubert had succeeded Spaun as head of the Orchestra. He came as a small boy to the Convict in 1812, when the heroes of the Napoleonic clash at Vienna in 1809 were rejoicing over the mis-adventures of Moscow. Schubert was then a student of considerable influence at the Convict. He had come to be acknowledged by Principal Lang, and by those about him, as abnormal in his musical gifts. Ruziczka, the thorough-bass master, declared that Franz Schubert knew more than he could teach him.

But Albert Stadler, coming in to the town Convict from the Convict at Kremsmünster as an obscure urchin in 1812, was able to assess him and his position at the time.[2]

" Schubert had already passed the stage of mutation, and had *a weak tenor voice*," Stadler said in recalling his musical association with Schubert at the Convict. " Every evening they had their orchestral practices, when they played two overtures and one symphony. Wenzel Ruziczka, the music master, conducted with the violin, and in his absence Schubert took his place, and played the violin very well. With the second violin Josef von Spaun often helped us as a guest. The violoncellos were Anton Holzapfel, an excellent musician and a friend of Schubert, and Max von Spaun. First flute, Franz Eckel; first clarinet, Josef Kleindl; tympani, Randhartinger.

" Although Schubert had already reached great artistic heights, he was very modest, and the last to recognize the important position he occupied. Simple and unpretentious, good-natured, somewhat neglectful of his outward appearance and the enemy of affectation, he was happiest in the company of his friends. Apparently phleg-matic, he had nevertheless an enthusiastic temperament, and was not lacking in wit and humour."

Soon after Stadler's arrival Schubert's voice broke. His work as an Imperial Chorister was done. It was on July 26th, 1812, that he

[1] Benedict Randhartinger: Letter to Luib.
[2] Albert Stadler: Letter to Luib from Salzburg in January, 1858.

sang there for the last time. There still exists in the Archives of the Court Chapel, now in the National Library, his copy of Peter von Winter's " Missa Nr. 1," on the fly-leaf of which is scribbled by a boy's hand : " Franz Schubert crowed for the last time, July 26, 1812."

It was in this year 1812 that the curtain of gloom fell across the Schubert household at the Säulengasse School. On May 28th, Frau Schubert, the mother of the genius that had yet to flower, died suddenly of typhus, the dread disease that was to destroy her son Franz in due season. " The good mother," as Franz referred to her in his diary four years later (June, 1816). She had been the silent but important influence in the household. She was not a woman of opinions, but a great mother to her sons. She was fond of Franz. One can imagine her little battle for Franz when the doctrinaire husband proclaimed his embargo against his entering the household because he had sold his soul to the impossible vocation of music. The greatest injustice the world did her was that she never knew of the genius of Franz. It is doubtful if she had even the least suspicion of it. And since she had no instinct for music it is equally doubtful if she would have recognized cleverness in him.

In the July following her death each of the children except Ignaz, the first-born, was credited in the public ground property register (*Grundbuch-territs*) with 204 florins as inheritance from the mother's share in the property of the school-house.

The disturbance of death passed, and the Schubert family fell once more into the accustomed routine of its life. Schoolmaster Schubert now had nearly three hundred pupils, and the loss of the woman who had aided him in the upbuilding of the school left him handicapped. Eleven months went by during which he carried on the school alone. Then on April 13th, 1813, he married again, and all the children, including Franz, were present at the wedding. Anna Kleyenböck was the daughter of a silk-manufacturer of Gumpendorf. She had just reached thirty, and the schoolmaster was fifty. But it was a happy mating. This second wife became exactly what the first had been. She fitted into the family plan, and became accustomed to the process of its ordered, uneventful life.

As the years passed this stepmother conceived a deep sympathy for Franz, even if she did not understand him. The acclaim given to him which produced a latent pride in his father drew a corresponding pride from her. Franz was irresponsible. He seemed to be drifting on an impossible course, but he was saluted, however vagrant a craft he appeared to her, and that was enough.

28

Ultimately when Schoolmaster Schubert moved to a school in the Rossau, and a slightly increased stipend and the earnings from his music-copying enabled him to save a little money, he handed this to his second wife, who always put those savings in a stocking.

Franz reached the heights and depths of poverty-stricken genius. His publishers debased themselves in plundering him, and gave him scarcely enough for the meanest livelihood. Then on occasions he would come to the school in the Rossau and say to his stepmother:

" Anything in the stocking, mother? "

It was very seldom that the stocking failed him.

CHAPTER IV

The Beginning of the Circle

(1814)

SCHUBERT'S prospects of earning his living by music must have appeared extremely remote to him in 1812. He had been gathered now into the family circle again, and to adventure beyond it was to court starvation. It may have been the Schoolmaster who decided the measure of life for Franz. He complained bitterly that his son spent too much time in composition; he must turn his wilful mind to a means that would at least yield food.

At the end of October, 1812, Schubert left the Convict, and in 1813 entered the normal school of St. Anna to undergo training as a teacher. A year later, when seventeen years of age, he was summoned to enlist as a conscript. The nation had been drained of its manhood by war, and now its assessment of a man was his value for military service. Franz was undersized, stumpy, awkward. He was very blind without his steel spectacles, and he did not respond quickly to anything in everyday life. His movements were slow and thoughtful, and as a conscript it is very doubtful if he would have been worth the price of his uniform to the nation.

Three times did the State issue conscription papers against him. Three times did it make abortive attempts to kill him on the battle-field. But in 1814 he entered the Säulengasse School as an assistant teacher, a step probably taken to avoid the exigencies of conscription.

Teaching was hateful to him, but he remained in the school for three years, as true to the family tradition as he could be in his fashion. To an active mind made passive by suppression to the monotony of teaching, the school must have been a prison-house. The room on the ground-floor in which he taught was dark, with a beetling ceiling. Crammed as it was with children in whom he had no interest, and whom he instructed with the rote of a parrot, it could only have been a place of suffering to him. The outer passage on which the window opened was narrow—so narrow that any breeze the Danube lent to Vienna in the heat of summer would fail to find its way to this secluded place.

In the Säulengasse School Franz was a figure in conflict. The children crowded by the law into this small room—children who sat in the dim light of an oil lamp on a winter's afternoon staring at the teacher who did not pretend to understand them, must have wondered sometimes for what end they had been delivered into the hands of this Gorgon. In family conclave—at the dinner-table when the school was discussed, Franz sank at once into dullness and disinterest. He was out of place, a fugitive whom the family had rescued for the sake of affection from the disgusting brutalities and distortions of the normal in a vice-ridden army. Schoolmaster Schubert and Ignaz had everything in common; Franz nothing with either. He and they were held together by blood, not by the mind.

It was the solitude of Schubert at this stage that brought him into close touch with the Grob family—three people of good breeding and certain means that ensured not only comfort but moderate luxury. Widow Grob, a woman still in middle life, had a silk-weaving business near the church in the Lichtenthal district, and owned her house. Her daughter Theresa had a remarkable soprano voice that could go up to " d''' " She was plain, but had a pleasant expression. Her mouth was large and ugly. But she was well-grown, full of figure, with a fresh, round child-like face.[1] Heinrich, the son, played the pianoforte, violin and 'cello.

Between 1813 and 1820 Schubert appeared regularly at the Grobs' house. All musical people of standing in the Lichtenthal district knew the Grobs, and took part in their musical evenings. Salieri went there, so did Holzer the organist of the church. The Grobs understood Schubert, and estimated him at his proper value. To this warming influence the spirit in prison responded.

In 1814 Schubert composed his first Mass in " F." He began it on May 17th and completed it on July 22nd.[2] That the work was

---

[1] Holzapfel, who knew her, thus describes her in a letter to Luib.

[2] An interesting point about this Mass is the characteristic form of the Credo. Alfred Schering, in his excellent monograph, " Messe und Requiem seit Haydn und Mozart," was the first to point out that " Schubert used *before* Beethoven that form which must be looked upon as the classical form. Already the Credo

brought into being under the influence of the Grobs and rehearsed at their house there is no reason to doubt. It was not produced until Sunday, October 16th, when it was given at the Lichtenthal church, Theresa Grob singing the soprano part exquisitely to an enchanted audience. Salieri boasted after the performance that Schubert was his pupil. Even Schoolmaster Schubert was so proud of this first work of importance by his son that he forgot his former annoyance at these ceaseless compositions and gave him a five-octave piano.

Theresa was only fourteen years of age when she sang in Schubert's Mass, but her voice rapidly matured until she was recognized as one of the most beautiful amateur sopranos in the district. When she merged into young womanhood she exercised a closer influence upon Franz. Her voice enthralled him, her musical understanding gave him what other friendship lacked. He composed ceaselessly. In spite of the hours he was compelled to spend in teaching, no fewer than 146 songs came from him the year following the production of the Mass, suggesting that some divine well of melody had been struck that would go on for ever.

The old friends of the Convict visited him occasionally at the Säulengasse School. Stadler, Holzapfel. But they only met the scowl of Schoolmaster Schubert, who saw in these calls a method of hindering Franz in his school duties. Spaun, too, would pay him periodical visits, and produce from his pocket a packet of music manuscript paper, a welcome gift to one so poor that he lacked frequently the groschen necessary to buy it.

The ring of suppression was tightened, but the victim would not change his faith. He drew more closely into himself. He became morose and quickly roused to anger by the stupidity of pupils. Naturally inactive in all things, save in that Art which was his life, he became more inactive. He took no exercise. When he went out of the school it was only to go to another house.

His friends, unbidden beyond the door of the school-house, returned to other means of keeping alive the friendship with Franz. " Our meetings at the Convict," says Stadler,[1] " were arranged so that he often visited us on Sundays and holidays, but this, too, met

of the Mass in F has the form of the respective movement of Beethoven's *Missa Solemnis;* the principal subject only returns at the *Et in Spiritum,* while Beethoven's Mass in C (1807) has still the older form. Naturally Schubert's Masses were not known to the former. Thus two great minds arrived independently at the right thing."

[1] Albert Stadler: Letter to Luib.

with difficulties. His reported appearance was not agreeable to the Director, and still less if he remained for any length of time. On Sundays we also had to attend the afternoon service in the adjoining University church, which always lasted a little over half an hour. If Schubert happened to be there at that time we used to lock him in the *Kamerade* (our living and studying room), and give him a few pieces of music manuscript paper, and any volume of poems which happened to come to hand, so that he could pass the time meanwhile. When we returned from church we generally found something ready which he would willingly present to one of us. Such smaller compositions *in flagranti* I possess still in autograph.... He brought to us faithfully what he composed at home, and we then hurried, with or without him, into one of the remotest rooms which had a pianoforte. He or I played, Holzapfel sang; we were full of admiration and ecstasy. They were beautiful times; noble enjoyments of youth! And when we thus gave vent to our feelings, he sat perfectly quiet at the instrument, smiled or told a joke. But all the while he was pleased that we had understood him."

The passion for friendship lived in Schubert. He could not exist without friends. He became discontented with his work if his friends were not within immediate reach. We can trace in this desire for understanding—understanding that was part of no vanity—the development of his relations with Theresa Grob. Theresa gave him her faith, and her artistry, and youth provoked this companionship into something more. Schubert slowly, and perhaps without knowledge of it, fell in love with her. He wrote no violent love letters. He dedicated no music to her.

Holzapfel says[1] that this love was deeply locked in his breast and very intense, and that it unquestionably had a great influence on his early compositions.

He wrote music for Theresa, even if he failed—probably because of his shyness—to complete the honour with his dedication. A *Salve Regina* and *Tantum Ergo* which he composed expressly for her appear to be lost. But a book of songs in his handwriting which belonged to Theresa Grob has lately come to light. It may have had a secret dedication to her, and some of these songs are still unpublished. It is in the possession of the descendants of her brother Heinrich, who justifiably refuse to part with it, and have so far objected to publication.[2] Schubert most certainly composed

[1] Holzapfel: Letter to Luib.
[2] Professor O. E. Deutsch: " Schubert und die Frauen."

for Theresa his *Ave in " C."* This may be identical with the lost
Ave Maria in " E Flat Major " which, according to Kottmaneck,
the composer Fried. W. Fenta found, together wits some other
Schubert manuscripts, in the Lichtenthal Choir where he played the
violoncello, and sometimes the organ, for many years from 1862.[1]

Hüttenbrenner later declared that Schubert had " an overruling
antipathy to the daughters of Eve." But this is scarcely correct.
That his love for Theresa Grob was the great passion is beyond
question. He had other amours, but they passed and left no wounds.
That a period in his more mature years was given to Caroline
Esterhazy is certain. He declared at a later stage that he would
gladly have married Theresa but that his Art kept him a pauper.
His shyness, his awkward personality, could never have made of
Schubert a good lover. He was born only to express love in the
most perfect form in music. What he never could say, he could put
into notes more expressive than the words of any other lover in the
whole history of human love-making. Schubert was the supreme
lover who could not find utterance except in his music.

Schubert's love for Theresa Grob was steadfast and unspoken
in fidelity until 1820. He had then reached the age of twenty-three.
All his compositions were doubtless heard by her before they were
given performance in wider circles. " To hear and see him play his
own pianoforte compositions," wrote Albert Stadler,[2] was a great
experience. A beautiful touch, quite steady hand, clear neat playing
full of soul and feeling. He belonged to the old school of good
pianists whose fingers do not crash down on the poor keys with
the swoop of a hawk." In two years he composed 250 songs. His
beautiful *Gretchen at the Spinning-Wheel* was written hurriedly in
an afternoon at the age of seventeen. The first movement of the
Quartet in " B Flat " (Op. 168) was composed in four and a half
hours at the same age. He delivered gem after gem with only the
encouragement of a few boisterous friends, and that of his love for
a girl three years younger than himself.

At a later stage, Hüttenbrenner related a conversation which
he had with Schubert on one of those rare occasions when he talked
about the secrets of his heart. He wrote: " During a country walk
which I took with Schubert in 1821 I asked him if he had ever been
in love. Because he showed himself to be so cold and unresponsive
towards the fair sex, I formed the opinion that he disliked women.

[1] Professor O. E. Deutsch: "Schuberts Herzeleid."
[2] Albert Stadler: Letter to Luib.

' Oh, no,' he replied. ' I loved one with all my heart, and she loved me in return. She was somewhat younger than I, and she sang the soprano solos magnificently and with deep feeling in a Mass I composed. She was not beautiful, and her face was marked with small-pox, but she was good—good to the heart. For three years I hoped to marry her, but I could find no situation, which caused both of us great sorrow. She then married another man, because her parent wished it. I still love her, but since then no other can please me so well or better. The fact is, she was not destined for me.' "

In 1820 Theresa married a master-baker named Bergman. What lay behind this marriage no one can define, but it was greatly distasteful to her. Possibly the widow foresaw that a marriage with an impoverished musician could lead only to distress. Frau Grob had brought her daughter up to view life from the angle of comfort. She had always been affluent. She had that smug complacency which comfort acquired without struggle inevitably breeds. Theresa hampered with the debts of the home—she who had never known the meaning of debt! To the widow the very notion was horrifying. Bergman was rich, whilst Schubert was crippled by penury. It was the hopelessness of the situation that compelled the marriage. Theresa lived with the master-baker, a commercial person with no inclinations towards Art—a man much older than herself—until he was gathered to his fathers, leaving her to survive him by twenty years. But from the time of the marriage Schubert was never seen at the Grobs' house again.

What was to become known as the Schubert circle—one of the most remarquable and brilliant circles that ever came about through the magnetic charm of a single personality—owed its inception to the meeting of Schubert with Johann Mayrhofer in 1814. Schubert had just completed the Mass in " F," which, rehearsed at the Grobs', was awaiting the Lichtenthal church performance. This Mass in " F " he knew to be achievement, the discovery of his own strength. For some time he had lived with the Mass in " F." It shut out all other thoughts, and absorbed him utterly.

Now whilst he waited to hear it sung, not by some wonderful choir in a great cathedral, but by a group of singers in a Viennese suburban church, someone brought him Mayrhofer's poem *Am See*. He set it in a day. To Youth at seventeen waiting for the performance of a first Mass—what was the setting of a song? He would have set as many songs as they chose to give him, so furious was his energy. He was enduring all the ecstasies, the terrors of genius in early fruition, which believes completely in itself, is satisfied with work well done, yet fears performance.

Some friend, to whom record has given no name, brought Mayrhofer's poem to Schubert. Franz read it over, mumbled, read it again. " It is beautiful," he said. He stared vacantly at the wall opposite. Then he said again: " It is very beautiful." The music had even now begun to shape its mystical bars across his mind.

Mayrhofer was ten years older than Schubert. He was employed in the Censor's office, a strange creature of moods. He was true to the ways of the poet, and reckless to any ordered plan. Whatever life offered to him—opportunity or the lack of it, success or failure— he accepted as destiny. He had great fits of melancholy. For the purpose of the Censor he must have been as great a comedian as the Censor himself. He would have suppressed the most banal domestic comedy, and given freedom to a work of Art of dangerous morality. His blue eyes, deeply set as if in large wells in his head, looked out upon a world mysterious, and built for the certain purpose of sadness. This same unknown friend, probably Spaun, took Schubert to Mayrhofer's rooms, created a friendship, and began, all unknowing, the circle. Schober, the gallant of ladies, followed Vogl the singer, Gahy, Enderes, Bauernfeld, the painter Schwind—individuals of differing personality but temperamentally akin to Schubert. Men of brilliance, all of them.

Schubert stood 5 ft. 1 in. in his socks. He was never a talker because he could not talk well, and he was aware of this defect. He could talk on nothing save music, and then he seldom spoke until someone had dropped badly on a wrong note. He would sit, smoking a pipe, grinning, nodding his head, his face a mask. But about him was the aura of personality. All these Schubertians, as they came one by one with their homage, felt the magic influence of that personality.

Mayrhofer had been born at Steyr in 1787, and was at school with Anton Spaun, who described him as a gentle youth, very pure, very amiable. Mayrhofer had been the little quiet boy, rather precocious, aggressive in his immature opinions, who was taken home to the Spaun household. The Spaun boys were permitted to bring a colleague to dinner on Sunday whenever they had completed their Friday preparation at school without fault. Thus did Mayrhofer, who was to write forty-seven songs which Schubert was to set, find a link with Schubert through the Spauns.

He was welcomed in the Spaun household. He was vivacious and witty. His conversation was intellectual with an unstudied intellectuality, and his dress old-fashioned. He was shy and awkward until he began slowly to understand that a dinner-table had not gathered to laugh at him. In boyhood he began to write poetry—poetry hidden as secretly as it was written. He wrote a poem to a girl whom he did not know, but whom he had seen crying at a window in the house opposite. His father, intending him for the Church, made him a member of the College of St. Florian, where, instead of studying the theory of religion, Mayrhofer spent his time completing what was already a remarkable knowledge of ancient Greek. Then he abjured the Church and decided to enter the tobacco trade. Again he replanned his life. His enthusiasm— and Mayrhofer was always a creature of enthusiasm—rose afresh to a new ideal. Someone gave him a copy of an essay by the famous Pater Abraham a Sancta Clara entitled "Der Tabaker—Luder— Narr." Mayrhofer read it, and decided against tobacco.

He went to Vienna as a law student and shared a little room with Spaun. He was terribly poor but somehow failed to notice it. His mind lived in the clouds beyond the reach of suffering. Bread being necessary to the writing of poetry, he obtained some pupils, but discarded them in the end because he could not endure the coarseness of the parents! All he wanted was sufficient money to buy tobacco, for he smoked a pipe ceaselessly. His heart was brave to face hunger if he had tobacco. Tailors never bothered him because he never bothered tailors. He was serenely happy in a state of semi-starvation, living in a pig-sty of a place which he describes as being " in a dark, dingy street; the house and furniture in bad repair, the ceiling beginning to bulge, the light hindered by a large building opposite, and part of the furniture an antiquated piano and a disreputable bookcase."[1]

Mayrhofer was all temperament, and he met a kindred soul in Schubert. When the latter set *Am See*, Mayrhofer invited him to visit him at his room. It was scarcely a place of inspiration. There was the decrepit piano, a guitar, many pipes, and many scattered papers; disorder and poverty rather obtrusive, and Mayrhofer in excited enthusiasm in a place that was stored with all the wreckage of unfulfilled dreams. He was passionately fond of music, and in this he found his link with Schubert. Without a loaf of bread in the house, he would spend the residue of what his pockets held to

[1] Mayrhofer: Memoirs.

37

get into the gallery of the Kärntnerthor Theatre to hear an opera by Gluck or Mozart.[1]

Mayrhofer was picturesque in his poverty without knowing it, and a man in complete subjection to his thoughts. He was revolutionary, and declaimed upon the hurt done by the world to those who served it with their brains. But he was a revolutionary who hated the sight of blood; it made him faint. When Warsaw fell during the Polish revolution, he jumped into the Danube and was dragged out, all contrition, by some fishermen. What impulse made him commit this foolishness he could never explain. Heated, nervous, a little frightened, he fought off all discussion of the incident after it had happened. Above all things, he lived in fear of cholera. It was a fear that stalked him as some dread shadow. He knew he would die of cholera; he was sure of it.

Such was his terror of cholera that when the disease swept across Vienna, as it did at intervals, destroying the citizens of an entire street, he became frenzied with fear. He would even refuse a glass of beer lest the germs of cholera lurked somewhere within it. He plunged into deep fits of depression, when he could write nothing and wished to talk to no one. He would shut himself up in his room and remain there for weeks, terrified lest the epidemic should enter through the closely-locked door. At such times he ate little, drank practically nothing, and, when the scourge had passed, emerged like a scarecrow, ragged and weather-swept, that seemed glad of the sun.

Mayrhofer in 1815 influenced Schubert unquestionably. To Franz, Mayrhofer was a not unkind temperamental reproduction of himself. He was a creature who juggled with poverty, and Schubert always juggled with poverty. Mayrhofer loved the sadness of old clothes; Schubert hated the acclaiming presence of new ones, even if the nuisance was seldom inflicted upon him. When their friendship blended them, and they grew ripe in the understanding of each other through their hardships, a great partnership was formed. Mayrhofer always declared that he liked his poems the better after Schubert had set them. Thus was the " atmosphere " of the Schubert circle made ready.

---

[1] Kreissle, in his life of Schubert, describes Mayrhofer as having a vulgar face, which description Spaun declared when he read it could only have come from someone who did not know him. "He had an intellectual face," Spaun stated, "lively, beautiful blue eyes, a fine, well-shaped nose and a handsome mouth with a satirical expression. One could not call the face beautiful, but it was intelligent and attractive."

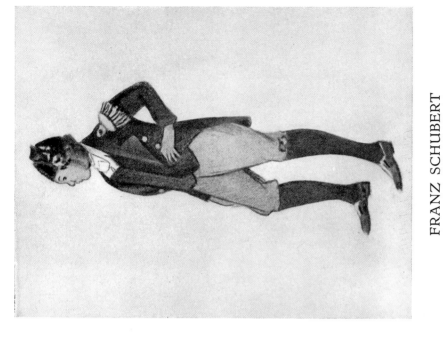

FRANZ SCHUBERT
in the dress he wore at the Convict, aged 14

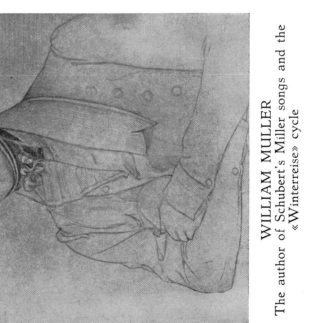

WILLIAM MULLER
The author of Schubert's Miller songs and the
«Winterreise» cycle

FERDINAND SCHUBERT

SCHUBERT'S ELDEST BROTHER, IGNAZ

The meeting with Mayrhofer led Schubert more certainly to the mission of his life. It made him a secret revolutionary in the Säulengasse School. It formed in his mind a nebulous vision of independence.

Ultimately this notion of freedom began to occupy a definite place in his mind. He stilltaught the urchins crowded like sardines in a box in that ground-floor room. He sat late correcting their examination papers in the solitude of this room with its turgid light.

But his mind was set on freedom—Mayrhofer's influence was unconscious and subtle. Schober came with his wild ideals, his great schemes—how many years too soon for the genius of his friend!

The Schubert circle had begun to form.

CHAPTER V

The Mystery of "Prometheus"

(1816)

DURING the year 1815 Schubert set to music no fewer than 189 different works. He composed the *Erl-King* in a few hours in the school-house on the last day of the year. He was engaged in the composition when Spaun called to see him, and that evening they took the song completed to the Convict, and there it was sung and acclaimed by Schubert's friends.

The old Court organist, Ruziczka, then played over the song, but without singing it, and was deeply moved. When someone wanted to take exception to a recurring dissonance, Ruziczka explained, as he played the song again, how in this place the dissonance was necessary to agree with the text. He declared it to be beautiful, and happily conceived.

Despite this initial enthusiasm of Schubert's friends, the *Erl-King* might well have been still-born. At the end of the evening it was put away in a drawer. Here it lay until, on 1st December, 1820, Gymnich sang it at the Sonnleithners' for the first time. At a later day Schubert met the singer Vogl, who sang it into fame.[1] Nevertheless, eight years had to pass before it was given to the public. When, later, he sent a copy to Goethe, Schubert altered the rapid triplet figures of the accompaniment to eight quavers in a bar for the right hand.[2]

If Schubert produced fewer works in 1816—131 as against 189 during the previous year—many were of greater length and impor-

---

[1] The *Erl-King* exists in four versions, three differing only slightly, the fourth showing the quavers instead of triplets.
[2] Anton Holzapfel: Letter to Luib.

tance. His school duties were occupying a great portion of his time and harassing his musical life. But in April he made a desperate effort to break away. A vacancy as director and teacher had occurred at the Government School of Music at Laibach. It was not an important post—the salary was only five hundred florins a year—but at least it would prove some relief from teaching the kindergarten class in his father's school. Those hateful children whose ears he wished to box.

He therefore wrote to the Town Governor in Vienna:

Most Honoured Imperial Royal Town Governor.

The writer humbly implores you to grant him the vacant position as director of music at Laibach.

He gives the following grounds for his request:

1. He is a pupil of the Imperial and Royal Convict, and has been an Imperial and Royal chorister at Court; a student in composition under Herr von Salieri, first Imperial and Royal Court Capellmeister, on whose friendly advice he applies for the vacant post.

2. In every branch of composition he has acquired such knowledge and ability in the playing of the organ, violin, and in singing, that according to the enclosed certificate he is declared to be the most capable among all the petitioners for this position.

3. He undertakes to use his abilities to their utmost extent and prove himself worthy if his request is graciously granted.

FRANZ SCHUBERT.
Temporarily School Assistant at his
father's School in Vienna.
Himmelpfortgrund Nr. 10.

The testimonials which Schubert sent with his application were from Salieri and Josef Spendou, chief Inspector of Schools. The request from one thus qualified and backed by men of importance should have been hard to refuse. But it was refused, and the appointment given to a man named Franz Sokol, of quite inferior qualities, who was already living at Laibach.[1]

---

[1] Various biographers have declared that Schubert lost the post at Laibach because Salieri purposely gave him so poor a testimonial that it was tantamount to an act of treachery committed in the interest of an applicant whom he favoured. It is an entirely baseless statement, scarcely worth recording. The first acrimony would seem to have been aroused when Salieri warned Schubert against setting any words by Goethe, and it was Schubert who made the breach.

41

Personal preference and bribery now controlled all the appointments made under Government in Vienna, and this was merely another instance of its corruption. In the previous August Schoolmaster Schubert had attempted to better himself by applying to Prelate Andreas of the Scottish Monastery for the post of teacher at their German School. He stated that, apart from the subjects of the first and second class, he had given special lessons also to those of the third class, and sent up pupils every year for their examinations at the Royal Normal head-school at St. Anne's who had passed with success. He enclosed testimonials of some importance, one from the local pastor named Langer. But the application was refused.

These refusals were frequently made under cover of the most stupid excuses. Shortly before Franz was negatived for the School at Laibach, Spaun, who was now occupying an ill-paid post in a Government office, decided to apply for a vacancy in the Ministry of Finance. He sought the aid of Dr. Lang, of the Convict, who secured for him the backing of Privy Councillor Von Collin. This official knew Spaun well, and was acquainted with his qualities. He approached Count Wallis, head of the Council of State, by whom the vacancy was to be filled. Wallis, no doubt, had his own favourite candidate for the post. His reply to Von Collin was that he would do what he could for Spaun, but he must point out that the applicant could not spell properly, as was proved by his letter of application.

Whatever Spaun's defects may have been, ignorance of orthography was not one of them. Wallis produced the letter, and pointed out that Spaun had written " Koennen " (can) instead of *Können* (with ö). Von Collin replied that surely this was not so great a defect as to lose a good man the post, especially as in Linz, from which town Spaun had emigrated, the form of spelling in use was that employed by Spaun. Wallis was adamant.

But for this, Spaun would have been appointed. This ignorance —this sublime ignorance must not be tolerated! It was necessary to teach Spaun never to write " oe " for " ö " again![1] A pedantry very characteristic of the official life of Austria at this time. The State Lottery was reorganized in the country shortly after this episode, and Spaun became practically sole manager of the institutions between 1815 and 1817, with an addition of 800 florins a

---

[1] Spaun: Memoirs.

42

year to his salary. The evil of Wallis therefore proved a blessing
in disguise.

Spaun's attachment to Schubert was unyielding. As he climbed
up the political ladder the splendid pauper beneath him became
more dearly cherished. He helped Schubert continually. Busy man
of affairs as he became, he always had time to write letters to his
friend. His passion for music, begun in the Convict, followed him
through the years. He was never absent from the Opera and always
a familiar figure at the Concerts.

On one occasion he took Schubert to hear Gluck's *Iphigenia in
Tauris*. When they left the theatre at the end of the performance
Schubert was chattering excitedly. He was beside himself with the
influence of great music. Anything more beautiful, he said, could
not be given on earth. He declared that the voice of Anna Milder
penetrated to his heart. He regretted that he did not know Vogl
so that he might fall at his feet in admiration of his achievement
as Orestes.

In the street they met the poet Körner, a little man no taller
than Schubert, and he asked the pair to sup with him at the
" Blumenstock " in the Ballgasse.

" While we were still revelling in the enjoyment of what we had
heard," wrote Spaun,[1] " a University professor at a neighbouring
table jeered at our enthusiasm, and declared that Milder had crowed
like a cock; she could not sing as she did not know how to execute
runs and trills, and Orestes had feet like an elephant! Our rage
at these impudent utterances knew no bounds. Körner and Schubert
jumped up in their temper, and the latter in doing so upset his full
glass of beer. The altercation became very heated, and would have
led to hostilities if others had not come in to soothe the passions. '

In all his troubles Schubert never lost his high spirits. Spaun
gives us a little picture of the Schubert of those days:[2]

" He accepted unhesitatingly the offer of a friend [Spaun
himself] to share for many years the jovial supper which usually
lasted till after midnight. When it became very late he did not go
home, but contented himself with a modest accommodation in my
room, where he often slept without taking off his spectacles, to
which he was so much accustomed. In the morning he would sit
down at the table clad only in his shirt and pants, and compose the
most beautiful things, mostly songs, and sometimes also the most

---

[1] Spaun: Memoirs.   [2] *Ibid.*

lovely German dances and Ecossaises which were then the fashion for us dance-loving couples. Gahy would play these dances with such fire and spirit that they quite aroused the dancers. Schubert himself never danced."

Spaun, more than any of Schubert's friends, was responsible for the enlargement of that coterie known as the " Schubertians." The meeting with Mayrhofer, the advent of Schober had been the small beginnings of a circle of thought in a city dying of dullness. But Schubert, Mayrhofer and Schober were people comparatively unknown. They met in secret, they were unacknowledged in public. They wanted a big figure, and they found Professor Watteroth.

The Professor was a man of brilliance in Vienna. He was a prolific writer and strongly assertive in his opinions. He defended the Protestants, and thereby opened up for his discomfiture a Catholic hornets'-nest. A Viennese Cardinal strove to ban one of his books, and a storm of contrary opinions circled like a blast of wind about Watteroth's head. It changed him not at all. He wrote his remarkable books on history; then, as if in sheer frolic, would put out a work which aroused a chorus of controversy anew. The students loved and acclaimed him.

Spaun, in order to return to his native town of Linz in 1809, had to pass certain law examinations. He visited the Professor in his house in the Erdberg district—the house in which Schubert was to produce his *Prometheus* in 1816. Spaun and the Professor walked round and round the garden in earnest conversation. Suddenly one of them was struck by a horse-chestnut. A few moments later another missile reached its mark. Looking up, they saw the Professor's daughter Wilhelmine, aged nine, hidden among the leaves of the tree.[1] Wilhelmine ultimately married Josef Witteczek, who rose to high office in the Government and became one of the most ardent of Schubert's admirers in Vienna. When the composer died, Witteczek spent a large sum of money in collecting his printed and unprinted compositions. Indeed he formed the first real Schubert collection, and left it, on his death, to Spaun, who, in his turn, bequeathed it to the Society of the Friends of Music in Vienna.

Spaun met Witteczek in a restaurant, and a speaking acquaintance ripened quickly into friendship. Witteczek had then gone to live at Professor Watteroth's house in Erdberg, a large rectangular building with a cool garden at the back—a house which is practically the same to-day as it was when Schubert sought it in 1816.

[1] Professor O. E. Deutsch: " Ein Schuberthaus in Erdberg."

Witteczek occupied three rooms on the left-hand side of the gate, and when two more rooms became vacant he besought Spaun to change his residence.

These details are necessary, for they show how small domestic happenings can shape, unknowingly, the formation of something that will be remembered. In these trifling events lay the widening of the Schubert circle. Spaun took up residence at Professor Watteroth's house early in 1816, and he lived there until 1820. Before the Spring of the former year had burst into Summer Franz Schubert was installed in the same house. That he was living there in May is proved by the inscription on such portions as are still preserved of 12 Deutsche and 6 Ecossaises, which runs: " Als Arrestant in meinem Zimmer in Erdberg, 1 May, 1816. . . . Gott sey Lob und Dank." (" As prisoner in my room in Erdberg, 1 May, 1816. . . . Praise and thanks to God.") His friends had played a practical joke and locked him in.

The Watteroth home rapidly became a meeting-place for lovers of Art. Presently Mayrhofer also left his lodgings and took up his abode there. The quality of the weekly concerts became widely known. Here in this Vienna where, under official oppression, Art was striving to live, was a house that gathered beneath its roof all the rising intellect of the time. The Watteroths entertained well— the Professor was a man of considerable wealth, and he was emulating in a more modest fashion the example of Cardinal Otto-boni at the time of Handel's visit to Rome.

While the Professor kept open house for Art, it was Spaun who gathered in its lovers and made for Schubert many of the most faithful friends of his life at this period. He introduced Franz Schober to Schubert, and so began a friendship that was to have a definite influence—if at times a baleful influence—to Josef Gahy, the brilliant performer on the pianoforte, Karl Enderes, the poet Matthäus Collin, Caroline Pichler, Kupelwieser, the recognized head of Viennese Art, and, at a later date, the brilliant young painter Moritz von Schwind.

The rooms which Schubert and his friends occupied in the Watteroth house are situated in the left wing in the court of the house, probably on the second floor under the side-tower. Here, within a few weeks of his arrival, Schubert composed his *Prometheus* cantata. A note in his diary reads:

" June 17, 1816. On this day I composed for the first time for money. To wit, a Cantata, for the name-day celebration of Professor Watteroth, by Dräxler. The fee is 100 florins." (Viennese currency=£4.)

A writer named Philipp Dräxler had, at the request of a number of friends, composed the poem of *Prometheus* during a walking tour at Baden. Schubert set it in a day as the diary note suggests, and the rehearsals were carried out in a hall of the old University. The performance should have been given on July 12th, in the garden of the Watteroth house, but the weather was bad and it was postponed until the 24th.[1]

Whether the genius of Schubert, now ripening so rapidly, was displayed to full advantage in *Prometheus,* no one can say, for the music is lost. It was a work designed for two solo voices—soprano and bass—with chorus and orchestra, and consisted of a duet, two choruses for mixed voices, and one chorus for male voices (the disciples of *Prometheus*). The latter was in the form of a slow funeral march, very original and interesting in form. The Cantata, which was followed by other pieces of music, lasted, according to Sonnleithner, who was present, three-quarters of an hour. Three years later Sonnleithner had the Cantata with pianoforte accompaniment performed in his house, and himself sang the part of Prometheus.[2] In 1820 it was to have been performed in the Augarten, but Schubert withdrew it because of insufficient rehearsals. It was, however, performed early in 1828, but, during his last illness later in the year, Schubert sent the manuscript to a friend, and it disappeared. This mystery work of Schubert's life had gone for ever.

The *coterie,* to a great extent harboured in the Watteroth house, brought emancipation to Schubert from the school. Schober is often credited with having persuaded Schubert to change the school for the life of an ill-paid composer, but the decision was Schubert's alone, and inspired by none. He was now nineteen and recognized by the intellect of Vienna, or the greater portion of it. Since he had need for but little, he decided to take the supreme decision and live, not by teaching, but by the melodies of his brain. For a time he gave music lessons in order to make a little money, but the work was so distasteful that he quickly cast this life-line from him. He swam out to the open sea of his imagining.

[1] Kreissle is wrong in his surmise that the Watteroth festivities were given for the younger son Hermann, who died shortly afterwards. He deduces this from the fact that the 12th of July—the day planned for the performance—is the day of St. Hermann, and not of St. Heinrich, the name of the father. Heinrich the *Protestant* name-day is on the 12th of July.

[2] For information concerning the Watteroth house and the gatherings there I am largely indebted to Professor Otto Erich Deutsch, with whom I visited the place.

CHAPTER VI

Schubert meets Vogl

WHEN Schubert left the school in the Säulengasse it was Schober who had offered him sanctuary and the assistance of his spare funds. Professor Watteroth was then beyond his ken. That he should take up his residence at the Professor's house, and come under the influence of the brilliant people who assembled there, would have seemed to him, had it been suggested, not improbable, but impossible.

The individuality of Schubert had scarcely begun to form. His musical cleverness at the Convict had been almost forgotten by his burial in the Säulengasse School. The personality, so certainly shaping itself in the later days at the Convict, had been obscured in the schoolmaster hack. School friends who had admired his musical brilliance at the Convict were beginning to lose touch with him. They were departing on their several ways in search of the serious business of life. The Convict now held only new faces. Schubert might walk into the old music-room there, and the urchins wrestling with the first rudiments of music knew him not at all. Of all his friends, only Spaun and Schober were, at this period, seriously conscious of the fact that Schubert was genius bound down and in danger of suffering destruction in the merciless prisondom of school-teaching.

Schubert left the school of his own free will—as the Schoolmaster said—to starve. And the Schoolmaster was nearly right. The story that Franz was dismissed for clouting the ears of his small pupils is difficult to believe. Schubert was too stupidly sensitive to bully the utterly weak; the Schoolmaster too human in his family affections to cast out to starvation and possible damnation a son—even a disappointing son—of his own loins.

47

Apart from the composers whom he loved—his Mozart, Handel, Gluck and Beethoven—Schubert had no idolatries at this age. But his veneration of Vogl, the Court singer, was deep and sincere. Vogl was the most brilliant baritone of his epoch, and in dramatic parts he was supreme. To a writer of songs such as Schubert the appeal of Vogl was limitless. He was a master of expression, and beautiful to look upon, but he had distasteful mannerisms whilst singing which irritated the musicians. He played with his monocle in an affected manner, was conscious—very conscious of his supreme ability and his fine appearance.

Vogl was ever a creature of romance. His life was a romance. That he was the greatest singer of Schubert's songs in the Schubertian age is not surprising, for he understood and expressed what the composer put into every note.

He was the son of an Austrian farmer. As a youth he was entered at the Monastery of Kremsmünster as a choir-boy, where his musical qualities attracted attention. He was well grounded in the classics, then for the dull routine of the law, but Süssmayer, who completed Mozart's *Requiem*, persuaded him to forsake the law and become a singer. As he grew into manhood he became a giant in stature with the features of a Greek god. The quality of his voice and his powers as an actor attracted attention. Only by a miracle did Vogl escape the death-in-life of a Government office. Just as he was about to be prematurely buried by the law, Süssmayer heard him sing, and engaged him for the Court opera.

From that moment Vogl became one of the dramatic figures in Central European music. He had no struggles; he knew no poverties. Society in a wave of enthusiasm drew him within its innermost circles. He was in request as a teacher of singing to the best families in Vienna, and he drew big fees. Moreover, he became the confidential friend in these families, for in addition to the endowment of great artistic gifts from the gods he had been given the equally valuable gift of personality. His conversation held those at a dinner-table mute to listen. He had deep thoughtful eyes; and he would break off a discussion to follow something that had come into his mind. Those who listened waited awhile in a room of silence, till presently he emerged from his dream and picked up the thread of what he had been saying exactly where he had laid it down.

His reputation spread widely, rapidly, but he remained unspoiled. While his admirers clamoured, he went on reading the classics. He would sit in his dressing-room at the Opera, dressed in the garb for his part, reading Plato, the Old and New Testaments, the gospels of the stoics, Marcus Aurelius's "Meditations," Epictetus's "Enchiridion," Thomas à Kempis, Tauler, a German mystic of the fourteenth century. He translated "The Imitation of Christ," and had copies of the translation distributed among his congenial friends. He used to extract the main thoughts and principal ideas from the classics, both Greek and Latin, and translated them on loose pieces of stout paper.[1] For Plato's "Discourses" he used oblong large octavo, while the shorter phrases from Epictetus, from "De Imitatione," "Medulla," etc., were written on more compact 16mo. Then he would have these extracts bound in little volumes.[2] After exhausting rehearsals at the Opera he made it a custom to hire a carriage to the outskirts of Vienna, there to walk for a while, taking one of these books as his companion. While other actors let loose the flood of free licentious conversation in the theatre, Vogl sat dressed for his part among them, unseeing and unaware, reading his Greek.

He was not a figure of pose. His mind could detach itself from all that was happening around. In many ways he was a man of great religious impulse and a mystic. Steinbüchel, who was the keeper of the Imperial Collection of Coins in Vienna at the period, and Vogl's close friend, relates how he took a long walk with him in 1817 over the hills beyond Perzing, one of the Viennese suburbs, and on this occasion Vogl talked for hours about personal immortality.[3] He revelled in the writings of the French clairvoyants.[4] He himself was a clairvoyant. He seemed to throw aside his personality at times, and sink into moods of deep brooding. It may be that this clairvoyance was something of which he was conscious, and which he recognized in Schubert, for he wrote of Schubert's

[1] Bauernfeld in "Alt Wien" says that he saw a work of Epictetus copied by Vogl's clear hand in four languages, Greek, Latin, English and German.

[2] MS. papers of Anton Steinbüchel.   [3] *Ibid.*

[4] The meeting between Steinbüchel and Vogl, which led to a great friendship, occurred in a romantic manner. In the Steinbüchel manuscript papers is the story of it. He says that "in 1816 Count Haugwitz, a big landowner and industrial magnate of Moravia, appeared one day and asked me to show him the collection. When we came to the cameos the Count and his friends sat down, and I began to enlarge on the beauty of the wonderful treasures. Turning to a gentleman, whose noble head and bearing had attracted my attention while the others had seemed aloof and disinterested, I said to him: 'You see, Baron——' I thought I had heard the others address him thus. I saw his friends staring at him in bewilderment, and the Count smilingly interrupted with the words: 'Is it possible that you do not know the great Court singer Vogl?' The Count was a musical enthusiast, and my mistake was a crime in his eyes."

songs in his diary: " These truly divine inspirations; these expressions of musical clairvoyance." Moreover, he told Stadler that many of Schubert's compositions were the result of clairvoyance.

He related that on one occasion, whilst a choir boy at the Kremsmünster, he had attended the funeral of another choir boy. During the service he distinctly saw the soul of the boy rise from the catafalque, he said, and he had fainted at the sight.[1]

This religious fervour and mysticism was a governing factor in Vogl's life. On one occasion he was giving singing lessons to a very beautiful, well-educated Viennese girl. When teaching her a song where the Mother, the Queen of Heaven, appears, he explained to her the deep significance and higher meaning of the word " Mother," so that she might grasp its right import, and give to it the correct expression in singing. He said that his remarks must have made a deep impression on the girl's mind, for, though some twenty years had passed, he could still see the beautiful expression on her face, and hear the sweet tone of her voice, as in the innocence of her heart she exclaimed: " Make me a mother! " It was this girl who eventually married the painter Overbeck.[2]

This was the Vogl who was to figure so prominently in Schubert's life. His chambers became the meeting-place of the artistic figures of Vienna. Every morning those small rooms were crowded —artists, poets, musicians and the higher members of the aristocracy had ready admission. They took their *déjeuner* in these apartments. They engaged their wit ruthlessly at the expense of their host, who never took offence. But if they committed the blunder of talking scandal they were asked to leave.

It was Franz Schober who brought about the meeting between Schubert and Vogl in 1817. Vogl had the burden of twenty-five more years than Schubert. He was acclaimed, a maker of money, a god in his world, whilst Schubert was known to comparatively few. Whenever Vogl had sung in opera, Schubert at the price of a few groschen had sat in the gallery, absorbed, carried out of himself by his singing. The first time Schubert saw Vogl off the stage was at a restaurant in the Schlossergässel, but they did not speak to one another. The ardent persistence of Schober ultimately made Vogl interested in Schubert's work. In the home of Schober's mother the singer first heard the work of Schubert, because Franz had no piano in his rooms. Schober arranged their meeting. By that act, this irresponsible soul paid the greatest service to his friend.

---

[1] MS. papers of Anton Steinbüchel.   [2] *Ibid.*

Vogl picked up *Ganymed*, then threw it aside. The *Augenlied* followed, and when Vogl had hummed it over he exclaimed " Not bad." Then he looked over the pages of the *Erl-King*. He had discovered a gem. Presently he turned to Schubert and said: " There is good stuff in you, but you are too little of an actor, and not enough of a charlatan! You are wasting your fine thoughts instead of developing them."

Vogl was extremely popular with the Emperor Franz and travelled everywhere with the Court. It was while he was with the Court at Laxenburg at the time when Napoleon was dethroning so many royal families that he heard the Emperor Franz say very quietly: " Well, I suppose they will at least leave me a farm! "[1] After Vogl resigned from the Opera he became a *Lieder* singer, but previously he had frequently said that he would have given up singing altogether, but that Schubert's songs made him go on. He sang the *Erl-King, Der Kampf*, the *Group out of Tartarus* and the *Wanderer* continuously, though very often in the big houses of Society he needed much coaxing to persuade him to sing at all. Spaun declares that when Vogl sang Schubert's songs the ladies would crowd round him, fascinated by the beauty of his voice and his appearance, and would completely ignore the composer.

Schubert persistently refused to alter a note he had written; he would destroy a manuscript rather than change a bar. But such was Vogl's influence over him that now—under protest, it is true—we find Schubert altering his songs in order that they might better suit the compass of Vogl's voice. Occasionally Vogl altered them himself and Schubert was dilatory in reproach. So closely had these two temperamental opposites grown together that Vogl in his turn submitted to inconveniences forced upon him by Schubert which he would have tolerated from no other man. He disliked being kept waiting five minutes; yet he would make the Opera curtain half an hour late in rising because he had not reached the theatre. In spite of his own peculiar habits he hated any form of inefficiency. The floundering of little people—hacks, he called them—at some of the theatres drew from him terrible brutality. He was always brutal except towards those who did not flatter him.[2] But when Schubert kept him waiting for a performance, and then did not come at all, Vogl merely shrugged his shoulders and said: " We

---

[1] MS. papers of Anton Steinbüchel.
[2] Dr. Adam Haller: Letter to Luib.

must all bend before Schubert's genius, and if he does not come we must creep after him on our knees."[1]

How Schubert found the means to live at this period cannot be said. He was certainly living rent-free with Schober, but his bills, even if of small proportions, could not for ever lie undisturbed in the small drawer where he put them. There were occasional loans from his father and his friends—loans always honourably repaid. The stocking at the Rossau school was also helpful at times. Schober continually helped him, and there are records in plenty of dinners provided for Schubert by Spaun and his other intimates.

In the year under review—1817—he completed sixty-eight works, including the setting of thirteen songs by Mayrhofer and four by Schiller, three Overtures and Symphony No. 6. Early in 1818 came *The Trout,* which he dedicated to his friend Josef Hüttenbrenner. He sent him the manuscript immediately after it was composed, a huge blot on the first page, and written at the foot the following explanation:

" Dearest friend, I am extremely glad that you like my songs. As proof of my most devoted friendship I am sending you one which I have just composed at midnight whilst staying with Anselm Hüttenbrenner. I wish I were in touch with you with a glass of punch. By a stroke of bad luck just as I intended to strew sand over this thing I was in a hurry, and, being very sleepy, picked up the ink-stand, and poured it all unthinking over the manuscript. Vale "[2]

A little later Schubert wrote and dedicated his *Mourning Waltz* to Anselm Hüttenbrenner, in whose house he was staying. Hüttenbrenner was at that time living with a bookseller on the Kohlmarkt. There was no monetary reward for the composer, but then his happy disposition could uphold the humour of life, and create forgetfulness for the unpaid bills. He wrote on this manuscript: " Composed for my coffee, wine and punch-brother, Anselm Hüttenbrenner, world-famous composer, Vienna, March 14, 1818 A.D., in his own imperial apartment, thirty florins monthly, Viennese currency." Schubert was fond of such dedicatory jests. On the manuscript of his *Life's Song* is this quaint dedication: ' To the apartment of Herr Schober."

Another famous song of Schubert's which dates from this year is *Der Jüngling und der Tod,* the words of which have been

---

[1] Dr. Adam Haller: Letter to Luib.
[2] See facsimile of this manuscript. It was written at midnight, 21st February, 1818.

attributed by some to Kreissle and by others to Anton Spaun. But Anton Spaun, a very able historian, never wrote a serious poem, and indeed was incapable of doing so. He was a person of peculiar habits, who suffered from very indifferent health although he had all the appearance of being robust. Schubert's friendship for him was sincere, but as Anton grew older he became eccentric with a manner of eccentricity which Franz did not pretend to understand. For instance, the year before Schubert's death, he began to collect the folk songs of Upper Austria, and he dragged about a young assistant-schoolmaster of Fraunkirchen with his fiddle on the pastures and slopes of the Alps, where the fiddler was compelled to play the songs after the cowherdesses. Sometimes these girls in their " jodels " taxed the fiddler to the utmost. Moreover, he was weak on the legs, and the long mountain climbs put a severe strain on him, but Anton's florins helped to overcome the difficulty.[1]

When apart from his friends, Schubert withdrew into long moods of thoughtfulness that were scarcely depression. It was perhaps at such times that he became acutely aware of his sorry state as measured by the worldly scale. In 1816 he had begun to keep a diary, and he jotted down odd thoughts in it as they occurred to him in these hours of solitude. He also wrote snatches of rather poor verse.

" A man endures misfortune without complaint," he wrote in the diary, " but he feels it the more acutely. Why does God endow us with compassion?

" Happy is the man who finds a true friend, and far happier he who finds that true friend in his wife.

" The greatest misfortune of the wise man and the greatest unhappiness of the fool are based upon convention.

" Easy mind; light heart. A mind that is too easy hides a heart that is too heavy.

" The world resembles a stage on which every man is playing a part. Approval or blame will follow in the world to come. A part is handed out [to an actor], thus we also have our parts handed out to us, and who shall decide for himself whether he has acted well or badly? The manager is to be blamed who distributes parts to his players which they are unable to act."

For many years he kept this diary alive with his views of the world as he saw it. But after his death a dealer in autographs secured it, and sold it, page by page, as a literary curiosity, an act

[1] Wilhelm von Chézy: " Erinnerungen aus meinem Leben."

of vandalism that caused the loss of this record of Schubert's thoughts during his most strenuous years.

Throughout 1817 Rossini's music was being constantly performed in Vienna, and, as a new importation from Naples, attracted attention and criticism. It interested Schubert, but the statement that he became a warm admirer of Rossini is, in the opinion of Spaun, only partly true. He liked *Il Barbiere*, and was enraptured with the last act of *Otello* when, at a later date, the work appeared in Vienna. But, as a whole, the operas left him unmoved. Many of the Italian singers of that time—notably Lablache—Schubert admired greatly, but he did not share the extraordinary applause poured upon them for their performance in *Nozze di Figaro*.

The influence of Rossini on the Viennese capital did not pass him unobserved. After an evening at *Tancred* he declared—possibly with some conceit—that it was not a very difficult thing to write music in the style of Rossini, and he produced within six months two Italian overtures. More than once in later years a thought, suggestive of Rossini, occurred in Schubert's compositions. In his music may also be traced occasional and more certain impressions of Mozart and Haydn. But neither the one nor the other disturbed or changed that individuality which has left a heritage of music marked by his own personality.

FRANZ VON SCHOBER
The closest of Schubert's friends
from the painting by L. Kupelwieser

THERESA GROB
A portrait painted in later life

CROWDING FOR A SCHUBERT CONCERT

THE SCHUBERTIANS ACTING A CHARADE AT
ATZENBRUGG
from the painting by L. Kupelwieser

CHAPTER VII

Schubert and the Esterhazys

(1818)

*I*N the opening months of 1818 Schubert's position became difficult in the extreme. He had no money; he was earning no money. At the age of twenty-one he had no income whatever. He had ceased to give music lessons because he hated the work, and these lessons—poor though the pittance they brought him—at least provided him with food. With his characteristic stubbornness he refused to pursue a means of living which he found odious. Had he not already been victimized too long in his father's school by the plague of earning means of existence? Now, save for the generosity of his friends, and an occasional loan from his father, he did not possess a coin.

In the late Spring he was introduced by Johann Unger to Count Esterhazy. Unger, the father of the famous operatic singer Caroline Unger, knew Schubert well; he was the author of Schubert's *Nightingale*. He saw in Schubert a genius crippled and starved. Unger understood music. He had suffered much and was familiar with the suffering which came to those who composed in a pleasure-loving capital.

The object of the meeting was made clear at the outset. The Count gave amateur concerts in his luxurious house on the Herren-gasse, and at his castle at Zelész in Hungary. He sang a good bass, and his Countess, the most accomplished in a family of rather inefficient amateurs, was a contralto of sufficient quality to be attractive. There were three children, Marie aged thirteen, Caroline now nine, and Albert threatened with enforced musical instruction at five.

Schubert appeared to Count Esterhazy as a brilliant person whom he could secure cheaply. His proposition was brief. He would feed Schubert at his house in Vienna during the winter; he would feed and house him at his castle at Zelész during the summer; and he would pay him two gulden a lesson to teach his children music. He preyed on Schubert's poverty. What could a man, tied by poverty to Vienna, desire more than the summer months at a Hungarian castle, and to be paid the respectable fee of two gulden a lesson into the bargain! Was he not being taken out of the awful sameness of Viennese life, and given a few gulden when he had not a groschen to settle a bill? He was to be transported to Hungary and housed, not in the Castle itself, but in the bailiff's house. The professional brilliance of Schubert was reckoned so cheaply by Count Esterhazy that he housed him with his servants, took him into the Castle *salon* when he desired music, then returned him somewhat tired at the end of the evening—the servile menial—to the society of a bailiff and his grooms, to the smell of horsedung. Yet Schubert accepted the offer. In July he went with the family to Zelész.

He had banished himself, suppressed himself anew, for the price of two gulden a lesson. Judas had sold his Master for thirty pieces of silver, and Schubert sold his Art for something less under the impetus of poverty. He rebelled against his imprisonment at Zelész. He was living with the spiritually dead and kept alive by his composing.

"Nobody here cares for true art," he wrote soon after his arrival, "unless it be the Countess." He had begun to feel the weight of his yoke. He yearned for Vienna, for his friends. He had the home-sickness of a boy at his first school.

"Dearest, most faithful friends," he wrote to Schober and his companions at the beginning of August, "How could I ever forget you—you who are all the world to me. Spaun, Schober, Mayrhofer, Senn—how are you? Feeling well? I am exceedingly well. I am composing like a god, as if it simply had to be done as it has been done.

"Mayrhofer's *Solitude* is finished, and I consider it to be one of the best things I ever wrote, since I am without worry. . . . Now I am alive for once, God be praised, it was time, or I should have been a spoilt musician. Schober, please deliver my respects to Herr Vogl. I shall be writing to him very soon. If it is possible, please endeavour to make him realize that he would be doing me a great kindness if he would sing one of my songs at the Kunz concert in November. Any song he chooses. My regards to all my friends. My most sincere respects to your mother and sister. Please write to me soon. Every letter of the alphabet coming from you is precious to me.

" Your ever faithful friend,
" FRANZ S."

The stimulating novelty of Zelész began to disappear. Vienna was life. Zelész was a slow but certain process of death. He worked ceaselessly to prevent the sterilization of his brain in solitude. In Vienna at least he had associates of brilliance. And now the little stupid things of life began to irritate him. The silly people he had never observed before became striking figures on his immediate horizon.

He wrote to Vienna describing those who were his daily associates. " You have no conception of what the parson here is like. As bigoted as an old farm-yard cow, and as stupid as a thoroughbred donkey, and as rough as a buffalo. Such is the intelligence of his sermons." Then after more vituperation: " He picks up a skull in the pulpit and says: ' Look at that with your freckled faces! That is what you will be like one day! '

" Our castle," he went on, " is not imposing, but is well built, and surrounded by a very fine garden. I live in the bailiff's house. It is fairly quiet except for forty geese which gabble in chorus so that you cannot hear yourself speak. . . . The rent collector suits his post very well, for he is a man of great insight into his sacks and bags. The doctor is really skilful. . . . The surgeon, whom I like the best, is a respectable old gentleman of seventy-five. . . . The cook is a bit gay, the lady's maid is thirty, the kitchen-maid is very pretty and often keeps me company;[1] the nurse is a good old soul and the butler is my rival."

He wrote to his brother Ferdinand:

" It is 11.30 p.m., and your Requiem is finished. It has made me sad, for I sang it with all my heart. Whatever is missing, please add. . . . My foot has gone to sleep, and I am very angry about it. If the idiot could write, he would not sleep. . . .

---

[1] Kreissle asserts that Schubert had an *affaire* with one of the servants, his opinion probably being based on this letter. But Spaun, criticizing Kreissle's biography when it appeared, wrote (Memoirs): "The story that Schubert carried on with a girl in the household is vicious, idle gossip, quite unworthy of Schubert's noble character."

" Good morning, old fellow. I have slept in company with my foot and am continuing this letter at eight o'clock on the 25th [August]. I want to ask a favour of you. Give my love to my dear parents, my brothers and sisters, and my friends, not forgetting Karl. . . . Please stir up my town friends and make them write to me. Tell my mother that my washing is being looked after exceedingly well. If I could have some more linen I would be very glad of some handkerchiefs, neckerchiefs and stockings. I am also badly in want of two pairs of trousers. Hart can take the measurements for them whenever he likes. I would send the money for them at once. For the month of July I have received two hundred florins, including travelling money. . . ."

Schubert gave his music lessons, and, if not impressed with the musical standard of the household, he took part gladly in the family concerts. When the Count's relative Baron Schönstein, who held various high appointments under Government and eventually became Minister of Finance, arrived at Zelész, its musical life became more interesting. The Baron possessed a baritone voice which rivalled that of Vogl in quality. Indeed he was said to have been a singer of such distinction that, had the lack of landed property compelled him to earn his living, he would have found wealth by his voice. To the exile from his accustomed associations Schönstein was a comrade sent by God. A friendship between them ripened swiftly, and whenever Schubert stayed at Zelész in later years the Baron appeared. He looked to Schubert as the Master, adored this stumpy little comrade, and when Vogl, drawing into age, began to surrender his voice to the years, it was the Baron who took his place in the *salons*.

In spite of his loneliness, the sense of absence from those who understood him, Schubert's compositions at Zelész were few. His *Einsamkeit, Das Abendroth,* and some exercises for one of his pupils were the greater part. At the end of the year he returned with the family to Vienna. He attended in the Herrengasse house daily to give the music lessons and remained an integral part of the family life.

Louis Schlösser, who made Schubert's acquaintance on his return to Vienna, shows us Schubert subjecting himself to these titled amateurs, giving way to their petty fads, and yet, in subjection, demonstrating his superiority. Only Schubert's poverty can explain his loyalty to the Esterhazys. They were people indolently rich. They paid the price of mediocrity for Schubert's genius. Having bought him by the cruelty of patronage, they relegated him to the servants' hall. It is one of the most remarkable points in Schubert's life that he endured these people. He refused music lessons in Vienna to accept them at two gulden from a titled snob. It was the last thing which, in the ordinary way, he would have done. He disliked the aristocracy. He disliked bought music. But a poor man can adorn a snob by further self-suppression.

" I knew," says Schlösser,[1] " that Schubert did not live in extravagant circumstances, yet when I visited him I was surprised at the absence of every comfort. The large room on the ground floor which he occupied was more like the workshop of an artisan than the study of a composer. I saw a piano covered with piles of music; string instruments, music-stands, the necessary chairs and table were all mixed up in disorder. Apart from these things, no signs of comfort of any kind. That was the young master artist's *home*, whence emanated such rich treasures of a soul flowing with all the deepest emotions. In this obscure dwelling Franz Schubert received the most distinguished visitors, especially Hungarian nobles whose national airs he often utilized in his compositions.

" I heard the sound of a piano from outside the room, therefore I opened the door very gently so as not to disturb him. But he saw me and got up. I begged him to continue playing, and he then let me hear the variations of the Impromptu in ' B Flat Major 2/4.' "

On one occasion Schlösser asked Schubert to be his guest for the day, and they drove to the most renowned restaurant in the town. Schlösser had ordered an exquisite dinner and the best wine in the cellar. To Schubert this was a gala night. All the worries of the world disappeared in a wonderful evening. He ate and drank with zest, and, as he did so, regaled Schlösser with stories of his life at the Convict. Occasionally he would produce a little note-book and scribble down something even as he talked. A musical theme had crossed his mind, and he wished to note it ere it was lost. It was not a pose. It was his continual habit.

" While we were conversing merrily," Schlösser said, " a servant dressed in a rich livery approached the table, and handed Schubert a letter from Count Esterhazy. Schubert opened it, read it slowly, then said to the servant: ' Tell your master I will come.'

" Then he handed the letter to me. It ran as follows: ' The musical fuel of my cousin Stefan has caught fire again and flamed

[1] Louis Schlösser: " Aus Franz Schuberts Leben."

up into an art product which only you will be able to decipher. I shall expect you soon.' "

Schlösser asked Schubert for an explanation.

" Have you never in your life," said Schubert, " met with a man who, endowed with the happiest gifts of music, has, through want of experience, knowledge and the ability for self-criticism, fallen into a mad passion for music so that he thinks he is a great composer? He—Count Stefan—writes down any mad thing his unbridled imagination dictates. No one can make head or tail of it. He cannot play it to anybody. It is simply chaos, which he considers sublime and equal to the work of Beethoven. He comes from time to time from Hungary to visit his relatives, the Esterhazys, in Vienna, in order that I may play his supposed masterpieces to him."

' But," said Schlösser, " how can you play what you say is chaos? '

" Let me go on," replied Schubert. " On a former occasion I found that this fantastical enthusiast had mistaken a Duo by Pixis and Bohn, Variations for pianoforte and violin, for the Variations of Beethoven's *Kreutzer Sonata*. It was clear to me, therefore, that I might count upon the chance that he could not distinguish between one piece of music and another. So it happened. I had taken note of the time and key of his own piece. Then I began to prelude arpeggios. Then I introduced some rhythmical sentences. And then, when I noticed no change of expression on the face of my pseudo-composer and that he even answered questions as to whether I was interpreting his music correctly with an affirming nod of his head, I bravely continued to improvise and play variations, and turned over the leaves of his music to make it appear as if I were playing from it. He had not the remotest idea that I was playing something totally different from the black notes that stared me in the face."

" But how could you dare risk such an indiscretion? " Schlösser inquired.

" It was done with the knowledge and consent of Count Esterhazy and the family," Schubert answered. " They would not deprive their good-natured cousin of a self-deception that made him so happy. Stefan himself was swimming in a sea of beatitude when, at the end of playing, they greeted him with ' Bravo! Bravissimo! ' All the same, I feel this deception weighing on my conscience, and I am quite determined to make a frank confession of the whole manoeuvre to him. From what I know of the character of Stefan, he will bear me no grudge. He will treat it as a Carnival joke. Now once more the experiment is to be repeated against my will, I have given my word, and I am too much indebted to the house to refuse. But, after that, *never again.*"

Schubert then asked Schlösser to accompany him to the Esterhazys' house. He told him that there was no restraint in the family, and that, as musical tutor, he was at liberty to take anyone there who was really interested in music.

With this assurance Schlösser went. He found Count Stefan a handsome cavalier who talked volubly about Beethoven and Mozart, but was careful not to go beyond generalities. He was obviously a man of intelligence. Then Schubert broke into the conversation. Count Stefan became suddenly silent as if exhausted by the mental exertion of talking. Presently he began again with a rush of nonsense. The fellow was a charlatan. Schubert, leaning towards Schlösser, said under his breath: " There are two contrary impulses which govern this man's brain—the one sane, and the other eccentric. They alternate at regular intervals, whereupon the normal state sets in again."

Meanwhile the piano had been opened, and the volume of music placed ready for Schubert. The Count saw his opportunity. He came forward and rather nervously asked for indulgence for a new fantasia which he had composed, and which their friend Schubert would now play to them at sight.

Schlösser caught a glimpse of the music.

" What did I see? " he exclaimed. " A forest of queer figures which, like black snakes, were winding in and out of the staves. And this unreadable manuscript Schubert was supposed to decipher! "

Schubert put the manuscript on the piano, sat down, and, after a casual glance at it, began to play. Schlösser declares that he never heard Schubert improvise as he did on that occasion. " Strings of melodic pearls of the greatest beauty rolled from the keys, and gradually took the form of a Romance of exquisite tenderness, alternated with episodes and enriched with wonderful modulations, all of which were kept in the nature of a Fantasia so as not to arouse the Count's suspicions. These gentle lyric melodies formed the introduction to an Allegro *con fuoco,* wild and full of the strongest colouring."

Schubert had, as was so often the case in the ecstasy of inspiration, forgotten the object of his playing. So absorbed was he that he had even overlooked the Count and the music before him. The

Count began to suspect that something was wrong. He got up quickly from his seat, his eyes flashing with anger, and his movement brought Schubert back to realities. Schubert regained his self-control at once, and began to turn the pages as he played, which for some moments he had forgotten to do. The Count subsided on to his chair again. He became still and serious, wrapped in the beauty of what he believed to be his own music. The crisis passed; the music ceased. Schubert turned round smiling at the company from the music-stool. The Count was the first to express his approval, but not without a touch of irony.

" A few minutes later," says Schlösser, " Schubert went up to the Count, and, with evident emotion, asked humbly for forgiveness for the deception he had practised upon him, not with evil intent as it might appear. He explained that his eye had caught a particular passage in the Count's Fantasia which had attracted him and led him on, and he pleaded guilty to having borrowed another man's idea and dressed it up.

" ' Why,' Schubert asked the Count, ' should the composer be more guilty than the poet who warms to fantasy by a strange flame, making an idea that inspires him the subject of his own very different treatment? And more than that I did not do.'

" It was a fine and resourceful turn of Schubert's delicate feeling. All who heard him pleading could scarcely suppress their laughter, for no one had ever heard Schubert make such a long and impassioned speech before. It was quite impossible for anyone to be angry with him. Presently the disillusioned Count put out his hand to Schubert in cordial and frank forgiveness. Schubert, relieved from the oppressive burden of his conscience, sat down again at the pianoforte and played some of his ' Deutsche ' in the way in which only he could play them."

When Schubert returned to Vienna with the Esterhazys at the end of 1818 he went to live with Mayrhofer in his rooms at 420 Wipplingerstrasse, and there he remained until 1820. At the same time Schober and his mother moved to the Göttweigerhof, and there Schubert joined them again in 1822.

Schubert still attended at the Esterhazys' house in the Herrenstrasse to give lessons to the children. But after the luxury of Zelész, the Wipplingerstrasse rooms must have afforded rough comfort. Yet he was probably far happier with Mayrhofer than he had ever been at Zelész—Mayrhofer with his strange moods of depression and quiet, smoking pipe after pipe through endless hours, and engrossed in the novels on which he spent all his spare kreutzers. But the atmosphere of Mayrhofer's rooms, the companionship of a kindred soul in Art, was more important to Schubert. The beer-houses, where he ate and drank with Mayrhofer and other friends, and where he performed endless pranks, beheld him now again. He smothered Mayrhofer's sitting-room—already a reflection of the discord of an untidy mind—with a scattering of manuscripts and odd pieces of clothing. Fortunately the twain had a landlady who understood the peculiarity common to the habits of genius of creating an eruption in any room. She was a French widow named Sans-souci, and her son had been at the Convict at the same time as Schubert. If they had moved in different circles there, they had known the same iron discipline, the same semi-starvation, the coldness and brutality of a place designed to make youth suffer.

Schubert had already composed over two hundred works, not one of which had yet found the glory of print. The only money he had earned by his composing was the £4 he received for *Prometheus*. The applause of a few friends was the sole reward he had received for the dozens of scores now tumbled loosely into drawers. He could not live on applause. But publishers did not seek him, and he did not seek the publishers, well aware, perhaps, that they were not prone to take risks save over the works of those who had not already established their place in music, and that then they only bought at villainous prices.

The currency in Vienna again became disturbed by the rumour that the Government intended to raise the value of the copper-coinage. People began hoarding their money. A disastrous state of affairs was thereby produced which hit the poor, and Schubert among them, badly. The trades-people made tokens cut out of playing cards, marked with a seal and the amount which they represented. These they handed to their customers as change for a bank or treasury note, and the tokens were only redeemable by further purchases made at the same shop. Soon the value of the tokens became rubbed out. On a token for 30 kreutzers, for example, the 0 disappeared and the shopman would only redeem it for 3 kreutzers.[1]

In spite of this new diversion of the currency which only tended to make his financial stress more acute, Schubert continued to compose his notes unimpaired by his troubles. He composed his *Wanderer* to Schlegel's words in February, 1819, in a single

[1] Dr. Karl Wagner: From "Neuer Krakauer Schreibkalender."

afternoon. This was not the *immortal* Wanderer, composed in 1816 to Schmidt's words which Vogl sang for many years until age left him infirm, sitting in a chair, but on special occasions willing to sing it again to a circle of friends. It was in Mayrhofer's rooms that Schubert composed his operetta *Die Zwillingsbrüder* in the first days of 1819. A few months later the same rooms saw the birth of the *Zauberharfe*. The union of these two blithe spirits was complete. Schubert was setting the verse of Mayrhofer as rapidly as the pen— and it was not a slow pen—of the poet set it down. Mayrhofer, in the intimacy of their friendship, nicknamed him "Schwammerl" (Fatty) because of his appearance [1], and for a long time Schubert was thus greeted by his friends. But Mayrhofer had another nick-name of his own for Schubert—a name which was the result of those two years together. He called him "Kanevas" *(Kann er was?* —Can he do anything?), which was the first question Schubert asked when a stranger was brought into the room.

It may have been the descent of Rossini with his operas on Vienna which made Schubert turn towards opera again in 1819. He believed all through his life that he was born to write a great opera. The circumstances of his times, the brutal wrongs done to him by music publishers, may have obscured in his mind any belief that he stood alone as the greatest song-writer. How could a man believe in his songs when a publisher paid him a mere tenpence apiece for them? It is so easy in view of the assessment of his genius made by Time to wonder why the scales of blindness lay across his eyes, to wonder why he grasped at opera when the song of an afternoon, a song written on a beer-table, a song written in the late watches of the night, could be so full of beauty; but a song which, in his day, could not buy him to-morrow's meal.

The success of Rossini, the success of good opera at this period, was to a suffering creature who believed in himself a temptation to seek the same path. It was in Mayrhofer's rooms that this brave soul sat down solemnly to write opera, to take the greatest chance any unknown musician could take. He gambled the talents he possessed against the hundred chances—the intrigue and bribery, the decision to exploit only well-known composers, which seemed to be the sole attitude of managers towards one to the world unknown.

---

[1] When Kreissle published his biography of Schubert, Spaun took exception to his remarks about Schubert's fat, and declared that they were quite inaccurate. He said (Memoirs): "The description in the biography would picture Schubert as a lump of fat. This is entirely wrong. Schubert had a firm, compact body, but of fat and a big stomach *(Schmerbauch)* not a sign. His youthful friend, Moritz Schwind [the painter], surpassed him already at that time in circumference."

CHAPTER VIII

Opera and Ludlam's Cave

(1819)

*N*O sooner had Schubert decided to compose for the theatre than he set to work. On January 19th, 1819, he completed the setting of *Die Zwillingsbrüder* (The Twins), from a translation by Hofmann of a wretched French Vaudeville *Les Deux Valentins,* and in June it was produced at the Kärntnerthor Theatre.

There were four principal theatres in Vienna at this time the Theatre An-der-Wien, the building of which was begun in the year of Schubert's birth by Schickaneder, author of the libretto of *The Magic Flute,* with funds supplied by a wealthy Viennese merchant named Zitterbarth. The interior was decorated with cornflower-blue and silver. The Kärntnerthor, the Leopoldstädter, and the Josefstädter followed in importance. The An-der-Wien became in the space of three years what was, for the age, a playhouse of magnificence and luxury devoted mainly to the production of spectacular pieces. It had the largest stage in Europe, which could accommodate five hundred people and fifty horses, and from which there was direct access to the street for the admission of the horses employed in the productions. At times the theatre was given over to ballet on an elaborate scale, to the production of fairy stories in which innumerable children were engaged. Here Schubert was to produce his *Zauberharfe* (The Magic Harp) in 1820.

The Leopoldstädter Theatre was mainly devoted to comedy and farce. Great stars of comedy of the time had emerged from it— Anton Hasenhut, Josef Kortheuer and Theresa Krones, whose beauty was famous throughout Europe, even if her private life did not permit of investigation. In later years Wenzel Müller, the conductor, wrote all the music for the theatre for a long period, and

65

took an important part in the development of the national Viennese music before Lanner and Strauss. The Josefstädter Theatre was the home of sensationalism, and was patronized chiefly by those students and youths who possessed the kreutzers for admission.

When Schubert's *Die Zwillingsbrüder* was produced at the Kärntnerthor in June it ran but for six nights in spite of the fact that Vogl doubled the parts of the twins. The piece was no more than an overture and ten numbers, and the story mere drivel, so stupid, indeed, that only the wild impulse of Schubert to reach the theatre could have made him compose it. It was followed by a ballet, " The Two Aunts; or Once Upon a Time and Now." Several biographers state that Schubert did not sit through the first performance, but this is not correct. He did not answer the call of the first-nighters at the end of the performance for the composer. Vogl had to come before the curtain and announce that the composer had left the house. Schubert feared to appear because he was not wearing evening clothes. He did not possess them.

Anselm Hüttenbrenner relates what happened. " I was sitting with Schubert in the top gallery. He was very happy when the Overture of his work was received with great applause, and the songs which Vogl had to sing were equally favoured. At the end Schubert was called for repeatedly, but he refused to go on to the stage as he had only a wornout coat on. I quickly took off my black dress coat, and tried to persuade him to put it on and go before the curtain, for it would have been very much to his advantage. But he was undecided and shy. As the applause continued it was announced that Schubert was not present, and Schubert listened with a smile. After that we went together to Lenkay's *Gasthaus* (tavern) in the Liliengasse, where we celebrated the success of the operetta with some pints of Nesmüller wine."[1]

" In the ordinary way Schubert always drank Bavarian beer at the *Schwarze Katze* (Black Cat) in Annastrasse," says Anselm Hüttenbrenner, " or at the *Schnecke* (Snail), near St. Peter's, and smoked a good deal while doing so. When we had more money we drank wine, or if circumstances were particularly happy we had punch at the Weihburggasse."[2]

[1] Karl Rosenbaum, husband of the prima donna Theresa Gassmann, wrote in his diary (Deutsch II, 69): " The operetta has nothing to recommend it, but Schubert's friends made a good deal of noise, the opposing party hissed, and at the end stormed for a long time until Herr Vogl appeared and said: ' Schubert is not present; I thank you in his name.' "

[2] Anselm Hüttenbrenner: " Reminiscences."

The Press, like the public, did not care for *Die Zwillingsbrüder*. It chided Schubert gently, it gave him a little patronizing advice about his composing. The principal critic *(Allgemeine Musikalische Zeitung)* said the best he could of the work: " It proves that he has a talented head full of power and inventive genius, the chief things by which all else can be acquired. It proves, however, at the same time that he has more talent for tragedy than comedy, where- fore we advise him strongly to choose the former, at least for the present. The music possesses much originality, many interesting episodes *(Parthien)*, and is correct in its declamation, but the senti- ments *(Empfindungen)* of the simple country folk are conceived too heavily. Herr Schubert ties himself too much to the detail of his text; which chases him and his hearers through a maze of modula- tions, and never permits of a moment's rest. He wants to express the sounds of words instead of painting the *whole* character of the *whole* piece, which Mozart proves to be the only means to reach the highest object of Art. . . . The end gave occasion to a party war. Schubert's friends wanted to call him, while ' many serpents ' made themselves heard in opposition to this. But the greater part of the audience remained passive in the quarrel, which really did not concern Art, for the auhtor had deserved neither one nor the other, but merely encouragement."

Schubert took the hint. He turned to tragedy. Hermann Neefe, the scene-painter and son of the conductor of the Bonn Court Orchestra, who had taught Beethoven, came to him and urged him to write a new opera. More than that, he brought with him Demmer, the stage manager of the An-der-Wien Theatre, which implied some security for the production of the Opera if Schubert would under- take it. Again Schubert, in no way deterred by the storm of criticism which had raged about the text of *Die Zwillingsbrüder*, went to Hofmann for his *libretto*. In a short space of time Hofmann produced *Die Zauberharfe*, and Schubert, alive to the new chance for operatic success, set it in a fortnight. But when it was produced he received nothing for his work. The theatre was struggling with a lean exchequer, and the 500 florins which had been promised to him were never paid, for the management went into bankruptcy.

Neefe painted remarkable scenery for this Opera, and Demmer certainly produced it on a lavish scale, but a few brilliant numbers failed to carry it to success. After a brief run it was laid aside, only to be brought out afresh and played on occasion, till towards the end of 1821 it fell into the limbo of forgotten things. In a measure

67

it shows Schubert groping for operatic expression, striving towards the conquest of the operatic stage, which he felt he had the power to capture.

The *Allgemeine Musikalische Zeitung* again pointed out to Schubert the error of his ways, and said of *Die Zauberharfe:* " If one takes into account that this is the first attempt of the young composer in a higher form (*Gattung*), one must accord full justice to so praiseworthy an endeavour to remain original, and to reach, in this the only possible manner, a high place in Art. A closer knowledge of the mysteries of the stage, and useful experience concerning the effect of large orchestral masses, will in time become the surest guides and teach him to escape the dangerous precipices (*Klippen*) which present themselves unavoidably to every young artist. The eye will be perfectly satisfied in this drama by the stage decorations, which are most wonderfully effective."

The versatility of Schubert persisted. The interruption of opera, and the hopes he had for his own work in operatic form did not spoil the music of differing order which swelled within him. Songs continued to pour out over loose sheets of paper, most of them to be pushed into a drawer as soon as completed. In addition to the *Wanderer, Abendbilder, Das Mädchen*—another of Schlegel's poems—*Berthas Lied in der Nacht* and *Himmels-funken* were all composed during the same month. He worked at a furious pace. On the manuscript of the *Overture à quatre mains* in " F " he wrote: " Written in three hours in the room of Herr Josef Hüttenbrenner at the Civic Hospital. Lost my dinner on account of it."

In a letter written from Vienna at this time to Anselm Hüttenbrenner, who was at Graz, Schubert reveals a happy state of mind at the prospects before him.

"DEAR OLD FRIEND,

" Are you still alive? I have to ask this question considering the length of time that has passed since you left us, during which you have not written to us, but have treated us faithlessly. . . .

" Why are you sticking so closely to this abominable Graz? Does it possess some magic circle for you which is keeping you from the rest of the world? I had a presentiment when you left that you would not return soon. You have composed two symphonies which are so excellent that I hear nothing but good about them everywhere. You might send some news to your old friend. . . .

" I expect you have heard that I am doing pretty well. With all my heart I hope that you fare equally well.

" Contrive to be my friend and do not forget

" Your

" SCHUBERT."

This reference to " doing pretty well " does not necessarily mean that he was in receipt of any definite income. He was possibly referring to his prospects, for the letter was written on January 21st, two days after he had completed *Die Zwillingsbrüder,* and the possibility of theatrical production of his work carried his spirits high. He had every right to believe that he was at the door of success which had opened so willingly to the young Rossini. He foresaw the chance of public recognition.

But that he was able to make a little money is certain, because in the summer he went off to Steyr on a holiday with Vogl and paid his own travelling expenses. *Die Zwillingsbrüder* had then come and gone, so brief in its run as to be no more than an episode in the life of theatrical Vienna. That it provided a few florins for the composer is certain, and he spent them on this holiday. The association with Vogl had now developed into a close intimacy.

At Steyr Vogl stayed with his relatives and with Sylvester Paumgartner, a great musical enthusiast, a good 'cellist, and the owner of a remarkable musical library and collection of musical instruments. Schubert became the guest of Dr. Albert Schellman, a barrister in the town, and an excellent amateur pianist. He also stayed with Josef von Koller, a wealthy merchant, who devoted much time and money to music. Stadler was present at Steyr, and he describes[1] one of the musical evenings at Koller's.

" In Josef v. Koller's house at Steyr we usually had music after an evening walk, or after the day's work was done. The very talented daughter Josefine, Schubert, Vogl and I enjoyed the most agreeable hours in the alternate performance of Schubert's songs and pianoforte pieces, and also many operatic pieces of Vogl's most brilliant period. An interesting episode I remember was the attempt—among ourselves, of course—to sing the *Erl-King a tre.* Schubert sang the father, Vogl the Erl-King, Josefine the child, while I accompanied. After the music we had supper and remained merrily together for a few hours."

On these musical occasions the host, and not Schubert, was

---

[1] Anton Stadler: Letter to Luib.

69

usually the accompanist of Vogl. Ebner, who married Schellman's daughter, states, on the authority of his wife, that when Schubert was staying with Vogl in her parents' house, he took the " Forte-piano " into his room, so that they had to miss their dancing during his stay. Vogl found that Schubert would not accommodate himself to the arbitrary manner in which he sang his songs (with ritardandos, rubatos and embellishments), and as he, the great singer and ex-perienced artiste, would not give in to the composer, they *agreed* that Dr. Schellman should be Vogl's accompanist, since he was an excellent pianist and willing to accommodate himself to Vogl's whims and fancies.[1]

A few months previously Schubert had reproached Anselm Hüttenbrenner for being a bad correspondent, but there was no worse correspondent alive than Franz himself. He ignored letters for months. He lost more than one friend through this indolent pen that could only write music. His brother Ferdinand, who adored him, wrote continuously begging for news. Schoolmaster Schubert would chide his son for his shortcomings as a correspondent and commend him always to God. Ignaz usually preserved a reproachful silence. But we find Franz writing one of his few letters from Steyr to brother Ferdinand (July 15th, 1819).

" DEAR BROTHER,

" I trust this letter will reach you in Vienna, and that you are feeling well. I am writing now to ask you to send the *Stabat Mater* as quickly as you can, as we are very anxious to perform it there. I have been very well, but the weather is wretched. Yester-day we had a thunderstorm, and the lightning killed a girl and injured two men.

" There are eight girls in the house in which I am living, and practically all of them are good looking. You can realize that I am kept busy. Herr v. Koller, with whom Vogl and myself dine every evening, has a very pretty daughter. She plays the piano rather well, and intends to sing a number of songs. . . .

"Your ever true brother,
" FRANZ."

From Steyr Vogl and Schubert passed on to Linz. They stayed with Spaun's brother-in-law, Anton Ottenwald, and with Emil Gottscheer—two homes devoted to music. Another of Schubert's

[1] Authority: Professor Otto Erich Deutsch.

THE FIRST PAGE OF THE SCORE OF "DIE FORELLE"

(THE TROUT)

The blot in the corner was caused by Schubert picking up the ink instead of the sandbox to dry the page, due to the fact that he had completed the composition very late at night and was tired

KATHI FRÖHLICH

ANNA FRÖHLICH

JOSEFINE FRÖHLICH

BARBARA FRÖHLICH

THE FOUR GRACES

spasmodic letters went to Vienna—this time to Mayrhofer on behalf of a friend. Schubert could always bring himself to write a letter in the interests of kindness.

"Linz,

"*Aug. 19th, 1819.*

"DEAR MAYRHOFER,

"If you are feeling as well as I am, then you are in excellent health. I was at Spaun's home, and met Kenner, Kreil and Forstmayer, made the acquaintance of Spaun's mother and of Ottenwald. I sang his cradle song, which I had set to music. . . .

"I recommend the bearer of this letter to you. He is a student from Kremsmünster named Kahl, and he is passing through Vienna on his way to Idria, where his parents reside. I beg you to let him have my bed during his stay in Vienna. I should be very glad if you would look after him, for he is a decent, kindly creature. . . . We have been celebrating Vogl's birthday with a cantata. Stadler wrote the words, which I set to music. It was a success. Good-bye till the middle of September.

"Your friend,

"FRANZ SCHUBERT.

"Herr v. Vogl sends his regards to you. Best love to Spaun."

Schubert returned to Vienna with Vogl in the Autumn of 1819 and resought his old haunts. He would dine frequently at a little restaurant in the Schlossergässchen, a narrow and crooked lane between the Graben and the Stefansplatz, which has since disappeared. It was in this restaurant that he first saw Vogl off the stage, a year or more before Schober brought them together. Vogl was dining at an adjacent table. He knew nothing of Schubert, nor could he foresee that the young man who watched him so intently and with such admiration was to be the friend of later years and the maker of his best songs.

In an upper room of the restaurant there met regularly one of the most brilliant gatherings of young men ever brought into contact by bohemianism and art. They had a club there called Ludlam's Cave. This club had been originated in 1810 among the dancers and actors of the town by Castelli, dramatist, editor of a musical paper, and writer of poetry. Schubert set two of his songs and also his *libretto* of *The Conspirators*, translated from the French, but the title was altered to *The Domestic War* for fear of the Censor. At first these people met in a beer-house "Zum Fliegenden

Rössl" (the Flying Horse) near the Kärntnerthor. Castelli was head of the Club, which to a large extent was always made up of irresponsibles, and had not yet included in its activities serious discussion and encouragement of the Art of the day. He taught them to speak on their hands and fingers, and fined those who did not know the signs. One day he delivered a humorous sermon while the dancer Reinoldi, hidden under a large cloak behind his back, accompanied him with gestures of his hands. They instituted an order known as the " Rostbratel Orden," the decoration of which consisted of a cardboard disc, on which was drawn a joint of roast-beef, and the disc was worn hanging by a green ribbon.[1]

The police of Vienna grew suspicious. They thrived on suspicion in those days. They scented Jacobin intrigue and propaganda. Regular reports were sent into police head-quarters about the mad behaviour of Castelli and his satellites. They became more fearful. They were quite certain that this gang of irresponsible young men contained the germs of a dangerous secret society which would operate against the State. They decided to confiscate the funds and all the belongings of the Society, even though they could not bring the slightest proof of any misdoing against its members.

The Society had to move. A little later it reappeared in the hostelry " Zum Blumen Stöckchen " (the Flowering Plant). Now music and debate in some measure displaced the playing of pranks. They sang solos and community songs, and had long and heated discussions on Art. Julius, afterwards Sir Julius, Benedict, was one of its members. When the Society adjourned for the night they had an orgy of bell-pulling at the houses down the street. People were summoned from their beds thereby to see the miscreants disappearing into the dark lanes.

It happened that at this time the Danish poet Oehlenschläger produced a fairy play called *Ludlams Höhle* (Ludlam's Cave). All the members of the Society attended the performance, after which they adjourned to the restaurant above mentioned, where Schubert often took his meals. The landlord was genial, the beer was good. The members remained there half the night and resolved to adopt the place. They named it Ludlam's Cave.

Ludlam's Cave could be identified in the dark lane by the figure of a nude Bacchus riding on a cask over the door. One entered by a low door, passed up a narrow winding staircase into a large but dim guest-room. The room was long, very full of tobacco smoke,

[1] Castelli: Memoirs.

and possessed but one window. In the centre of the room was a long table with chairs around it. The Court actor, Carl Schwartz, a tall powerfully-built man with a big stomach, a very red face and bushy grey hair, was then appointed Calif of the Society. Because of Schwartz's colouring he was called " The Red Moor," and this led to the Society's motto, " Red is black, and black is red." When Schwartz was asked the meaning of the Society's motto he replied: " What is the colour of my face? Red. And what is my name? Schwartz (black)." When asked why he had been elected as head of the Society he answered quite frankly: " Because I am the most dense man in it, and have a daughter." Both these qualifications had been fixed by Statute as essential for the Calif.[1]

Ludlam's Cave rapidly became famous. It drew to its gatherings all the brilliant young men in Vienna, among them Grillparzer the poet, Rückert, von Zedlitz, Sapphir, Carl Maria von Weber, Ignaz Moscheles, Julius Benedict, Rellstab, and many others. There were in all a hundred members, and most of them appeared regularly at the Cave. The members were called " bodies," and were allowed to bring aspirants for membership who were called " shadows." Moreover, the Society ran five papers in Vienna, in one of which, *Die Wische*, Calif Schwartz published all his jokes.[2] The poets of the Cave wrote special songs, which its musicians set to music. On one occasion a prize was offered for a tragi-comedy in three acts, of which three authors wrote one act each, and this nonsense opera with several choruses was composed by Karl Blum and Moscheles.

Schubert was thus drawn into Ludlam's Cave, and became a " Shadow." He was at length put up for membership. But before the election could take place the police, with the same lack of justification as before, descended once again on the Society, confiscated its funds and wiped out in a night the most brilliant intellectual society Vienna has ever known. They locked up the Club's officials in prison, and brought them up for justice in the morning. And, to the credit of Vienna be it said, they got it. The trial caused great hilarity among the judges; the police were laughed at. They had determined to expel Castelli from the country and heavily fine his associates, instead of which the prisoners were set free, hailed as good fellows by the Court, but advised to dissolve their Society.

So Ludlam's Cave came to an end. The Chief of Police, von Perza, who thought he had achieved a coup, was so chagrined by

---

[1] Castelli: Memoirs.   [2] *Ibid.*

the laughter hurled at him for his foolishness that he committed suicide by throwing himself out of an upper-floor window.

As for Calif Carl Schwartz, he never recovered from the passing of Ludlam's Cave. When a little later he lay on his death-bed he exclaimed with an air of finality: " It is all over with me, my friend. I cannot, and do not wish to live any longer, because Ludlam is no more."[1] And the day before his death he gave a ball!

The destruction of Ludlam's Cave killed its Calif. Grillparzer the poet, his artistic soul aflame at the affront to a Society of men of intellect, angrily shook the dust of Vienna from his shoes and went for a time to another land, to Germany, to write his poetry.

[1] Castelli: Memoirs.

CHAPTER IX

Schubert and the Four Graces

(1820-1)

SCHUBERT was changing. The years 1820 and 1821 reveal a definite inward change in him. Outwardly he was the same. His musical ardour nevertheless drew new enthusiasm from an inexhaustible storehouse. The restless gaiety which his friends had known so long—the gaiety of a joyous personality whom they loved—appeared to be unspoiled. But a riper knowledge had come to him, much of it the result of suffering. He was given to periodical fits of gloom which he carefully concealed from those about him. At the end of 1820, when none of his works had been printed, when his *Zwillingsbrüder* had faded away in dismal fashion, he could have foreseen no future that would relieve the pressure of debt. Only the obscurity of clouds up to the far horizon.

He had moods of intense religious feeling. The religious music of Bach and Handel, the profound thought of Mozart in his serious themes moved him deeply. In February he composed in the space of a fortnight his Easter Cantata *Lazarus, or The Feast of the Resurrection,* a work in three parts based on the libretto of a theological professor, one Niemeyer of Halle. It was performed in April, and then the manuscript disappeared. His songs became fewer. He composed seventeen in 1820, but the beauty and richness of feeling of his work seemed to increase. His *Der Jüngling auf dem Hügel, Die Sterne,* his *Waldesnacht* all demonstrate the emotion of the year's bringing. He also began a new opera *Sakuntala,* sketched out two acts of it and then, disgusted with the poor libretto, put it aside fo ever.

His circle was growing. The Fröhlich sisters became attached to him, and began to exploit his music. With them came Grillparzer.

75

A year later Schwind, the painter, came into the circle, and he, in his turn, brought in Bauernfeld.

Examine the members of the Schubert circle, the differing personalities and the conflicting temperaments. It would require more than the common bond of friendship to make of these opposites a *coterie* so united. Spaun, level-headed and true to the mission of making the best of life. Vogl, captious, overweening in manner, reading his classics and his Bible whilst awaiting his cue at the Opera, and experiencing a life of adulation on the one hand, and of severe self-discipline on the other. Mayrhofer drawing the closer into the deeps of gloom as the years passed, awaking to sudden flashes of light, and at such times writing verse of moderate beauty. Schober the man of good looks, accomplished and idle, who found time only for the pleasure of life. Hüttenbrenner as sound and practical as Spaun. Grillparzer the dramatist, all pride and moods, the classic writer of his Austria. The lesser members of the circle were equally diverse in their personalities, but were men of cleverness. It was impossible for a person of mediocrity to enter the circle, however attractive his personality.

Genius alone could not have drawn to itself and welded such a circle of differing personality and activity. Without Schubert, most of these people would not have been in common touch. Broadly speaking, they were diverse in their thoughts. Their ambitions and ideals sought differing horizons. It was the extraordinary personality of Schubert that blended them. The richness of his mental gifts adorned his poverty, but it was the secret lodestone of his heart that brought these friends together and held them.

Schubert's mentality attracted to himself those of artistic nature, who strove for the Art in which they believed, and were content to suffer for it. Schober was the sole exception. He possessed a brilliant intellect and squandered his intellectuality. In days that were to come he certainly led the feet of Schubert towards paths they might never have sought or found alone. But he earned the forgiveness of posterity by the fact that he helped Schubert for some years after he left the Convict. Not only had he given him food and shelter, but by his assurance he had kept bright the courage in him.

" My work has been conceived by my understanding of music and by my suffering. It is the latter that seems to interest the world least," Schubert wrote bitterly in his diary. How truly he expressed himself in a confession intended for no eyes but his own.

And yet at this very time the Fates were arranging a better order of things for him. For a long time he had been on intimate terms with Dr. Ignaz von Sonnleithner, a lawyer who was also a professor of commercial science, and with his son Leopold.

The Professor himself had a good bass voice, he sang operatic parts, both light and serious, with great feeling. He had always moved in musical circles; he had walked with the immortals. Haydn and Mozart had been his friends, and, later, Beethoven and Salieri. They had been intimates. They had taught him how to perform their work. How proud his memories, when ageing and infirm, his mind wandered to those giants he had known, whose masterpieces he had viewed in the making! His wife Anna was also a lover of music, though a poor performer. But the flame of music was kept burning in the Sonnleithner house. Their son Leopold had been a school colleague of Schubert's. They had shared the same birth-year. Small wonder then that Schubert with his talents was readily taken into the Sonnleithner circle and assessed at his proper value.

The Sonnleithners' house in the Gundelhof was one of the best-known musical houses in Vienna. The real artists sang there, and from time to time foreign singers of repute appeared. Every Friday during the summer months, and at least once a fortnight during winter, more than a hundred people assembled at the Sonnleithners' for music. Reissiger, the composer, took part in some of these evenings. One after another, Schubert's songs were copied out and sung at the Sonnleithners'. They gave his *Prometheus,* the only performance since it was produced in the garden of Professor Watteroth's house four years previously; and it was at the Sonnleithners' that a talented amateur, Gymnich, sang the *Erl-King,* accompanied by Anna Fröhlich. Schubert's *Gretchen am Spinnrad, Das Dörfchen,* and indeed most of his more popular songs were sung there.

Schubert's friendship with the Sonnleithners had led to his meeting with the Fröhlich sisters in 1820. They were four brilliant women, who, without the benefit of higher education, became famous for their artistic talents. Their father had been a vintner—a bad vintner. Through indolence and bad management the business had failed and was closed. Fröhlich then drew aside in poverty and watched his daughters make a living.

Anna Fröhlich, the elder of the sisters, was three years senior to Schubert. She was short and was nicknamed the Gnome, very beautiful in the Italian style, with black eyes, vivacious and affectionate. She loved laughter, but had a habit of suddenly breaking into tears of violent emotion.[1] She had been taught music by Hummel, and when the *Konservatorium*, which had been founded by the Society of Friends of Music, was opened in Vienna in 1819 she became a teacher there. The second Fröhlich, Barbara, possessed talents in another direction. Although musically she was as brilliant as her sisters, she became a painter and was trained by Daffinger, many of whose pictures she copied. She soon became noted for her paintings of flowers, and ultimately married Ferdinand Bogner, the flute player.

The two younger sisters, Kathi and Josefine, are perhaps the more interesting. Kathi, three years younger than Schubert, was clever, lively and full of feeling, rather " touchy " but beautiful. She was slender of figure, with oval face and eyes of the deepest black. So attractive was she that the Emperor Franz had noticed her at play when she was a small child, and catching her up had stroked her long black curls. Josefine lacked the beauty of her sister, but developed a graceful soprano voice and went on the concert stage in Vienna. Soon after her meeting with Schubert she had an ambition for opera. She appeared at the Kärntnerthor Theatre in *Il Seraglio*, but only with moderate success. She played at Copenhagen, at Dresden, Venice and Milan, and sang Italian operatic music in all the renowned drawing-rooms of Vienna. Success did not spoil her. She made her own clothes, darned her own stockings, and saved every kreutzer she could. When she came back from the Opera she would diligently sit down to mend her linen. But at the end of it all came disappointment. She failed to reach the ultimate triumph of opera. Her voice began to lose its mellowness; she saw younger singers rise and surpass her. Her last appearance in Milan convinced her that she was a failure. Then she gave up public singing and devoted the rest of her time to teaching.

The Fröhlich sisters kept open house to all interested in music. The sounds of instruments or singing continued regularly far into the small hours of the morning. They entertained in simple fashion and chattered ceaselessly. During the next two years Schubert visited the house regularly, and a few months after he came under the influence of the Fröhlichs the poet Grillparzer joined them as the result of a meeting which took place at a musical evening given by the Geymüller family. It was a fortunate meeting for all

[1] This is how Theodor von Karajan, who was in Grillparzer's office described her.

concerned. In Grillparzer, Schubert found a friend. In Kathi Fröhlich, Grillparzer discovered the passion of his life.

Grillparzer was not attracted by Kathi Fröhlich at their first meeting. He disliked her manner of speech, and he regarded her rather as a curiosity than as a woman of flame. There was no suggestion here of the great fire that was to blaze so soon. But at their second meeting their temperaments seemed to blend, and again it was at a musical party that they came together. Schubert was playing the piano, and when he finished the poet got up and walked across to where Kathi Fröhlich was sitting. He looked long and silently into her black eyes, as if the magic fingers of Schubert on the keyboard had expressed something in common between them, had aroused some chord of understanding, and brought two passionate forces together. He asked for her birthday-book and wrote in it: " For hearts and for minds the moment is supreme."[1] He wrote impassioned letters to his friends about the beauty of Kathi. He expressed the wonder of her in his poem, "All-Presence." His " Libussa " is a portrait of her. His poem " *Still sass sie da, die Lieblichste von allen* " gives a picture in words of Kathi sitting listening to Schubert's music.

The romance with Kathi Fröhlich gave an added beauty to Grillparzer's work. His poetry came from him with greater fluency: he seemed to exist in some ethereal realm of dreams. Poem after poem of brilliance was found ready for Schubert's music when Franz visited the Fröhlichs' house.

Two years later Grillparzer resolved to marry Kathi. They began to buy furniture. But strange and conflicting emotions were stirring in the poet. He became restless; he gave himself to moods of jealousy. Dark clouds of suspicion and distrust obstructed his thoughts and drove him from his work. He evoked deep despairs, sharp and senseless irritation as he thought of Kathi with all sorts of imaginary lovers. Then sanity would succeed these delusions, only to be broken again by a mood uglier than its predecessor. Gradually, almost unconsciously, the lovers were drawing apart, though in Kathi the devotion to Grillparzer never wavered. The more strenuously Grillparzer endeavoured to escape from the thrall of his love for Kathi Fröhlich, the greater became his anguish. He endured mental suffering of the most desperate kind. He ate little, and sleep deserted him. His pen, which so willingly became his comrade for expression in the hours of mental exaltation, almost

---

[1] Hans Sittenburger: " Grillparzer und Die Frauen."

refused its office; and such work as he produced—his ' Tristitia ex Ponto," for example—reflects his mournful mood. He sat brooding in his chair for hours. We glimpse something of the stress that held him in his poem " Thoughts at a Window," written at Grinzing in the summer of 1822, wherein he sees in the threatening clouds of an approaching thunderstorm an analogy with the existing circum-stances of his life.

Eventually the romance which had brought such fine thought into beautiful expression was broken off by Grillparzer in a letter to Josefine, not to the woman he had adored. He stated—and it was no more than an excuse—that he had heard that Kathi had an affair with a man at Achau. The news almost destroyed Kathi. She was demented. She feared to meet Grillparzer, and to avoid him she accompanied Josefine on a concert tour to Milan. The furniture that had been purchased for the home they were going to set up was dispersed. They had written love letters to each other, although they lived in the same house. Bundles of these letters that had been stored with such reverence went on the fire. In the madness of his emotion Grillparzer became feverishly attracted by another woman named Marie Smolenz, but after a few months of unstable belief in a newly-created life, he came back to the only ruler of his thoughts—Kathi.

During this *débâcle* of her love, Kathi had written abundant letters to her sisters, beseeching them to use every means that would make for the comfort of the man who had discarded her. She disclosed the secrets of a heart that beat still for the poet, knowing that those secrets would be passed on to the person for whom they were intended.

The inevitable happened. Grillparzer could live without her no longer. He was suffering. His work had become indifferent to him, when he was able to work at all. Kathi Fröhlich, in her turn, jilted another man who had offered her marriage, and returned to Vienna, to Grillparzer. But the old fires had burned low, and some beautiful phœnix was arising from the ashes. Gone the furniture and the motive that prompted its purchase. Gone all desire of marriage. Instead there grew up between these two a wonderful friendship that never languished, that stood firm against the comment of a critical world, and the test of years. Grillparzer would depart on some journey through Europe and send no word to Kathi of his welfare. Kathi, when she knew where he could be found, would refrain from writing to him for fear of disturbing or troubling him.

" All that is good in me I have from him," she declared.[1] Life could offer no greater devotion.

Ultimately Grillparzer went to live with the Fröhlich sisters. A strange and difficult man. He had moods of violent depression brought about by a sense of failure to reach his ideals. He was struggling for spiritual freedom, mental freedom which he felt he could not attain. At such times days would pass and he would not speak. " To really exist in a dual form was forbidden to me by my solitude," he said on one occasion. " I must love all four," he added, referring to the sisters. " I cannot love singly." But it was only Kathi who was pursuing him with her love.

Grillparzer, still in a Government office when Kathi Fröhlich returned, was bored to extinction by the monotonous life, but he realized that a poet who lives in moods can be a sad fellow to himself save for continual occupation. He usually came home grumbling. He was peevish, then the cloud across his mind would disappear, the sweet disposition of the man would show itself, and one would get a glimpse of a fine soul.

" God greet you, girls! " he would exclaim as he came in at evening with the blackness of night in his face. " Damnation and hell to it! Where's Anna? "

Anna: " Greet you God, Grillparzer, why are you so disagreeable? "

Grillparzer: " Who would not be disagreeable? Hell to it all! That's right, laugh at me that I am such a fool as to remain in a Government office. I can stand it no longer. Come, Anna, sit down with me, and let us play a piece for four hands, and mind you pay attention."

So he played. Played to his mood, now too slow, now too fast. He would jump up angrily and begin to sing a scale, ten times, a hundred times. Then he would exclaim: " The whole lot of you don't know anything. I go on singing for years and years, and I do not sing a scrap better."

Then Kathi would exclaim under her breath:

" It's age, Grillparzer, age! "

" Who talks about age? " is the blunt challenge. " Who's old? I am older than any of you, but you can learn from me what strength and vitality is." And hurrying into the next room he would throw himself down on the couch in despair.[2]

---

[1] Grillparzer Annals: August Sauer Essay.
[2] *Ibid.*

The associations with the Fröhlichs and Grillparzer were of the utmost importance in the development of Schubert. Evenings of his music were held regularly in the Fröhlich household. Grillparzer, under the thrall of Kathi, had reached the fullest richness of his writing.

" When Schubert was introduced to us," said Anna Fröhlich,[1] " he used to come to the musical evenings which I was then giving at our rooms. I can see Schubert now. He had folded his hands in deep emotion as if in prayer, and pressed them to his mouth, as he was accustomed to do when he listened to anything beautiful. Then he exclaimed: ' Oh God, what a treat this is! ' Presently he added suddenly: ' I know what I am going to do! '

" Within a few days he brought me the quartetto *Gott ist mein Hirt*, and soon afterwards, the quartetto *Gott in der Natur*. Apart from these two things he composed for me the *Serenade*, and then *Miriam's Song of Victory*. The latter was really written for Josefine, or, perhaps I ought to say, for all four of us."

It was Anna Fröhlich who secured for Schubert the commission to write *Der Schicksalslenker*. Baroness Geymüller wished to have a song set to music, and she expressed this wish to Anna Fröhlich, who approached Schubert and asked him to set the words. For this Schubert received fifty florins.

" Poor Schubert," she said. " His was a magnificent soul. He was never jealous or grudging to others, as is the case with so many people. On the contrary, he was overjoyed when beautiful music was performed. He folded his hands and placed them against his mouth, and sat there as if in ecstasy. The purity of his mind, the lack of all thought of guile, are beyond expression. Often he would sit down with us on the sofa and rub his hands and say: ' To-day I have composed something with which I believe I have been really successful.' "

The Fröhlich sisters at this period were the only women who shared Schubert's thoughts. In their rooms he sat for hours, linked to them by the bonds of music. His poverty did not shame him. Never in the whole of his life did his poverty shame him, unless it happened on that night when in the company of Anselm Hüttenbrenner he had sat in the gallery of the theatre, ashamed to take his call on the stage because he was not wearing respectable clothes. The garments which he wore were never of any account. He was

---

[1] From a manuscript in the possession of Professor Otto Erich Deutsch: " From Grillparzer's House," by Frau Gerhard von Breuning.

entirely out of date in all fashions, because he probably never knew that such a thing as fashion existed. A suit was mere clothing designed for the definite purpose of hiding nakedness. It ceased to function only when he suddenly became aware of its disreputable appearance; for he disliked being untidy.

The consciousness to Schubert of his poverty came to him at times in waves of acute feeling. It was despair, not shame. He reproached, not himself, but a world that could not, would not understand him. The overpowering moods of depression assailed him for an hour, killed his spirit, gnawed at his courage, till Mayr-hofer or Spaun took him out to dinner at a *Gasthaus*. Then his secret fears, the timidity of humility which his poverty often brought to him, disappeared.

The musical functions held at the Sonnleithners' and the Fröh-lichs' were making Schubert's work known to a rapidly widening circle. On Ash Wednesday, March 7th, 1821, the Sonnleithners gave a concert at the Kärntnerthor Theatre in the cause of charity. At his function Vogl sang the *Erl-King*, accompanied by Anselm Hüttenbrenner because Schubert was too shy to appear on the plat-form. Now for the first time Vienna publicly heard the *Erl-King*, apart from the semi-private performances at the Sonnleithners' house. There was such a storm of applause that Vogl had to sing the song again.

It was Leopold von Sonnleithner who first endeavoured to get the music engraved, and he was encouraged in this by Anna Fröh-lich. He discussed the matter with Gymnich, whose singing of the *Erl-King* had aroused so much enthusiasm. They decided to leave nothing undone that would assist towards the production of some of Schubert's songs. The *Erl-King* was offered to two publishers, Diabelli and Haslinger, and refused by both. They not only flatly declared that they would pay nothing for the song, but, since Schubert was unknown among the music-sellers, it would not pay them to engrave the score.

To get the work of this immortal published at all it had to be done by private subscription! The attitude of these music-publishers was not one of over-caution only, but also showed lack of any discernment. The *Erl-King* was well known at the time to a certain circle in which those who understood music moved, but the publishers defied the opinion of that circle. They pronounced the *Erl-King* to be worth nothing.

Leopold von Sonnleithner, to his eternal credit, thought otherwise. The ignorance of the publishers and their mulish refusals caused him to seek other means of making Schubert known through the medium of print. Four men, of whom Leopold von Sonnleithner and Gymnich were two, put up sufficient money to pay the cost of engraving the collection of Schubert's songs, copies of which the first-mentioned possessed. This committee then heaped coals of fire on the head of Diabelli by giving him an order to print the first part of the songs at their expense. They printed exactly one hundred copies.

The printed music arrived in time for a musical evening at the Kiesewetters'.[1] Anna Fröhlich, who was present, states[2] that Leopold von Sonnleithner put the whole parcel on the pianoforte and said: "If any one wishes to possess these songs, he can buy them in these books."

The whole edition was subscribed for on the spot, which provided the money necessary to ensure the publication of the second volume. Anna Fröhlich bought one of these books at the Kiesewetters' that evening, and ultimately gave it, a little tattered and torn, to the Mozarteum at Salzburg. The *Erl-King,* the first work published, was dedicated to Count Moritz Dietrichstein, head of the music at the Viennese Court. The second work to be engraved was *Gretchen at the Spinning Wheel,* which the composer now dedicated to Reichsgraf Moritz von Fries.

Schubert's delight at the launching of his work was boundless. A future had opened out to him; a path appeared, however misty and obscure, in what had been so far a wilderness. The works as they were published were bought up immediately. All copies of the earlier books were autographed by Schubert "Sch.," and when in due course other books of the songs followed they were autographed "Scht." in the lower right-hand corner of the back page.

Out of the money derived by the sale of these songs Leopold von Sonnleithner states that he and the other friends paid Schubert's arrears of rent, his shoemaker's and tailors' bills, all his arrears at the restaurant and coffee houses, and in addition they handed over a substantial amount to him. Unfortunately he had no idea of economy, and "was often persuaded by his wine-house companions (mostly painters and poets and a few musicinas) to

---

[1] Both Kreissle and Grove declare that the music was first subscribed for at a soirée at Dr. Sonnleithner's house, but this is not so, as Anna Fröhlich testifies.

[2] From MS. in the possession of Professor Otto Erich Deutsch entitled " From Grillparzer's House," by Frau Gerhard von Breuning.

unnecessary expenditure the benefits whereof the others enjoyed more than he did." [1]

Schubert was now clear of debt. Indeed, for the first time in his life he was in funds, for he had averaged from the sale of each book 165 florins. The patrons to whom the works had been dedicated had also done what was expected of them.

" Now I must let you know," Schubert wrote to Spaun in November, " that my dedications have had this effect. The Patriarch [2] has given 12 and Fries 20 ducats at the instigation of Vogl, and I am benefiting by this. When you are writing to the Patriarch be so kind as to render my thanks due to him. Schober's opera has got as far as the 3rd Act. [3] I wish so much that you could be present at its production."

The music publishers began to show interest when the composer they had despised sold out his works almost as soon as they were published. In one year the *Erl-King* brought in 800 gulden. Then in a mad moment Schubert sold to Diabelli all the plates and rights in the published songs, and tied himself up to this Viennese Barabbas for the equivalent of seventy pounds. Diabelli had preyed on Schubert's poverty in an unguarded hour. He continued to thrive on Schubert. Respected personage as he considered himself to be in the world of music, he kept Schubert poor, and bloated his own private purse by so doing. He made out of the *Wanderer* alone during the next few years nearly three thousand pounds. A bonus, however small, to the composer who was suffering the flagellation of poverty would not have been amiss, but Diabelli was not prone to do such things. He went on plundering Schubert in his fashion.

Schubert's publishers always treated him as some underdog to whom the smallest bone was a gift from God. They changed the titles of his dances without even consulting him. They cut pieces out of his works without the courtesy of asking permission. When, on one occasion, Schubert heard his *Valse Triste* (*Trauerwalzer*) he recognized the music but not the title.

" What sort of a donkey ever composed a *valse triste!* " he exclaimed. [4]

---

[1] A. Farreau: "Leopold von Sonnleithner's Reminiscences of Schubert."
[2] Ladislaus Pyrker, Patriarch of Venice, to whom Schubert dedicated one of the parts published.
[3] *Alfonso and Estrella.*   [4] Spaun: ' 'Remarks on Kreissle."

CHAPTER X

Schubert's Illness

(1822)

INTIMATE as Schubert's associations with Schober had been, he seemed to conceive a still deeper affection for him during 1821. The links that bound them drew closer, the understanding became more complete. So intimate had the friendship become that Schubert blended their two names, and called Schober " Schobert." Schober's personality had a strange attraction. Women adored him in spite of his crooked legs. Men who quarrelled with him admitted to themselves that the fellow had a measure of attraction vouchsafed to few.

Schober was the most engaging man who never did anything, yet attempted everything. He was Swedish by birth, and Schubert's senior by a year. As a child he had watched through a telescope Lord Nelson's siege of Copenhagen. He had seen a Danish warship blow up under the hammering of the English guns. Then on the death of his father he was brought to Central Europe. He received a Scandinavian scholarship and eventually entered the Convict at Vienna, only to leave it two years before the arrival of Schubert. He was an adventurous soul. He studied for the law, but threw the law over in 1818 because it was too monotonous for him. He decided to pledge himself to all forms of Art. He painted, wrote poetry, plays, attended every first night, was seen in all the best musical *salons.*

He lived on the high tide of life, loved freely, and could not be troubled with hatred of anybody. Schober was all Romance, good looks, gay words, and he was ever fluent and cultured in conversation. He looked admirable in a drawing-room; he *was* admirable. He could never be anything else. He was not suited to the roughness of life, since he was a materialist gifted with a very artistic mind. A romantic mind.

Romance was in the blood of the Schobers. His sister, Ludwiga, had heard the Italian singer Siboni in Spontini's *La Vestale*, and had fallen in love with him. She went home and drew a portrait of Siboni from memory—a portrait so remarkable that it was engraved by David Weiss. Although Ludwiga was engaged to a high official in a Government office, she persisted in her pursuit of Siboni until he was compelled to marry her. Shortly afterwards Siboni shot his wife dead with a gun he was about to unload. It appeared to be an accident, but, since it was said that he had strangled a former wife, many attributed the second affair to an "Italian temperamental accident!" The Schobers in the course of events forgave Siboni his fumbling with a gun, and reaccepted him into the Schober household.[1] Possibly they regarded Ludwiga as a victim predestined by Fate to what had occurred.

In the Autumn of 1821 Schober and Schubert went together to Ochsenburg, where they stayed with Schober's uncle, Court-Councillor von Dankesreither. A Baroness Mink was hostess. The reputation of Schubert drew to the house the highest society of the countryside, and three baronesses were amongst those who came to the *Schubertiaden*, which were given in the same manner as those in Vienna. The *Schubertiaden* were musical evenings given at private houses for the express purpose of performing Schubert's music. Bauernfeld in his "Reminiscences of Old Vienna" says: "Then again there might come Schubert evenings so-called *Schubertiaden*, with many lively fellows, where the wine ran in rivers, and the exquisite Vogl regaled us with all the glorious songs, which poor Franz Schubert had to accompany until his stumpy fingers almost refused to act."

The music was often followed by parlour games, and the evening finished with a "Würstelball," so called from the little sausages (*Würstel*) which were served as refreshments at these entertainments. The "Würstelballs" were then very popular with the young people of Vienna.

"What with the balls and concerts we had a lot to do at Ochsenburg, in spite of which we were diligent," wrote Schober, referring to their work on *Alfonso and Estrella*. The hours not spent in work found them in the country; on long walks together, picnics, flirtations. Schubert, eternally shy of the petticoat, not

---

[1] Professor Otto Erich Deutsch: Lecture on Schober at Malmö.

because of any sloth in the stirring of sex, but because of the lack of expression in his words, was carried forward by Schober. Schober the gallant required no laggard in Schubert.

By the end of the year Schubert was back in Vienna. Schober had completed his third act of *Alfonso,* and his collaborator had set many of his recitatives. *Alfonso* is a lyrical poem, and if it is one of the best *libretti* Schubert ever set, it is at the same time the worst conceived for operatic production, by reason of the author's ignorance of operatic construction. This does not seem to have troubled Schubert, who completed the setting in the following February.

Christmas came, and Schubert spent the season with Anschütz, the greatest actor of his time. He was a man of simple tastes, but of unbreakable stubbornness in pursuit of his artistic ideals. There was a large house party. Dances went on long into the night, and at this period Schubert was composing dances extensively.

As this was the first Christmas Anschütz had spent in Vienna, he determined to spare no effort to make it a success. His first endeavour was to buy a Christmas-tree. Being fond of children, he had decided to get as many children as possible to the party. But to his surprise he found that in this Catholic city such things as Christmas-trees were unknown. Shopmen stared at him vaguely when he asked for them; wood-cutters had never heard of such trees. St. Nicholas—the English misplaced Santa Claus—whose feast is early in December, they knew as one by reason of whom children received presents. But of *Christmas* presents they knew nothing, and still less of *Christmas*-trees. Anschütz, however, persisted in his search for a Christmas-tree and continued his preparations. Since he was a well-known figure, these things were soon talked about. He got his tree. More than that, he started the Christmas-tree habit in Vienna.

" I may really say," he stated,[1] " that my entrance into Vienna has contributed not a little to the general acceptance and popularity of Christmas, for in the very next winter regular fir woods were dragged into Vienna, and every toy vendor and merchant arranged for the new demands of the market.

" This Christmas party was of peculiar interest to me, because it brought Schubert to my house for the first time. He was then one of the most active members of the Nonsense Society. It was through my brothers that he came to the house. His second visit

[1] Johann Anschütz: "Reminiscences from Notes and Verbal Conversations."

happened on an evening that was spent in quite a different way. I had asked some friends, Schubert among them, including a number of young men and women. My wife was young, and my brother Gustav was passionately fond of dancing, and soon the conversation turned on this subject. Schubert, who had already played a few pieces, sat at the piano and broke into dances. They all joined in the circle round him, laughing and drinking. Suddenly I was called away; a stranger was announced. It was a Commissioner of Police, who forbade us to go on with the dancing because it was Lent! When I went back to the room and announced what had happened everybody was alarmed. But Schubert remarked: 'He has done that on purpose. The fellow knows that I like playing dance music!'"

Months passed and the opera was no nearer production. Schubert, disappointed and angry, continued his work slowly. He set Mayrhofer's *Nachtviolen*. Summer arrived with no news of the opera. He produced his *Gott in der Natur* for the Fröhlich sisters, and in August he set Schober's *Todesmusik*. With the coming of the winter he turned again to his beloved Goethe, and set *Die Rose, Der Musensohn,* and several other poems—all of them in a month. His pen refused to keep still. All the buoyancy of spirit for the production of *Alfonso and Estrella* had been sapped and destroyed.

Shortly before Christmas, in sending to Spaun at Linz the dedication of three songs, he wrote:

" I have been composing a Fantasia, a piano duet which is also being engraved and is dedicated to a certain important personage. I have also been composing some new songs by Goethe, *The Return of the Muses, To a Departed One, At the River, Welcome and Farewell.* There is nothing to be done with the opera [*Alfonso*] at Vienna. I have demanded it back and received it. Vogl has left the theatre. I shall send it to Dresden, whence I have received an encouraging letter from Weber, or else to Berlin. My Mass is finished and will shortly be produced. I am still adhering to my old opinion that I should dedicate it to the Emperor or to the Empress, as I think the work is a success.

" How is your family? Do write news of them to me soon. I should be quite well if I were not so upset about this abominable affair of my opera, but I am not bothering any more in that direction in view of the fact that Vogl has left the theatre. . . .

" Your faithful friend,
"FRANZ SCHUBERT."

Schubert now seems to have come completely under the sway of Schober. He appeared to study Schober before all people. If he was not actually living with Schober, there was certainly a room in Schober's house which was kept for him. He became influenced by Schober's habits. But in spite of his excesses in other directions, Schober was not a drinker, and there is ample evidence that in the ordinary course of events Schubert did not drink heavily. Had he done so, the vast mass of work which he left as a heritage to the world could not have been composed. Without question there were times when Schubert knew excess, times when his condition was so parlous that he sought comfort in the cup, as a being under restraint and in despair may snatch at any momentary relief.

Towards the end of 1822 Schubert's illness manifested itself. There is little reason to doubt the nature of that illness. He had contracted venereal disease. To blame Schober for this, to heap upon his head blame for his friend's weakness, would be unsound. But his influence upon Schubert was malevolent.

Kreissle and others among Schubert's biographers have avoided stating the nature of Schubert's malady, but it is too important in its effect to be lightly passed over. Its continual recurrence throughout Schubert's remaining years, and at times when he believed himself to be cured, drove him to fits of great depression and impeded his work.[1]

The nature of his illness was without doubt known to his friends at the time. Josef Kenner, who was at the Convict with Schubert and knew both the composer and Schober well, is unyielding in placing the blame on the latter. After Schubert's death he wrote:[2]

" Among other friends, he [Schubert] fell under the spell of a seductively amiable young man of extraordinary talents [Schober] but lacking in moral character. With a firm hand to guide him, this friend might have achieved great things. With his brilliant sophisms he gained over Schubert a lasting and injurious influence. Anyone who knew Schubert was aware of the fact that he was composed of two differing natures. How powerfully the love of enjoyment dragged him down, and how he looked up to the counsel of friends whom he loved. They will understand his devotion to

---

[1] It is interesting to note that when Schubert's skull, together with that of Beethoven, was exhumed on October 12th, 1863, no indications were found that the disease had in any way affected it, or any other part of the skeleton. Nor did a second examination by the anatomist Tolest reveal any effects of the disease upon the bones when they were removed from the Währing to the Central Cemetery in 1888.

[2] Josef Kenner: Letter to Luib.

the false prophet who covered over the lure of the senses with a glittering veneer. Was it not this empty, vain person who drew into his meshes men of far stronger character? "

Kenner then refers in his letter to Schober's shifty, insincere character, which, at a later stage, estranged him from two of his intimate friends, Bauernfeld, whom the composer was to meet in 1825, and Moritz von Schwind, the young painter who became Schubert's friend in 1822 just before the illness developed. Though there was little doubt whom Kenner had pilloried in his indictment, Luib wrote to Kenner again. Luib intended to make himself Schubert's first biographer and he wished to be sure of his ground.

To this letter, Kenner replied[1] that, in his picture of the seducer of Schubert, he did mean Schober, with whom he was intimately acquainted from the time both he and Schubert were at the Convict in 1808.

He continued: " Later experiences proved that in the whole of the Schober family, under the guise of amiable sociability, even cordial friendship, there was moral turpitude. What wonder, then, that Franz chose the same path? . . . To his adherents Schober wanted to be the *one* prophet and god without rival. Whoever did not solely worship him after his manner was deemed incapable of rising to his mental heights, and those who finally turned away from him—no longer held by his phrases and tears—were people whom he persuaded himself he had dropped. With women he had no scruples, and he put them in two categories: those with whom he succeeded, and who he therefore thought were worthy of him, and those with whom he had no success."

Schubert's illness quickly reached a serious stage, and he was placed in the Vienna General Hospital at the beginning of 1823. All patients, whatever their maladies, were jumbled together in the common wards, with the exception of idiots, who were put in a separate ward for mental cases known as " The Fools' Tower." He was dieted very carefully, given special baths, and, it is believed, was treated with mercury. His hair began to fall out, and he was compelled to wear a wig. And yet, in spite of his suffering, the restricted life, the terrible depressions that descended upon him, it was in this hospital that he composed the first of the *Müllerlieder*.[2]

How many weeks Schubert remained in hospital cannot be said with certainty. In those days no records were kept of individual

[1] Kenner MS.: Letter to Luib from Ischl, May 22nd, 1858.
[2] Waldemar Schweisheimer: " Der kranke Schubert."

patients. But apparently he was back in his house by February 1823, for on the 28th he wrote to Ignaz von Mosel: " Forgive me that I must again bother you with a letter, as my health does not yet allow me to leave the house." No sooner did Schubert feel better health returning to him than he discarded his medicines, and set to work again with renewed vigour. He spared himself in nothing. He only considered his illness when the constantly recurring attacks drove him from his work and forced him to fresh despair. " Nobody understands another's sorrow," he wrote out of the bitterness of his depression, " and nobody another's joy. One always believes that he is going towards another, only to discover that one is only walking side by side. Oh, the torment of him who realizes this! "

In August he had sufficiently recovered to go to Steyr, and he wrote to Schober a letter reflecting the depression that now closed about his mind at periodical intervals. " I correspond diligently with Schäffer,[1] and I am fairly well. Whether I shall ever be *quite* well again I almost doubt."

November came and with it a letter from Moritz Schwind to Schober (Nov. 9th, 1823). . . . " The day before there was a kind of bacchanalia at the ' Crown.' We all dined there except Schubert, who was in bed that day. Schäffer and Bernard,[2] who visited him, assured us that he is on the road to recovery, and that in about four weeks' time he will probably be quite well again."

This forecast evidently matured, for at the end of the month Schubert took part in a *Schubertiade* at the house of Schober's mother. On New Year's Eve he and Dr. Bernard visited the painter Mohn, and announced themselves by throwing pebbles at his window, and Schwind drank " Bruderschaft " with the Doctor. Again the medicines were put aside as unnecessary. Again the old life was resumed. Again the enemy struck at him for the neglect of its presence in his body. He suffered from perpetual headaches— long and terrible bouts of headache. In February, 1824, close attention to the Doctor's ruling had mended things again, and Schwind wrote: " Schubert is enduring a fourteen days' fast and stops at home. He looks much better, is in very good spirits and comically hungry." By the end of the month Schubert's hair had grown again, and he was able for the first time to discard his wig.[3]

[1] Dr. August von Schäffer, his doctor.
[2] Both Dr. von Schäffer and Dr. Bernard were ardent Schubertians who used to attend the *Schubertiaden* at the " Hungarian Crown " in the Seilerstätte.
[3] The researches of Dr. Schweisheimer into Schubert's illness have been amplified and confirmed by Professor Otto Erich Deutsch, who is in possession of

From the moment when Schubert was first taken ill in 1822 until his death at the end of 1828, the effects of the malady never really left him. That he was aware of the hold which it had obtained upon him is revealed in a letter he wrote in 1824, when his opera *Fierrabras* was rejected, to his friend Kupelwieser, the painter. Referring to himself, he said: " Picture to yourself a man whose health can never be re-established, who from sheer despair makes matters worse instead of better; picture to yourself, I say, a man whose brilliant hopes have come to nothing."

From 1824 onwards his health to some extent improved, but the sickness within him revealed itself nevertheless, stealthily sapping at his strength, bringing to him with each return fresh and deeper despair. He tried to conceal the knowledge of his complaint, to hurl off depression in the gay company of his friends. Gloom entered the more readily into his composing, so that on one occasion the Vienna Musical Society sent a message to him beseeching him not to make his work so dismal.

If the illness did not change his nature, it provoked moods of irritability that came and as quickly passed. The irksomeness of penury became less possible to bear. The dishonesty of his publishers drove him to distraction. For the first time in his life he wrote sharp letters, but letters never undeserved. In February, 1823, when the first dangers of his illness had passed, he wrote to Diabelli asking for an account for the last two books he had published, and offering to sell him the copyright for 300 florins if he cared to buy them outright. The account when rendered surprised Franz, as it may well have done. Among other extortions they had charged him 100 florins for making a copy of *Alfonso and Estrella*.

Schubert wrote to Diabelli again:

" Vienna,
" To Cappi and Diabelli. " *Feb. 28th*, 1823.

" SIRS,

" Your letter certainly surprises me, as according to Mr. Cappi my account was settled. Since, from your behaviour when publishing my waltzes, I observed none too honest an intention on the part of my publishers, I could well understand the reason of your present action; while you yourselves will find a ready

contemporary documents and letters bearing on the matter, which came into his possession in 1914. This material he kindly placed at my disposal, and I am indebted to him for some of the above facts. I have, however, only dealt superficially with Schubert's illness in relation to the man and his work.

explanation why I have entered into a fixed contract with another publishing house. I do not understand what you mean by the reference to a debt of mine of 150 florins, Viennese currency, for according to your statement the copying of my opera is only 100 florins V.c. Be that as it may, the very unfair prices you have paid me for my former works, in addition to that for the *Fantasia,* a mere 50 florins V.c., has long since discharged the debt which you now most unjustly thrust upon me.

" Though I doubt that you possess any human understanding, I must draw your attention to my just claim to 20 copies of the last and 13 copies of the previous books, and to a still stronger claim for the 50 florins which you got out of me in such a very smart fashion. Reckon all this up, please, and you will find that my demand is not only greater than yours, but juster, though I should not have claimed it if you had not reminded me of it in such a disagreeable manner. As the debt was cleared up in this way long since, as you will assuredly see, there can be no discussion about allowing you to publish songs, which once again you could not undervalue sufficiently, while at present I receive 200 florins V.c. for a book, and Herr v. Steiner has repeatedly made me an offer for an edition of all my compositions. Finally, I must demand that you return to me all my manuscripts, both the engraved works, and those which have not been engraved up to the present.

" With esteem,
" FRANZ SCHUBERT."

For some reason—it may have been the dictate of a mood that came with his illness—he now began to shun the Fröhlichs. Between the years 1822 and 1824 he was never seen at their house; indeed it was not until a short time before his death that he resought their society. The sisters were no less ardent in their admiration, no less devoted in the constant performance of his work. But for the space of two years he held aloof, still setting Grillparzer's poems, but with no other link to the house of music. It was an absence without apparent cause or motive.

Then Kathi Fröhlich met Schubert one day in the street. Let her tell the story of that rediscovered friendship.[1]

" He used to come so often. But then he drifted into somewhat loose society, and moved for some time in other circles—not neces-

---

[1] From a manuscript in Professor Otto Erich Deutsch's possession, " From Grillparzer's House," by Frau von Breuning.

sarily bad, but in circles in which he let himself go too much. And he did let himself go too much. For instance, he went among other families, to one in the Landstrasse. One day an acquaintance of these people said to us: ' Yesterday we had to carry Schubert into another room. He had been drinking too much. . . .'

" Schubert got into debt. Then he did not come to see us for nearly two years. One day I met him in the street, and when he saluted me I gave him a significant side-glance, severe, reproachful. He looked at me bashfully, very shyly. I shall never forget his conscience-stricken appearance. He made his excuses for not having been to see us for so long. And I felt it was my duty to lecture him severely, and to tell him that his conduct and manner of living were not creditable. He promised me to make amends.

" A few days later there was a knock at the door. I was sitting at my window as usual. It was our long-missing Schubert. He opened the door a little, and, pushing his head through, said: ' Fräulein Kathi, may I come in? '

" ' Since when, then, is our house so strange to you? ' I asked him. ' You know very well that it has always been open to you.'

" ' Yes,' he answered. ' But I am a little timid. I have not forgotten that look you gave me in the street.' "

At intervals his illness distorted his outlook on life. Inwardly disturbed, he was outwardly the same. A plaint in a letter was all he revealed of his hurt. Malevolent intrigue that involved him left his natural benevolence unchanged. If he had changed, or become more sensitive, he was unaware of it. He seldom knew anger; he once confessed that anger was unknown to him.

It happened at Neustift-am-Walde. A jolting vehicle had drawn up in the middle of a meadow that was radiant with buttercups and daisies and multi-coloured wild flowers. All the passengers were jumping from the carriage, and Schubert was assisting a lady to alight. As he did so, he continued his conversation:

" Above all things, I must not get angry. For God's sake I must not get angry. For if I do get angry I knock all the teeth out of the mouth of the poor wretch who has angered me."

The little lady with the broad-brimmed hat decorated with flowers looked at him in frightened surprise.

" And have you often been angry? " she asked nervously.

" No," said Schubert. " Never yet! "

CHAPTER XI

The "Unfinished Symphony," "Fierrabras" and "Rosamunde"

(1823)

THE year 1823 produced the richest fruiting of Schubert's genius, and this in spite of his sickness of body. To this year belongs his opera *Fierrabras*, his *Rosamunde*, his *Schöne Müllerin* songs, and such works of beauty as *Der Zwerg* and *Du bist die Ruh'*.

The money which Schubert had received by the first publication of his songs had gone. During 1822-3, Josef Hüttenbrenner worked unceasingly for his friend, only to plough little more than furrows of sand. The fidelity of this younger Hüttenbrenner to Schubert was remarkable in the extravagance of its service. One would have expected such idolatry more readily from Anselm Hüttenbrenner, since he was the musician, the composer with the same tireless energy Schubert possessed. Anselm not only composed rapidly but well, and on one occasion Schubert used one of his themes for a set of variations After Schubert's *Erl-King* was produced, Anselm Hüttenbrenner also set the poem.

" Anselm," said Schubert one day when they were out walking together, " you produce your *Erl-King* and I'll withdraw mine."

" Franz, as long as I live no one will ever see my *Erl-King*," Anselm replied. It is said that he burned it, but that he wrote it out again from memory at some time between the years 1829 and 1832.

The fact remains, however, that after the success of the *Erl-King* in 1821, Anselm Hüttenbrenner had the audacity to write an *Erl-King* waltz. The work was very bitingly criticized in a satirical

96

poem in the *Allgemeine Musikalische Zeitung*, whereupon Schubert cut out the verses and sent them to Anselm by his brother Josef.[1]

Josef Hüttenbrenner's love of Schubert amounted to idolatry. So effusive was it that it became at times a nuisance to Schubert, who on one occasion exclaimed petulantly: "That one (Josef) is pleased with anything I do!" But he was unfailing in his affection for his disciple. Certainly Josef Hüttenbrenner, who was now employed at the Home Office at Vienna, struggled hard to mend Schubert's fortunes at the close of 1822 when the illness was developing at a rapid pace. He endeavoured to get Schubert's first opera *Des Teufels Lustschloss* (1814) produced. There seemed a remote chance that the effort would succeed. Beethoven's *Fidelio* had been revived after eight years, and the revival had completely killed the Rossini boom in Vienna. Operatic managers became aware that there were other pebbles than Rossini on the shore. The director of the Imperial Opera asked Beethoven for another opera, and Beethoven in his turn encouraged Grillparzer to finish *Melusina* hurriedly so that he might set it. But whilst the *libretto* was being completed, Beethoven received a commission for an opera from Count Brühl who controlled the Imperial Opera in Berlin. The master preferred to be heard in Berlin rather than in Vienna. He sent the Grillparzer *Melusina* to the Count, only to receive it back with an intimation that the theatre was already occupied by a ballet, *Undine*, which dealt with a similar subject, caused Beethoven to change his mind. He turned to other work and abandoned *Melusina* for ever.[2]

The time therefore appeared to be propitious for Schubert. Josef Hüttenbrenner now approached in turn the management of the theatre An-der-Wien, Count Gallenberg, the assistant of the Italian Domenico Barbaja, who was in control of the Kärntnerthor Theatre, Capellmeister Winter at Munich, and Director Holbein of the Prague Opera House, in an effort to get Schubert's opera performed. From each the reply was the same—the opera was not wanted. Hüttenbrenner, hot in his zeal, then wrote to Peters, the musical publisher at Leipzig, hoping thereby to make a more lucrative arrangement for Schubert than Franz now had with the swindling Diabelli. He wrote of Schubert: " Among the local newer composers Vienna possesses there is now a talent which is already attracting general attention, and has become a favourite with the

[1] Anselm Hüttenbrenner: "Reminiscences."
[2] Karl Kobald: "Schubert."

97

public here. In short, speaking without exaggeration, he is a second Beethoven—indeed this immortal man has already said of him (Schubert), 'This one will surpass me.'" Peters sent his blessing but no commissions for Schubert, whose work, he declared, was quite unknown in northern Germany.

Again Hüttenbrenner had failed, but that he was of some service to Schubert is suggested by a letter which Franz wrote to him in October, 1822, when Diabelli was making a copy of *Alfonso and Estrella*—the copy for which he wished to charge 100 florins.[1]

" Dear Friend,—Be so good as to bring out here to me one act of the Opera after the other for correction. I also wish that you would trouble yourself with getting my account from Diabelli up to date, as I am in want of money." Schubert was then living with Schober in the Göttweiher Hof.

Shortage of money, his illness, the failure of Josef Hüttenbrenner to secure anything of advantage for him could not suppress the flow of Schubert's music. Count Dietrichstein offered him the post of organist at the Court Chapel, but he declined it. He kept to his room; for awhile the familiar circles in the *Gasthaus* remembered him in absence. He was still working without the direct hope of any gain, even the return of a few florins for what he did. He composed his *Unfinished Symphony* in " B minor " as a gift to the town of Graz, which had elected him an honorary member of its musical society. At the same time the Society of the Friends of Music in Vienna, founded by Leopold Sonnleithner, had refused Schubert's admission to its circle as a viola player because he was a professional musician! Even the examples of the towns of Graz and Linz, which offered him the honorary memberships he had so eagerly accepted, did not draw from Vienna a corresponding *geste*. He remained " not without honour, save in his own country."

The manuscript of the *Unfinished Symphony* was sent to Graz, and, according to Josef Hüttenbrenner, it was given to his brother Anselm, who was living in the town at the time. Anselm Hüttenbrenner certainly had it, and for a long time kept it locked up in his desk. Many years later[2] Hüttenbrenner, in writing about his brother Anselm's collection of musical antographs, said: " He possesses a treasure in Schubert's ' B Minor ' Symphony, which we consider equal to the great symphony in ' C,' his instrumental swan-song, and to any by Beethoven. Only it is not finished. Schubert gave it

---

[1] Deutsch II, 139, No. 345.   [2] March 8th, 1860.

to me for Anselm in recognition of his sending him the honorary diploma of the Graz Musical Society through me."

Why should Schubert present Anselm Hüttenbrenner with a symphony as a reward for passing on an honour that had been conferred upon him? He had already written to the Graz Musical Society declaring that he would, in the fullness of time, present it with a symphony in recognition of the honour. The gift thus promised would scarcely be presented elsewhere. It was not Schubert's habit to make promises and disregard them, for he was, according to the written word of Hüttenbrenner, "the soul of honour." "I shall," he had explained to the Graz Musical Society, "take the liberty of sending the honoured Club one of my symphonies as soon as ever I can." Moreover, Anselm, in a letter to his brother Josef, referred to the Symphony, but when he enumerated his Schubert manuscripts in a later letter,[1] he made no mention of it whatever. He always declared that he had lent the Symphony to Herbeck, who kept it.[2]

When Schubert met Beethoven for the first time is problematical. It is attributed to this period, but we have only the evidence of Schubert's friend Schindler for a story which Hüttenbrenner afterwards denied. Often the composers had sat in the same beer-house, the old master surrounded by his circle of friends; the young one timid and aloof. Beethoven, the rugged and distant figure, now quite deaf, knew nothing of a young star rising on the horizon to follow him in full blaze. They had told him frequently about Schubert, but he did not heed. Why should he heed? A hundred heralded stars had been announced to him, all of them to disappear into the murk of mediocrity.

Schindler declares that Schubert, accompanied by his rapscallion publisher, on one occasion called at Beethoven's house with a copy of the Variations which he had dedicated to the master. So flurried was Schubert in the presence of a genius to whom he had given the devotion of a life that, when Beethoven pointed out certain technical errors in the manuscript and asked Schubert to write down the answer to his criticisms, Franz was paralysed with fear. His brain

---

[1] To Luib.

[2] The manuscript afterwards came into the possession of Nikolaus Dumba, together with a sketch of the scherzo, and it was eventually presented by him to the Society of the Friends of Music. The Symphony was never performed during Schubert's life-time, the first performance taking place in 1865 in Vienna under Herbeck.

failed to think; his pencil to write. He did not set down a word. Not till he reached the street did he recover himself.

Romance could not have shaped the story of that meeting more truly to its own ethics. But Hüttenbrenner destroyed the romance with a prosaic rejoinder. He declared that he accompanied Schubert to Beethoven's house when Schubert wished to present the copy of the Variations, that Beethoven was out, so he left the manuscript with the maid, like a tradesman delivering a parcel! Schindler, always a person of romantic mind, is probably wrong, since he was not there. Hüttenbrenner, who was on intimate terms with both composers, is the more reliable recorder.[1]

To some extent the same confusion exists with regard to the relations of Schubert and Weber. The former had met Weber during his stay in Vienna in 1822. Weber had declared that he would use his influence toward the production of Schubert's ill-fated *Alfonso and Estrella* in northern Germany. If he did, it was a lost effort, probably a misguided effort, since *Alfonso* had an impossible *libretto*. But in 1823 Weber returned to Vienna and—according to Spaun—promised to secure the production of *Alfonso*.

Schubert became a regular visitor at his house, and was accepted as a composer of unrecognized brilliance. The consumption which was to wear Weber's life away, to drive him to compose rapidly in the hope of being able to raise sufficient money to support those dependent upon him, had already set in.

The day after Weber's *Euryanthe* had been produced in Vienna, Schubert and Weber met.

" How do you like my Opera? " Weber asked.

Schubert, who was always frank, declared that a number of things had pleased him very much, but he liked the *Freischütz* better. He expressed the opinion that there was too little melody in the new opera. Weber received the remark very coldly, and there was no further talk of the production of Schubert's opera. " This the truthful Schubert told me himself," said Spaun. That Weber made the stinging retort, when referring to Schubert's opera, that " first puppies should always be drowned," would seem to be a legend without any authority to support it. Schubert certainly did value the *Freischütz* very highly, and his favourite piece in it was the male

---

[1] Spaun, in his criticism of Kreissle's biography of Schubert, gives yet a third version. He states that Schubert expressed his sorrow because Beethoven was so unapproachable, and that he *had never spoken to him*. When Schubert was told that Beethoven had in his last days found pleasure in his songs, he was overjoyed.

quartet or quintet at the beginning of the Opera. Indeed, he thought so well of it that he frequently walked round his room singing it to himself.

Thus did Schubert's and Weber's paths cross in 1823. Weber may have been sincere in his admiration of Schubert. He may have wished to help a fellow-artist, till the criticism of *Euryanthe* pushed that desire away. But he certainly did nothing to help a fellow-traveller on the difficult road. He had three years of life, a life of coughing, of struggle before him. He returned to Germany, then set out for London, saying that " he was going to London to die." He was right. He died in Sir George Smart's house in Great Portland Street at some time during the night of June 5th, 1825, and Smart had to force Weber's bedroom door open, and push his dead body away from it, before he could enter the room.[1]

The future for native opera in Vienna now seemed clear. Rossini had been driven out. Beethoven, in spite of the success of the revival of *Fidelio*, had left the operatic field. Weber with his *Euryanthe* had failed to capture from the Viennese any degree of enthusiasm, and he had departed with no greater laurels than a *succès d'estime* could provide. Barbaja at the Kärntnerthor Theatre with a contract which was running out, and which, with the decision against Italian influence in opera, would certainly not be renewed, was in search of a work that would bring back to his house some prosperity. He had hitherto shown no faith in Schubert. Josef Hüttenbrenner and others had acclaimed Schubert to him, only to give their praises to deaf ears. This man is a song-writer, declared Barbaja. What does he know of Opera? But he commissioned Schubert to write an opera for his house nevertheless.

Soon came *Fierrabras*. Josef Kupelwieser, the brother of Schubert's friend Leopold Kupelwieser, the painter, wrote the *libretto*. Schubert, swift to the new chance, composed the whole of the work, approximately one thousand pages of music, in four months, between May 23rd and September 25th, 1823. The opera when complete was delivered to Barbaja, who in the press of other things put it in a drawer and forgot it. The applications of Schubert for a verdict on his four months' work were ignored. *Fierrabras* had been buried in a common grave with other great failures before it had even been given the chance of life. Barbaja ultimately returned the opera stating that its production was impossible because of the

[1] Sir George Smart: Letter in " Sir Arthur Sullivan," p. 37. Herbert Sullivan and Newman Flower.

badness of the *libretto*. Four months' work had thus been thrown away. The enthusiasm for an opera which Schubert had regarded as being certain of production departed, and left him with a bundle of manuscript and no possible chance of production.

He began to feel the bitterness of his purgatory and expressed it in a letter to Leopold Kupelwieser, who was in Rome:

" Every night when I go to bed," he wrote, " I hope that I may never wake again, and every morning renews my grief. I live without pleasure or friends. Schwind pays me an occasional visit. Our reading union has been broken up through eating too many sausages, as you will have heard. It is to be dissolved in two days' time. Leides-dorf [his publisher] is a very good person, but is despondent, and his affairs and mine are in a very bad way. Therefore we never have any money. Your brother's opera (it was a pity he left the theatre) was declared to be impossible, and my music was not even taken into consideration. . . . In this way I have composed two operas quite uselessly. I have written only a few songs, but I have tried to compose something for instruments, two quartets for violins, viola and violoncello, and an octet. I want to write another quartet. In this manner I hope to prepare the way for my great symphony. The only news from Vienna is that Beethoven is to produce his new symphony in three parts with a new Mass and a new overture. God willing, I intend to give such a concert next year. I must finish now in order not to use up too much paper. . . .

" Your faithful friend,
" FRANZ SCHUBERT.
" Good-bye, Farewell! "

During a holiday in August he had written from Steyr to Scho-ber: " If I shall ever recover again seems rather doubtful. I am living a very simple life here, going for long walks, working much at my opera and reading Walter Scott."

The disappointment of *Fierrabras*, which opera, like his *Alfonso and Estrella*, he was never to hear performed, drove Schubert to fresh irritation. New operatic writers of mediocre talent came into Vienna and had their work produced at its theatres whilst he waited at the closed door. Unlike the Handel he admired, he had been forbidden the stage by bad *libretti*. His *Zwerg, Auf dem Wasser, Du bist die Ruh'* were composed in the month of October whilst he was awaiting Barbaja's decision on *Fierrabras*. At the end of the year—just before Christmas—he began *Rosamunde*. A work pro-duced to benefit an actress!

102

Kupelwieser, whose *libretto* of *Fierrabras* had proved such a fiasco, was the originator of *Rosamunde*. The Countess Chézy, who provided Schubert with the book—she had previously written the *libretto* of Weber's *Euryanthe*—recounts the happening.[1]

" A young friend of the name of Kupelwieser, brother of the famous painter, asked me for a drama, to which Franz Schubert would write the music. He was in love with a beautiful girl, Mdlle. Neumann, an actress of the Theatre An-der-Wien, and the drama was to be given for her benefit performance on December 20th, 1823."

Schubert had been as luckless with his new *librettist* as he had been with her predecessors. The book of *Rosamunde* was absurd. It lacked imagination and merit. It was badly written—the sort of jargon that might be conceived by an amateur for a drawing-room full of amateurs. Yet he seized upon it, blind to its disorder, blind to the fact that these impossible *libretti* were absorbing his energies uselessly and forcing him the deeper into poverty. He set *Rosamunde* in five days. The overture was that of the unperformed *Alfonso and Estrella*. In December it was produced at the Theatre An-der-Wien, a house quite unsuited to a work of this sort, since it was usually given up to spectacular drama. The overture met with such approval that it had to be repeated. Applause swept the theatre as the curtain fell at the close and loud calls for " Schubert " remained unanswered. Was *Rosamunde* going to carry the man who had striven so hard for a theatrical hearing to his goal after all? It seemed so.

Schwind, the young painter who had just joined the Schubert circle, wrote to Schober on the night of the performance, December 20th, 1823:

" I had been at home all day because of a cough, and in consequence I was unable to join with the others, so I sat alone in the gallery whilst they were in the pit. Schubert used the Over-ture which he had composed for *Estrella*, but he thought it was too noisy for *Estrella*, and he is going to compose a new one for that Opera. It met with general applause, to my great delight. . . . In the last act came a chorus of shepherds and huntsmen, and I never remember hearing its equal. . . . Madame Vogel sang another air in a most appalling manner. A subterranean chorus could not be heard, and the gesticulations of Herr Rott, who was brewing poison during it, did not allow it to come into existence."

[1] "Unvergessenes." Aus dem Leben Helmines von Chézy.

Whatever may have been Schubert's hopes for *Rosamunde*, they were quickly destroyed. One other performance of the work was given and it was dead. Wilhelmine von Chézy eventually decided to rewrite it and bring it out again, and in the following summer the revision was completed. Schubert wrote to her in August:

" Convinced of the value of *Rosamunde* from the moment I read it, I am very pleased that your honour has undertaken to correct, surely to the greatest advantage, a few unimportant shortcomings which only a spiteful public could censure. I should consider it a particular honour if you would let me have a copy of the manuscript when you have worked over it.

" As regards the price of the music, I don't think I can put it at less than 100 florins without depreciating the music itself. In case that price should be too high, I beg your honour to fix the price yourself, but at not much below the above-named figure, and to forward it to the subjoined address, as I am absent from Vienna.[1]

> " With greatest esteem,
> " Your most devoted
> "FRANZ SCHUBERT."

But *Rosamunde* remained in obscurity until 1867. In that year George Grove and Arthur Sullivan went to Vienna to search for the lost manuscript. Spina, the music publisher, who had succeeded Diabelli when he had been called to his fathers, welcomed the Englishmen with open arms. He gave them big cigars, and parcels containing manuscripts of unknown origin. He handed the Englishmen over to his friend Dr. Schneider, who possessed more parcels of unknown manuscripts. But the parcels contained only the work of those whom Fame had refused to know. As a last resource they hunted through a cupboard and unearthed more dust-strewn parcels. At the bottom of this cupboard was a heap of music books two feet high. They were the part books of the lost *Rosamunde*. Grove and Sullivan sat through the night copying them; they played leap-frog when they had completed their task at two in the morning.[2]

Rosamunde that was dead had come to life again. It had come to life for ever.

---

[1] Schubert was then making his second sojourn at Zelész with the Esterhazys.
[2] Sir Arthur Sullivan's Diary. " Sir Arthur Sullivan," by Herbert Sullivan and Newman Flower.

CHAPTER XII

Zelész Again

(1824)

THE Schubert circle was to some extent changing. Spaun was attached to it no longer, save by the slender links of correspondence, for he had departed from Vienna and settled in Linz. The parsimony and intrigues of the Government office in which he had slaved made him a disappointed and embittered man. When the State Lottery was reorganized it was placed under his charge, and, as stated, his purse had benefited to the extent of 800 florins a year. He saved the Government enormous expenses, and was granted another 500 florins a year, which he never received. On the way to Spaun the florins had found a resting-place in the pocket of another. Therefore, when the town of Linz offered him the post of assessor, he went to it gladly. Not until 1826 did Vienna see him again. He then returned to take up a profitable post under the Government that had formerly suppressed him.

Kupelwieser, the painter, was still in Rome. Schober, who had become engaged to Justina, the sister of Schubert's friend Bruchmann, had hurried to northern Europe in a mood of impulse. Bruchmann was a wealthy wholesale merchant in the Weinburggasse, who gave *Schubertiaden* at his house, attended not only by the Schubertians, but by some of the most talented and beautiful women in Vienna.

Schober had no object in making this journey. No means of earning a living had been offered to him. " Schober is engaged," wrote Schubert. " Will this bring trouble to his friends ? "

It did. Schober reached Breslau and went on the stage under the name of Torupson—after the name of the Swedish castle Torup in which he had been born. " I wish you good luck in your enterprise," Schubert wrote to him, " and assure you of my everlasting love. I shall miss you terribly."

The news of Schober's stage experiences—unfortunate they proved to be—filtered back to Vienna. The poet, the cultured dilettante among the mummers! Justina Bruchmann promptly jilted him. Possibly this meant little to Schober. There had been so many Justinas in his life. His world was full of Justinas. But it caused difficulty between members of the Schubert circle and the Bruchmann family which time failed to heal completely.

At the end of 1823 Schubert wrote to Schober again:

" Our party has lost its sustaining pillar in you. Bruchmann has not been the same person since he returned from his journey. . . . If he is absent, or, what is worse, ill, one hears nothing but ceaseless chatter about riding and fencing, horses and dogs, which is revolting. . . .

" How are you? Have you appeared before the eyes of the world? Let me hear something of you soon, I beg of you, and ease the longing I have for you. I hope to recover my health, which would cause me to forget many a suffering. Only you, dear Schober, I shall never forget, for no one could ever be to me what you have been.

" Your ever loving friend,

" FRANZ SCHUBERT."

But the loss to Schubert was to some extent compensated for by the advent of Moritz von Schwind, the painter. Schwind was six years younger than Schubert. He was nineteen. Slim, good to look upon, with an agreeable wellcut and typically German face, and a fresh complexion. He had long wavy hair, a moustache and pointed beard of a reddish blonde.[1] He was a romanticist, a dreamer, a music-lover. " One must have daily a mouthful of music," he said. Of all Schubert's friends few gave him greater fidelity. " As Schubert composes, so do I want to paint," Schwind once exclaimed to Bauernfeld.

The attachment between Schubert and Schwind grew rapidly into the deepest friendship, approaching the friendship that existed between Schubert and Schober. Yet Schober and Schwind were direct opposites. Schober was a triumph of personality. He was a scholar, unsound with only superficial knowledge, and the super-

[1] Bauernfeld: " Alt Wien."

ficiality of it as cleverly concealed. Vogl, with his deeper learning, was never *en rapport* with Schober, the artificiality of the latter was always obvious to him. Schwind was of a different calibre. He had the same merriment and joy of living, but his mind dwelt with serious things. Schubert and his friends called him " Cherubim." He was tender, almost feminine, yet always restless and given to long moods of thought during which he would speak to no one. He was very excitable. When sitting with Schubert and his friends, who were drinking whilst Schwind had resisted the appeal of wine and punch, he would suddenly awake from his brooding and assume a mood of unrestrained merriment and brilliant wit.[1] Then he became the boon companion of the Gasthaus. He was ready for any prank or adventure of the night. Or he would sit modelling a caricature of one of the Schubertians out of the tobacco someone had spilled on the *Gasthaus* table.

Temperamentally Schwind was closer to Schubert than almost any of the Schubertians. In the minds of both there existed an intense love for the beautiful. They walked together and ultimately lived together. Schubert jokingly called Schwind his sweetheart because he shared the secret places of his heart. " In Schwind I find my fullest understanding," he said. Moreover, they were fellow-strugglers in adversity. Vienna spurned the paintings of Schwind with the coldness it had heaped upon the music of Schubert. But Schwind continued to struggle until Vienna ultimately broke his heart and drove him out. Utterly discouraged, he eventually left the city and went to Munich, where he quickly sold for 1,200 thalers a picture for which Vienna would not give him a few hundred florins.

The lack of interest which Vienna had in these two great men would seem surprising. But the artistic life of the city had been destroyed or driven into dark corners by the ceaseless crushing of officialdom. How could a distracted populace, that lived under continual threat, impoverished by the variations of money values, that was able to exist only by constant battling with adversity, have been expected to heed the claim of genius, of artistic brilliance that helped not at all towards solving the problem of living?

From 1819 to 1826 Schwind lived with his mother, sisters and brothers in the Moonshine House (Mondschein Haus auf der Wieden No. 102), a building of some pretensions which had belonged to his grandfather. There was a fine view from its windows, over

---

[1] Bauernfeld : " Alt Wien."

the *glacis,* to the Wiener Wald. At the back of the house was a garden courtyard, so that the property formed a rural island in the heart of Vienna. It became a meeting-place for the Schubertians— Schober when he returned from his wanderings was constantly there. Kenner, Lachner [1] Kupelwieser attended regularly, and Schubert was never absent. The Moonshine House became widely discussed. Its windows glowed with light till the small hours of the morning. The sound of roystering and music went on till Vienna stirred in its sleep with the coming of dawn. They produced humorous plays there, and, in their serious hours, works of musical importance. They practised physical exercises and played games. So attached did Schubert become to Schwind and the Moonshine House that he went to live at the house next door (Frühwirt Haus), and he remained there until Schwind left the Moonshine House in 1826. Schubert, Schwind and Schober then decided to live together.

One of Schubert's most beautiful songs, *Hark! Hark! the Lark!* was the outcome of a Schubertian gathering at the Moonshine House. Schwind wished to draw Schubert's portrait. But Franz, restless as ever, refused to keep still. Persuasions proved of no avail. Someone then gave Schubert a copy of Shakespeare. Looking through it, he came upon *Cymbeline,* and the words of the song so captivated him that he immediately proceeded to set it to music. Schwind ruled some lines on a piece of paper for Schubert's use, saying as he did so that they were the most valuable drawing he had ever made. And while Schubert composed Schwind made his picture.

The departure of Schober on his travels had left Schubert in difficulty for rooms. But he eventually took a room at No. 100 auf der Wieden [2] on the second storey, and to reach it he had to climb up several flights of stairs. It was often as difficult to find the money to pay the rent for these rooms, amounting to twenty-five florins a month, as it was to discover publishers ready to publish his songs—and pay for them.

On one occasion when he was walking with Randhartinger he explained the difficulty, and his companion lent him 15 gulden (12s. 6d.) to clear the rent. After he had done so they chanced to pass a music-shop, and Schubert exclaimed:

[1] It was in Lachner's rooms in a garden house on the Landstrasse behind the Home for Army Pensioners that Lachner and Schubert played for the first time the Fantasia in " F Minor " (Op. 106) The Great Octet (Op. 166) and the Quartet in " D Minor " were also performed there.

[2] The Frühwirt House.

" Look here, these people have any number of my things, and you might get your money back at once if they would only pay me a little of what they owe me. I have often been to them about my royalties, but every time they said that they had so many expenses, and that my compositions sold very slowly. Do you know, I'm not going to enter that shop again." [1]

It was undoubtedly Schubert's poverty at this period that induced him to go in May, 1824, to Zelész again with the Esterhazys, who paid him five hundred florins for a stay of five months. He was practically assured now that all chance of the production of his two operas had gone for ever. The small flow of money that had come from the first publication of his songs had ceased. Such songs as he now sold were paid for after long delays, and then the receipts were insufficient even to cover his rent. With only four years of his life to run, at a time when his genius never displayed greater brilliance, the very means to live by that genius were denied to him. His letter to Kupelwieser written two months before his departure for Zelész (see page 102) shows the distress of his mind.

Zelész certainly improved his health. Removed from the night life of the *Gasthaus*, the rooms hung heavily with smoke, the constant beer-drinking, his energies stirred anew. But the quietude of Zelész, the absence of convivial companions brought only rest-lessness and home-sickness as it had done before. This is apparent in a letter which he wrote to Schober at Breslau during the summer:

" DEAR SCHOBER,

" I hear you are not happy. You have to sleep off the plague of despair—so Schwind tells me. Although I regret so much hearing this, I am, however, not surprised, as it is the fate of every rational being in this miserable world. And what should we do with happiness since misfortune is the only spur we have left to us? If only you, Schwind, Kuppel and I were together, then misfortunes would not bother us. As it is, we are separated, each of us in a separate corner. That is my trouble. I should like to say with Goethe: ' Who can bring back to me but one hour of that sweet time!' That time when we used to sit together so comfortably, and each revealed to the other the offspring of his Art, not without dread, as he awaited anxiously the verdict which love and truth would pronounce; that time when each inspired the other, and thus all were animated by a mutual striving to attain beauty.

[1] Dahms: " Schubert."

" I am sitting here, far away in Hungary, where I have un-fortunately allowed myself to be drawn for the second time; nor is there a single person to whom I can speak a sane word. Since you went away I have scarcely composed any songs, but have attempted some compositions for the orchestra. Heaven only knows what will happen to my Operas!

" Although I have been feeling quite well for the past five months, I am often depressed. This is brought about by your absence and Kuppel's, so at times I spend rather wretched days. In one of these sad hours when I was feeling the inactivity and un-importance of our own times most acutely I wrote the enclosed poetry, which I am sending you, because I know that you will reprove my weakness with love and sympathy. . . .

" Till now I have fared badly with Leidesdorf. He cannot pay, nobody buys anything, neither my compositions nor those of other composers, only trumpery work being the fashion.

" I have told you about my present position, and am longing to hear of yours. I wish you were coming to Vienna soon. And now good-bye, and write to me as soon as possible.

" Your

SCHUBERT.

" Farewell! "

Apart from the concerts at Zelész, Schubert apparently gave little time to music. He composed there some waltzes, and the music for the house quartet to Fouqué's " Prayer before Battle." One morning in early September the Countess Esterhazy brought Schubert the words, and that evening the composition was sung from the manuscript at the pianoforte.

His *Divertissement à la Hongroise* (Op. 54) was undoubtedly composed during the second visit to Zelész, and technical reasons support this view. It is said that the opening subject which reappears in the middle, and again at the end, is a melody which Schubert heard a maid singing in the kitchen when he was returning from a walk with Baron Schönstein, for the Baron was staying at the Castle, as had been the case during Schubert's former visit. On the other hand Remenyi, the violinist who arranged the piece for solo violin and string quartet, denies the presence in it of Hungarian folk tunes or gypsy music.

Schubert's visit to Zelész in 1824 would have been forgotten as an episode, had it not been for his love affair with Caroline Ester-

110

hazy. She had now reached seventeen years of age, and was most attractive. But it is difficult to believe that the affair was more than a passing romance—the outcome of the lonely surroundings at Zelész. Schubert, as her teacher, had seen Caroline Esterhazy regularly in Vienna, but throughout this time there was no suggestion of any affection between them. Had such affection occurred, why did he not refer to it in his letters? Moreover, the difference in station made such a match impossible. But it is conceivable that at Zelész, where according to his letters he was unhappy, he found in Caroline Esterhazy something more than a friend who compensated him for his lost friends of Vienna and filled the hours of his loneliness. On one occasion she asked him why he had dedicated none of his compositions to her. To this he quickly replied, " *Wozu denn, Ihnen ist ja ohnehin alles gewidmet.*" ("Why, everything is dedicated to you as it is.") He did indeed dedicate to her his Fantasia in " F Minor " (Op. 103), and on the autograph of two unpublished dances is the inscription in his handwriting " *Für die Comtesse Caroline.*" But at some later date, and for some reason unknown, the dedication was struck out in thick strokes by himself.

In a letter written to Schwind in August he refers to the attraction of a certain star, undoubtedly a reference to Caroline Esterhazy.

" Dear Schwind,—At last a letter from Schubert, you will exclaim, after these months! It is certainly a long time, but as my life has been simple in the extreme I have had little to write to you and the others. . . . How is Schober's enterprise faring? Is Kupelwieser in Vienna, or still in Rome? Does the reading circle still meet, or has it been dissolved? What are you doing?

" Thanks to God I remain quite well, and should be happy if you, Schober and Kupelwieser were here. As it is, in spite of the attraction of a certain star, I am longing for Vienna most terribly. I hope to see you again about the end of September. I have composed a long sonata and variations as piano duets. The latter meet with particular approbation here. As I do not trust the opinion of the Hungarians, I shall leave it for you and the Viennese to decide on their merits.

" How is Leidesdorf? Is he progressing, or is the dog losing his hair? I leave it to you to scold Leidesdorf in a thorough manner, as he did not answer my letter, nor did he send me what I asked for. What the devil is the meaning of this? The Miller songs are progressing very slowly too. Every three months one book is published.

" And now good-bye. My love to everybody you can think of. And (I warn you) do write to me soon or you can go to——.

" Your faithful friend,
" FRZ. SCHUBERT."

In a letter to his brother Ferdinand written a few weeks previously he vaguely hinted at a love affair at Steyr which it is of course impossible to reconcile with his attachment to Caroline Esterhazy. But Theresa Grob was married by this time. Did some memories of the old passion recur, and renew again the bitter disappointment? For no woman ever usurped her place in his heart. If Caroline Esterhazy really ever entered it she brought a benevolent soothing, as Bauernfeld declared in later years.

" We do not live any more in the happy times when everything seems to be surrounded with a youthful halo," Franz wrote to Ferdinand, " but we are fully aware of miserable reality, which I try to decorate with my imagination (thanks to God) as much as I can. You believe happiness to be derived from the place in which once you have been happy, but in truth it is centred in ourselves.

" I had an unpleasant disappointment, and renewed an experience here which I had already had at Steyr. But now I am able to find happiness and peace in my own soul. As proof of this may serve a great sonata and variations, dealing with a theme which I invented. . . .

" The quintets of that great ass Hugelthier I have brought with me by mistake, and I swear to God that he shall not have them back until he has apologized either by word of mouth or by letter for his vulgar rudeness. If ever an occasion arises to give a good piece of my mind to this dirty pig, I shall not fail to do it. But enough of this wretch. . . ."

That the relations between Schubert and Caroline Esterhazy had, for a time, become more intimate than those usual between master and pupil was a fact well known in the circle of his intimate friends. Proof of this is found in a letter, here published for the first time, which was written by Baron von Schönstein in his old age to Moritz von Schwind. It is in reference to the portrait of Caroline Esterhazy that is reproduced in this volume.

" Vienna, 28th April, 1863.

" DEAR FRIEND,

" In my last will and testament stood the following passage : ' The miniature picture by Teltscher, representing a lady in a blue

112

dress, I leave to the Professor of the Munich Royal Academy in friendly remembrance, and as a token of my veneration for a soulful master and friend who was full of genius.'

"It hardly needed more words to connect this passage with the memory of a man whom we both highly esteemed and whom posterity now praises, for the not-unsuccessful copy of the little picture, which is still in your possession[1], will at once present to you the person it portrays.[2]

"At the time when I set my earthly affairs in order I did not believe that I was destined to see the days of my life spun out very much longer, for since it had been overtaken by the worst of catastrophes it had become entirely joyless. As, however, Heaven seems to have determined that I shall now have to bear much longer that (existence) which long since has become a burden to me, I do not wish to withhold from you for any further time the thing with which I intended to give you a little pleasure. In cancelling therefore that passage in my testament, I send you herewith the legacy intended for you, as a *Donatio inter vivos*, with the request that you will give it a friendly reception.

"This year I shall hardly be able to visit my beloved Bavaria, and although of late, through the force of circumstances, I have not seen you, yet I am constantly hearing about you through my friends, and as what they tell me is usually agreeable news, I am heartily pleased with it. Remember me kindly to your wife, give my greetings to Lachner, and do not let your memory entirely forget

"Your old friend,
"SCHOENSTEIN." [3]

In the Autumn, Schubert returned to Vienna with the Esterhazys. From that moment the passion for Caroline, if indeed it was a passion, seemed to disappear. He continued to visit their house, which he could not have done had the secret between them assumed dangerous proportions. He played at their musical *salons*, sang and laughed with them. An amour born of loneliness had lived its butterfly day and perished as quickly.

Schubert did not go to Zelész again.

---

[1] From this it appears that Schwind had made a copy of the miniature for his famous picture "A Schubert Evening at Josef von Spaun's," in which the portrait of Caroline is *evidently* taken from Teltscher's miniature of her.

[2] Schönstein addresses Schwind throughout in the familiar "thou" (*Du*), showing the intimacy of their friendship.

[3] Translation from the original letter kindly lent by Frau Prof. von Ravenstein.

CHAPTER XIII

The Year of Promise

(1825)

BACK in Vienna, Schubert returned to his old haunts and discovered his lost gaiety. True the circle in which he resumed his accustomed place was smaller and lacked the kindred spirits of Spaun, Kupelwieser and Schober. Schubert also found that some of those remaining were not as ardent as they should be in serious endeavour, and he complained. But after the stillness of Zelész, the suppressed life at Zelész, the banishment which Zelész had inflicted upon him from a world in which things happened, he was a spirit freed from prison.

The year 1825 was to be a year of promise of better things. He made a little money, and when his pocket held a few coins he worked harder than ever. He paid his debts when he could with strict honour. Then he quickly spent the balance, and waited for poverty to pounce upon him from the next corner. He went to the theatre, he bought dinners and wines for his acqaintances who were enduring the bitter poverty that had been his most inseparable companion. He let the few coins he possessed slip through his fingers in thought-less generosity, and thoroughly enjoyed the goodness of God which had at last enabled him to give to those he loved.

During the year Schubert set seven of the songs from Scott's *Lady of the Lake*. Other songs, *Die junge Nonne, Im Wald, Der blinde Knabe, Auf der Bruck,* and many more followed each other quickly. He composed three sonatas and partly finished a fourth, and his Symphony No. 9. Nearly thirty different works came from his pen in this magic year. Anselm Hüttenbrenner states[1] that he

---

[1] Anselm Hüttenbrenner: "Reminiscences."

also wrote a Sonata in " C Sharp Major," which was so difficult that Schubert himself could not play it without some slight stumbling. He adds: " I practised hard at it for three weeks, and then played it to him in the presence of several friends. He dedicated it to me after that, and sent it to a foreign publisher, but received it back with the remark that they had not the courage to publish such a terribly difficult work, and that if they did it would have no more than a small sale."[1]

It even seemed as if something might be done at last for his luckless operas, for at the end of 1824 the great Prussian singer Anna Milder heard of Schubert through Vogl. Again Vogl had championed the genius of his friend. To Schubert a miracle seemed to happen. He received a letter from Anna Milder asking him if he would agree to one of his operas being produced in Berlin. A production in Berlin! He sent her *Alfonso and Estrella*, together with a copy of Suleika's second song, which he asked permission to dedicate to her.

Schubert's hopes endured only for three months. Early in 1825 the prodigal *Alfonso* came back. " It grieves me to tell you," wrote Anna Milder, " that the *libretto* is useless for the taste of audiences here, which are accustomed to great tragic or the French comic operas. You will see for yourself therefore that *Alfonso and Estrella* would have no chance of success here." Again *Alfonso*, a little more tattered, and probably regarded as more of an ugly duckling than before, went into the drawer.

The *Schubertiaden* continued, at Schwind's, at Jenger's, at Hüttenbrenner's; Schubert invariably at the piano and frequently playing duets with Gahy, whom he preferred above all others as partner in music of this kind. Sophie Müller, the great actress and singer, had now come to Vienna. She entertained lavishly and handed out invitations to her house like commands to Court. She was the friend of the Empress and widely sought in the higher reaches of Society. When she appeared at a dinner-table, rank counted for nothing since she represented all rank. She had the authority of a queen, and remained a simple woman. Schubert attracted her. That he was not known throughout the length and breadth of Europe was not so much a tragedy to her as an absurd blunder. " With such genius, recognition is so easy," she exclaimed.

---

[1] Professor Deutsch states: " Nothing is known about the Sonata in ' C Sharp Major,' its dedication or the offer to a foreign publisher. It is, however, unthinkable that Anselm Hüttenbrenner could have confused it with another pianoforte work."

It was not difficult to talk thus from the top of the mountain to those who toiled below. She made Schubert bring his songs to her as he composed them. One evening he nervously produced from his pocket the manuscript of *Die junge Nonne,* and she sang it at sight. It was in the Müller drawing-room, too, that Vogl first sang Schubert's setting of Walter Scott's songs.

In these crowded, overheated drawing-rooms, Schubert was now appearing regularly. Professor Watteroth, a revered figure, was a regular guest; Baron Schönstein sang, usually accompanied by Jenger. Sophie Müller and Nanette Schechner gave of their best. Only Beethoven kept outside in those secret and exclusive circles of his own. When on these occasions Schubert sang his own songs, he always accompanied himself. When others sang, it was Anselm Hüttenbrenner who accompanied, while Schubert sat in a corner of the room or in an adjoining chamber alone and listened. One evening he whispered in Hüttenbrenner's ear: "I say (Du!), I detest these women with their compliments. They understand nothing about music, and what they say to me they do not mean. Go, Anselm, and bring me, on the quiet, a little glass of wine."[1]

Then came Eduard von Bauernfeld. He was only twenty-three when Schwind introduced him to Schubert in 1825. A youth given to writing sonnets, a youth who bore in him all the promise of the brilliant writer he was to become. He had been well trained in music by Johann Schenk, who at one time had been Beethoven's master in Musical theory. Bauernfeld knew nothing of Schubert except by repute, although he had first heard him sing his own songs in 1822. "A few times I heard him singing his own songs," he writes. "His voice was somewhat midway between a soft tenor and a baritone. His style of singing was simple and natural, full of feeling, and without mannerisms."[2]

At the time of their meeting, Bauernfeld was a lawyer in his fourth year. He was sitting alone in his rooms one February evening when Moritz von Schwind came in accompanied by Schubert. It was the first time they had spoken. "We were soon on intimate terms," Bauernfeld said. "At Schwind's request I had to recite some of my mad youthful poems. Then we went to the piano, and Schubert sang and played duets. Later we went to a restaurant till long into the night."

So came into the circle the last and one of the best of the great Schubertians. From that time forward Schubert, Schwind and

---

[1] Anselm Hüttenbrenner: "Reminiscences."   [2] Bauernfeld: "Alt Wien."

Bauernfeld were constantly together. Their minds moved in a common orbit. A month after the meeting Bauernfeld slept at Schubert's rooms for the first time. " As a tobacco pipe was wanting, Moritz made me one out of Schubert's spectacle-case. Became on terms of ' Thou ' with Schubert over a glass of sugar-water. He wants an Opera libretto from me, and suggested the *Bezauberte Rose* (The Enchanted Rose; by Schulze). A Count Gleichen was in my mind. Visited the singer Vogl. Curious old bachelor. Reads Epictetus and is a treasury of agreeable foolery. Moritz behaved in an impertinent manner towards him. Schubert is always the same, always natural."[1]

A week later, after Schwind had painted portraits of himself and Bauernfeld on the signboard of a char-à-banc conductor, they went off to a *Schubertiade* which Bauernfeld declared was brought about by a little cask of *Rotzer* they had taken with them. They were a gay trio of adventurers, comrades in ambition and rich in dreams. When they ultimately decided to live together so as to reduce expenses, they made a common pool of their clothing, boots, hats, socks and all personal belongings, and wore each other's garments as the mood or necessity dictated.

Whilst they were living apart they frequently accompanied each other home after a *Gasthaus* night, and sometimes remained at Schubert's rooms till the morning. Schwind would usually throw himself down on the bare floor, wrapped in a leather coat.

On one occasion Schwind called at Schubert's rooms to take him for a walk and found him in bed. Franz got out and began to rummage in a drawer, pulling out socks, then throwing them viciously back again.

" What are you looking for, Franz? " Schwind inquired.

" It appears to me, Moritz, that they don't knit socks without holes in these days," Schubert answered.[2]

" Schubert is well, and, after a short period of inactivity, is at work again," Schwind had written to Schober at the beginning of the year. " He has been living for a short time in the house next to us where the beer-house is, on the second floor in a very pretty room. We see each other daily, and, as far as I can, I share his whole life with him. In the Spring we want to move to Dornbach into the house of a good friend of mine. Every week there is a

[1] Diaries, 1819-1848.
[2] Related by Frau Professorin von Ravenstein, Schwind's daughter, living at Karlsruhe.

Schubertiade, and Vogl sings. . . . The new Variations for four hands are something extraordinary. In eight variations these pages are developed quite independently and vividly, and yet each appears again to be the theme.

"At present he is composing songs. If only you would write an operetta on the subject of David and Abigail, or something of the kind, he would like to have the *libretto*, but with few words. You can imagine the thing quite well. The *Zürnende Diana* and *Nachtstück* have come out, and they are dedicated to Frau von Lascny, that is, the one *née* Buchwieser. What a woman! If she were not almost double my age, and unfortunately nearly always ill, I should have to leave Vienna, for I could not bear it. Schubert has known her for some time, but I only met her recently. She is pleased with my things and myself, as no one is apart from yourself. The first time I met her I was quite frightened by the way she spoke to me and treated me. It seemed as if there was nothing she did not know about me."

In Schubert there lived always the spirit of affection. Quarrel sprang up among the Schubertians at times, quarrel of little depth, that created no more than an atmosphere of almost feigned distrust and departed as quickly as it had come. But no barbs were hurled at Schubert; it was as if they feared to hurt a friend who, when he had any money, would give it all to get a laugh out of a comrade smitten by depression.

"Whoever happened to have any money paid for the other three," Bauernfeld said.[1] "It sometimes happened, however, that two had no money and the third—none at all! Naturally Schubert seemed to us a sort of Crœsus, sometimes swimming in silver when perchance he had sold a few songs, or even a whole cycle like the songs from Walter Scott, for which Artaria or Diabelli paid 500 florins (Vienna currency), which figure pleased him greatly. He intended to husband it well, but as usual it got no further than the good intention. At the beginning there was living in plenty, ' treating ' and spending money right and left. Then there came a period of lean days again. In short, it was a continued state of ebb and flow.

" To a return of the latter I owe the fact that I heard Paganini play.[2] The five florins (gulden) which this concert-corsair demanded were quite beyond the powers of my purse. That Schubert

---

[1] Bauernfeld: " Alt Wien."
[2] This took place in March, 1828, a few months before Schubert's death.

JENGER, ANSELM HUTTENBRENNER AND
SCHUBERT
From the tinted drawing by Josef Teltscher

JOHANN MAYRHOFER

VOGL

should hear him again was a matter of course, but he would not hear him again without me, and he was extremely angry when I refused to accept a ticket from him.

" ' Silly nonsense! ' he exclaimed. ' I have heard him once already, and was very annoyed that you were not there. I tell you such a fellow will never come again! I have money like chaff at present, so come along.' Saying this, he dragged me with him. Who would not have surrendered to such pleading?

" We heard then the infernally-heavenly fiddler whose fantasias Heine describes so beautifully. And we were no less transported by his wonderful Adagio than astounded by his devil-tricks, also not a little humorously interested by the incredible bowing and scraping of the demoniacal figure, which resembled a thin black puppet moved by wires. In the customary manner I was treated after the concert at a restaurant, and an extra bottle was drunk at the expense of enthusiasm.

" That was flood-tide. In contrast to that I entered the coffee-house near the Kärntnerthor Theatre early one afternoon, ordered a ' Mélange ' and half a dozen ' Kipfel ' (crescent rolls) with it. Very soon Schubert appeared and did likewise. We mutually admired our good appetite, which demonstrated itself so soon after dinner. ' The fact is, I really haven't eaten anything yet! ' Schubert said in a somewhat subdued tone. ' Neither have I! ' I laughed back. So we had both come to the coffee-house without a previous appointment and taken a ' Mélange ' on credit instead of our midday meal which neither of us could pay for. That was the time of our mutual ebb! "

In all things Schubert was ever the soul of generosity. Anselm Hüttenbrenner recalled how on one occasion he came to him and showed him the original score of Mozart's *Berg-Knappen* music in " F Major," consisting of an Allegro, a Minuet and Trio, an Adagio Cantabile, and a Presto. Schubert had received this work as a gift from a still surviving friend of Mozart's. He and Hüttenbrenner played over this symphony, scored for two violins, viola, two horns and contrabass, and were greatly amused by the many faults in composition of which Mozart had been intentionally guilty. Schubert then offered to halve the manuscript with Hüttenbrenner, so that both of them should possess a souvenir of the immortal composer. Hüttenbrenner refused. He protested against the tearing of the score and declined the half. Schubert then presented him with

I

the whole of the manuscript, and, to his shame, Hüttenbrenner took it.[1]

Schubert's passion for the poetry of Goethe is demonstrated by the fact that during his brief life he set over seventy of the master's songs. Goethe could not have had a greater tribute to his genius than the brilliant setting of his *Erl-King* by a boy of eighteen.

In all, the *Erl-King* has been given nearly forty settings but only that of Schubert remains to be remembered.

In the early Summer of 1825 Schubert resolved to send a set of his songs to Goethe, and he sent them with the following letter:

" YOUR EXCELLENCY,

" Should I succeed by the dedication of these compositions of your poetry in proving my unbounded reverence for your Excellency, or in gaining some notice of my unimportance, I should regard this desirable success as the most beautiful event of my life.

" With greatest esteem,

" Your most devoted servant,

"FRANZ SCHUBERT."

The master poet, sitting in state at Weimar, paid no heed. He did not even acknowledge the gift, or the greater honour of the dedication. He had his Zelter, whose setting of his songs he adored. Doubtless a deluge of settings of his works was part of the everlasting nuisance of his life. That he received the songs is certain from a remark he made in later years when somebody persuaded him that Schubert was a master in music. He said that he had disliked the form of Schubert's setting, which had left him unmoved. But when the great singer Wilhelmine Schröder (who at the age of fifteen was the playfellow and sweetheart of Bauernfeld and at sixteen took the part of Agathe in the first performance of the *Freischütz* in Vienna with phenomenal success) sang Schubert's setting of the *Erl-King* to him, he was overcome with emotion. It was then too late to make amends to Schubert. He had been dead two years. This was the great God who did not recognise genius when he saw it!

In spite of the rebuff from Goethe, Schubert continued to set his songs. No poet made such a profound impression upon him. Once when he was describing to Bauernfeld his adoration of Goethe's poetry he went on to explain what a deep effect his first reading of

[1] Anselm Hüttenbrenner: "Reminiscences."

120

the little poem *Rastlose Liebe* (Restless Love) had produced in him. " I think we all know it—that effect," he added significantly.

In March, Vogl went to Steyr, and Schubert, having a little money in hand, joined him there at the end of May. By his departure he missed the celebrations of the Schubertians which followed the return of Schober from his travels in June. Not that Schubert had forgotten him. " I am very anxious to meet Schober and Kupelwieser," Schubert wrote to Bauernfeld from Steyr, " the former in order to see what a man looks like whose plans have failed." There was a grim irony in the remark.

This holiday with Vogl was undoubtedly one of the happiest episodes in Schubert's life. With Steyr as their headquarters, they visited Linz, Gmunden, Salzburg. Schubert, in ecstasies with the scenery, wrote letters of excited description to brother Ferdinand and the Schubertians, composing his songs from the *Lady of the Lake*, which Vogl sang at the places they visited. With Stadler he stayed at the Schloss Steyregg, about an hour from the town, a house of great beauty on the banks of the Danube. One morning Schubert sang a melody from the *Magic Flute* whilst lying in bed, and asked Stadler if he could sing the second part to it. " Next morning," says Stadler,[1] " I was up early and wanted to show Schubert the beautiful view from an adjacent hill, but he would not stir; he preferred his bed, and he let me go alone."

From Linz, Schubert wrote to Spaun at Lemberg, in July:

" You can imagine how annoyed I am at having to write a letter to you since I am at Linz and you are at Lemberg! Here I am perspiring to death in this infernal heat. I have composed a whole book of new songs, and you are not here. Are you not ashamed of yourself? Linz without you is like a body without a soul, a rider without a head, soup without salt. If Jägermeyer had not such good beer, and if the wine on the Schlossberg were not drinkable I should hang myself on the Promenade with the inscription attached to me: ' He committed suicide because his soul had fled. . . .'

" From Schober we have heard some astounding things which seem to be comical.[2] To begin with, I read in a Viennese paper about a pseudonymous Torupson! What is the meaning of this? Surely he cannot have got married. That would be funny. . . .

[1] Stadler: " Reminiscences."

[2] Schubert seems to be unaware that Schober had already reached Vienna. That he had done so is proved by an entry in Bauernfeld's diary for June, 1825, in which he says: " Walk with Moritz [Schwind]. A few days later he announced to me the arrival of his most remarkable friend Schober."

" I only stayed a fortnight at Steyr, and then we (Vogl and I) went to Gmunden, where we spent six happy weeks. We were living at Traweger's, who possesses a splendid pianoforte and is, as you know, an ardent admirer of poor me."

Something of Schubert's life with the Trawegers is recorded in a letter written by the son of the house, Eduard, in later years.[1] Eduard was little more than four years of age at the time of Schubert's visit, but the details appear to have been clearly imprinted on his mind because his father had made the children fully realize the importance of the guest they were entertaining.

Young Traweger was suffering from diphtheria when Schubert arrived, and the doctor had ordered the use of leeches, but no one could persuade the restless child to allow them to be put on. The parent and the doctor failed utterly to pacify the patient, and Vogl's intervention was equally fruitless. The leeches remained in the basin.

Schubert then tried coaxing, at first with no success. But Eduard Traweger states that the importance of Schubert had been so deeply impressed upon him that at length he asked that Schubert himself should apply the leeches. Under the direction of the doctor, Schubert put on the leeches one by one, and when the operation was completed gave the boy a silver pencil-case as a souvenir. " I remember this as clearly as if it happened yesterday," said Traweger.

When Vogl sang and Schubert accompanied him, the boy was allowed to listen, and not infrequently the men present were so overcome that with tears running down their cheeks they embraced each other. Every morning when the boy awoke he ran into Schubert's room in his nightshirt and jumped into his bed. He had visited Vogl in the same way on one or two occasions. But the singer disturbed from his sleep scolded him and sent him away.

Schubert, on the contrary, was more accommodating. He had the heart of a child and understood children, a virtue one can hardly imagine in Vogl. Schubert would sit out in his dressing-gown, a long pipe in his mouth, and take the youthful Eduard on his knee, blow smoke at him, place his spectacles on the little fellow's nose, rub his whiskers against his face and allow the child to rummage with his fingers in his hair. On one occasion the boy proudly showed Schubert his attempts at writing as the result of his first lessons. Schubert then went to his table, which was littered with sheets of

[1] Eduard Traweger: Letter to Luib, 1858.

manuscript music, and picked up a leaden writing-stand which he prized to such an extent that he kept it in a glass case. He gave it to young Traweger, who took it with him when he went to the University.

Schubert then began to teach the boy to sing. He began with his *Guten Morgen, Schöne Müllerin,* and to coax him he would say: " Eduard, sing *Guten Morgen* and I will give you a shining penny." " Then," says Traweger, " I squeaked as loudly as I could." When friends were present the boy was shy and could not sing until Schubert took him between his knees and began to play the accompaniment.[1]

During Schubert's stay with the Trawegers, concerts were held continuously. Hofrath von Schiller, whom Schubert described as Emperor of the whole of Salzburg, arrived at the house, and the concerts assumed greater proportions than before.

" My new songs from Walter Scott's *Lady of the Lake* met with great approval," Schubert wrote to his father and stepmother. " They were greatly surprised at my piety which I expressed in a hymn to the Virgin (the *Ave Maria*), which apparently moved everybody and tends towards devotion. I believe it is because I never force myself to be devout except when I feel so inspired, and never compose hymns or prayers unless I feel within me real and true devotion."

Meanwhile Bauernfeld had written to him from Vienna, saying that his rent was unpaid, and suggesting that in future they should live together in order to curtail expenses.

Schubert replied: " Regarding my quarters in Frühwirt's house, I intend to keep them on, and have sent him word to that effect by way of my father's house. It may be that they have forgotten about it, or it may be that he is very fussy and anxious. Anyhow, be so kind, one or all of you together, to send him twenty-five florins, Viennese currency, and apprise him of the fact that I shall certainly be returning, about the end of October.

---

[1] Old Traweger collected all Schubert's letters and every scrap of paper that came from him. After his death these souvenirs were shown by his wife to the children, who were told that they must be kept with great care. Eduard Traweger, in later years, resolved to give them to the Society of the Friends of Music in Vienna, but learned from his sister Elise that, in moving from one place to another, they had been lost. Eduard Traweger went to the Vienna Convict as a choirboy in 1832, and whilst he was there the Choirmaster, Pater Georg Benedict, a native of Steyr, spent his holidays one year with the Traweger family. He looked over their music, picked out a considerable quantity, paid for it and took it away. It is believed that the Schubert letters and MSS. were thus secured by him.

" With regard to our living together, I should be very pleased, but, knowing the ways of bachelors and students, I should not care to be left sitting between two chairs in the end. Should we find a suitable place, I can always discover a means of leaving my landlord. The above-mentioned twenty-five florins he is to have for the month of October. I shall return them to you directly I arrive. . . .

" Schwind is like a wool-winder. He has written me two letters, of which one is more confused than the other. I have never known such a mixture of sense and nonsense. Unless he has been producing some very beautiful things in the meantime, he cannot be excused for writing such senseless twaddle. . . .

" Steiger and Hönig paid me a visit at Gmunden, which pleased me very much. If you had added a little to your common sense you would have done the same. But such is not to be expected of two boys [Bauernfeld and Schwind] who are as deeply in love as you are! How often you will have been miserable again and drowned your sorrows in punch or beer! ha! ha! ha! ha! Good-bye.

" Your SCHUBERT.

" Do write something sensible to me, some poetry with music in it for instance."

On the way back to Vienna in September, Schubert stayed at Salzburg. The majesty of its hills, the romance that enfolded its old houses impressed him deeply. The journey had put him in better health than he had known since the outbreak of his illness in 1822. His letters are those of a man light of heart who sees no shadow across the beauty of the world. Nature, its life, always stirred him profoundly. When in Vienna he loved to walk in the woods alone, and from these walks came the reflection of Nature in many songs.

In Salzburg he paid his tribute to Michael Haydn. He went to his devotions at the little corner in the Cathedral where the monument to Haydn is partly concealed. " I was thinking, if only your pure and clean mind could touch me, you dear Haydn," he wrote. " Even if I cannot be as pure and clean, nobody has a greater reverence for you than I have."

He reached Vienna in October. Schober had returned, impenitent, as gallant and attractive as ever. Kupelwieser was back, full of the glories of Rome and Naples. The Circle was complete again, save for Spaun, who was soon to return from Lemberg. The *Schubertiaden* were renewed, a warmer comradeship came to the nights at the *Gasthaus*.

At the end of the year Schubert had a fresh attack of illness. In consequence, he had to forgo Schober's New Year party, whereat Bauernfeld read a dramatic parody he had written about the Schubertians. In it Schober appeared as Pantaloon, Schwind as Harlequin, and Schubert as Pierrot. With Schubert the old trouble had broken out again. More medicine and abstinence.

Bauernfeld's diary for October may throw a little light upon the cause of Schubert's new attack.

" October, 1825.—Schubert is back. Wine and coffee-house. Life with our friends often till two and three in the morning.

" Schober is the worst in this. He has, of course, nothing to do, nor does he do anything. Moritz continually taunts him about his idleness."

Schubert had just come into twenty pounds as the result of the sale of the Walter Scott songs. And the Schubert who could never change himself paid his debts, including a loan from his father, and spent the balance.

CHAPTER XIV

Some Gasthaus Nights

NDER the shadows of St. Stefan's runs a little cobbled
street known as the Grünanker Gasse. The top of the
spire of the Cathedral rises sharp and clear—like a huge needle
pointed at the sky—over the roofs in this street on any moonlit
Viennese night. And in the middle of the street is the " Green
Anchor " (*Zum grünen Anker*).

Between 1825 and 1827 Schubert could be found in the " Green
Anchor " daily. He was there in the afternoons. With Schwind,
Schober and the rest of them, he was always there in the evenings.
In the same company, often augmented, he was usually there late
into the night. Of late years the " Green Anchor " has been an
Italian restaurant—the same building as that of the Schubert nights,
the same low-ceilinged rooms and boarded floors, the same apartments opening from one into the other. Over the crowded tables
hangs a pall of smoke undisturbed by draughts, just as in the nights
when Schubert and his friends sat in the corner with their wine and
beer, their ambitions and dreams.

From the " Green Anchor " they usually emerged very late, and
when Schubert, Schober and Schwind went to live together in 1826
their nights at the " Green Anchor " grew later still. Schwind
usually wore a coat with a wide black cape. When in the fullness
of the midnight hour they emerged into the narrow street he would
dance up and down the cobbles, flinging wide his cape and pre-
tending that he was a bat. They would perform pranks down the
street till they reached the Stefansplatz, where they danced awhile
and sang and serenaded the moon. Solitary foot passengers would
pause and stare at the mad frolics of youth.

After leaving the *Grünen Anker* or some other *Gasthaus*, they
frequently went to Bogner's coffee-house, which continued to be

Schubert's favourite coffee-house until his death. The " Green Anchor " was visited regularly; its beer remained as good; its atmosphere as convivial. The kindliness of the " Green Anchor " to those who sought the comradeship of the nightly meetings remained unimpaired. Moreover, it was a happy halting-place on the way to Bogner's.

The average events of a Schubertian evening when the fun was free, and the cares of the day seemed to disappear with the tobacco smoke, are recorded in the diary of one of the circle, von Hartmann.[1] This is how the diarist described what happened on January 13th, 1827.

" We went to the ' Anker,' where Spaun, Enderes, Gahy and Schober had foregathered, and also Derffel [Schober's uncle]. After we had been in there for a long time and at last considered it time to break up, we went on this glorious moonlight night to Bogner's coffee-house, where we danced and engaged in all manner of childish pranks. From there we danced over to the Stock-am-Eisen Square round the Stefan's Cathedral, which we gazed at. Then into the Goldschmiedgasse and made our demonstration at that coffee-house, also at the Peter and the coffee-house on the Graben. Then we went to Geringer's coffee-house in the Kohl-markt, where we said we would push Spaun in, as he was always averse to late coffee-house going. But to our surprise he went in as meekly as a lamb when we pushed open the door, and we all trooped in sedately behind him. We smoked and talked merrily. Finally we parted and went home at 12.30."

" Over a glass of wine or punch Schubert was most talkative," says Anselm Hüttenbrenner.[2] " His musical judgments were sharp, and he always hit the nail on the head. In this way he resembled Beethoven, who could be very sarcastic at times. If at a Society gathering music was discussed with knowledge, Schubert would listen with pleasure and rarely interrupt. But if an ill-informed amateur made statements which proved his ignorance Schubert's patience broke at once. He would go up to the jabberer and exclaim hotly: ' You'd better be quiet. You don't understand that, and you never will understand it! ' "

There was no coarseness, no debauchery in these *Gasthaus* gatherings. Laughter and excitability—perhaps a few more glasses of punch than prudence would have decreed, but seldom excess—

[1] Franz von Hartmann's Diary. Discovered by Professor Otto Erich Deutsch.
[2] Anselm Hüttenbrenner: " Reminiscences."

good humour and sublime faith in each other. " Schober stands mentally above us all, especially in conversation," wrote Bauernfeld in his diary on March 8th, 1826, " but a good deal in him is artificial. Moreover, his best powers threaten to be stifled by idleness. Schwind is a magnificent pure nature, only in a perpetual state of ferment as if he would use himself up. Schubert has the right mixture of the ideal and real. The earth is beautiful to him. Mayrhofer is simple and natural, although Schober asserts that he is a sort of secret intriguing plotter. And I? Ah! If only one might know oneself! Until I have created something worth while I am not a man."

" Mayrhofer was sullen, shy, and to strangers unapproachable," said William von Chézy,[1] whom Feuchtersleben introduced to the Circle one evening at Bogner's. " His very counterpart was the little broad-shouldered musician [Schubert], outwardly a lump of fat, but with eyes so sparkling that they revealed at once the inner fire. Unfortunately his urge for the fullness of life led him into those wrong paths (*Abwege*) whence there is usually no return, at least no healthy one. Conversion is not always identical with turning back, especially when, following the example of the old devil, one turns hermit. He took, shall I say? a certain pride in the accidents which befell him in his wild ways. . . . When the blood of the Vine glowed in him he did not rant, but moved into a quiet corner to give himself up to a comfortable frenzy. A smiling tyrant who, if he could do so, would destroy something, glasses for instance, or plates or cups. He used to sit there and grin and contract his eyelids, so that his eyes became very small."

Chézy was never a great favourite with the Schubertians, so there may have been motive behind the bitterness of his pen. Very different from the frank statement of Anselm Hüttenbrenner: " Schubert was absolutely honest, true and upright. And he lived at that time—be it said, between you and me—a much purer life than I did! "[2] Chézy's flagellation has small evidence to warrant its justice. Not that any of Schubert's disciples would have given the opinion that Franz was a saint, or that hidden behind that calm and benevolent exterior did not lurk the demon of temper, difficult to rouse, but, when roused, as difficult to exorcise.

It was certainly roused on one occasion when, with his friends,

---

[1] William von Chézy: " Erinnerungen." Chézy was the son of the Wilhelmine v. Chézy who had written the *libretto* of *Rosamunde*.
[2] Anselm Hüttenbrenner: " Reminiscences."

he was returning from a *Gasthaus* at Grinzing. Lachner and Bauernfeld had walked there to the festival of the "New Wine." "During the mornings," says Lachner,[1] "we played our compositions to one another and exchanged views about them with the greatest frankness, which taught us both a good deal. In the afternoon we went excursions together to Grinzing, Kloster Neuberg, etc., and very often did not return till after midnight, only to meet again early the next morning."

Schubert was very fond of new wine, and on this particular occasion he found all he wanted at Grinzing. They sat round the table drinking wine, and only returned to Vienna after night had descended. Bauernfeld, who lived in a distant suburb, now wanted to go home, but Schubert had no such intention. He took Bauernfeld and Lachner to a tavern. Then, as the night was young, he led the way to another tavern. When one in the morning struck a heated musical discussion was going on over the punch.

"Schubert," says Bauernfeld,[2] "drained one glass after another and worked himself up into a state of ecstasy, in which he was more eloquent than usual. He explained to Lachner and myself all his plans for the future. Then an evil genius brought to the *Gasthaus* some professional musicians, well-known members of the orchestra at the Opera.

"When these fellows appeared, Schubert stopped in the middle of his florid oration; his little eyes gleamed wildly from under his spectacles, which he was restlessly pushing up and down. As soon as the musicians saw the master they hurried up to him, took his hands, and smothered him with flattery. At lenght it was revealed that they were in urgent need of a new composition, with solo parts for their respective instruments; Master Schubert would no doubt be agreeable, etc.

"The master remained silent. Then, when they pressed him repeatedly, he exclaimed abruptly: 'No! For you I shall write nothing.'

"'Not for us? And why not, Herr Schubert?' inquired one. 'We are artists just as you are. None better known in Vienna.'

"'Artists!' Schubert shouted. He quickly emptied his glass of punch and rose from the table. He pushed his hat over one ear, and planted himself in front of the one much taller and the other more corpulent virtuoso in a threatening manner. 'Artists!' he repeated.

[1] Franz Lachner: Letter to Luib.
[2] Bauernfeld: "Alt Wien."

129

' Musical artisans! Nothing else. One bites into the brass mouth-piece of his wooden cudgel, and the other blows his cheeks out on a French horn. Do you call that Art? A craft which brings in money, and there it ends. You—artists! Don't you know what the great Lessing says: "How can a man do nothing all his life save bite into a piece of wood with holes in it?" That is what he said. Is it not so?' he inquired of his friends. ' That or something like it.'

" ' You want to be artists!' he continued to rave at the musicians. ' Tootlers and fiddlers you are, all of you. *I* am an artist! *I*. I am Franz Schubert whom all the world knows and acclaims. Who has made great and beautiful things. Eh, brother?' he said, turning to Lachner. ' The most beautiful cantatas and quartets, operas and symphonies! For I am not only a *Ländler* (dance) composer, as it says in the stupid newspapers, and as the silly people repeat—I am Schubert! Franz Schubert, so that you may know it, and when the word " artist " is mentioned, it refers to me, not to you worms and insects—you who demand solos which I shall never write for you. I know perfectly well why! You creeping and gnawing worms, whom my foot should crush—the foot of a man who reaches to the stars! *Sublimi feriam sidera vertice!* Trans-late that for them,' he added. ' To the stars! I say, while you poor blowing worms wriggle in the dust. And with the dust you will rot and be blown away.' "

The startled visitors stood there with open mouths. They had no answer, no challenge to hurl back. The torrent of abuse had smitten them into silence. The adored god was transformed into a devil out of hell. Lachner and Bauernfeld endeavoured to persuade Schubert to leave the place, and tried to assuage his anger. After some time they took him home.

" Next morning," says Bauernfeld,[1] " I hurried to see my friend, as his condition had caused me to feel some uneasiness. I found Schubert in bed, fast asleep, with his spectacles on as usual. His clothes lay strewn in wild disorder all over the room. A sea of ink had spread itself over the table from an overturned ink-stand, and on a single sheet of paper was written: ' At two o'clock in the night.' Then followed a few somewhat confused aphorisms. Violent mental explosions which, no doubt, he had written down after the turbulent scene of the night before. From them I extracted a curious passage which ran thus:

[1] Bauernfeld: " Alt Wien."

"'Enviable Nero, thou who wast so strong as to destroy a detestable people whilst playing on thy lyre and singing!'"

And so writing he had gone to sleep and forgotten the detestable people, presumably the musicians.

Bauernfeld waited in the room till Schubert awoke. "It's you!" said Schubert presently, adjusting his spectacles, and slowly putting out his hand.

"Slept enough?" Bauernfeld asked significantly.

"Nonsense!" exclaimed Schubert, and jumped out of bed laughing.

"What will people think of you?" Bauernfeld said in a censuring tone.

"The rogues! D'you know, they are the most intriguing rascals in the world? Especially towards me. They have deserved their lesson. I confess I repent it. But I suppose I shall write the solos they asked me for, and then they will still kiss my hands for the gift. I know those people!"

Such a scene with Schubert was not only rare, it was unprecedented. "It only happened on that one occasion, and when he was in an exceptional state of mind," said Bauernfeld. He never sought quarrels—only outrage or injustice too rank to be endured drew from him outward signs of loss of temper.

On another memorable *Gasthaus* night Schwind was the disturber. A year previously he had conceived a passion for Netty Hönig, a beautiful and accomplished girl, a pianoforte player of considerable brilliance. She frequently took part in the *Schubertiaden,* and it was at one of these functions that Schwind had met her. Schubert considered her to be one of the best female musicians in this company of clever people.

Schwind was nervous and undecided: "The sweet Netty I keep almost entirely to myself," he wrote to Schober. "Dear Schober, I am really not in love, but I feel happy when I am with her; why, I really don't know. And yet, in the end, it all amounts to the same thing."

His wooing then became more turbulent, and the slow progress of his passion drove him into moods of depression. "Schober and Schwind have quarrelled. Poor Moritz is suffering from love-sickness and finds no recognition of his art. Schubert without money like the rest of us," Bauernfeld graphically wrote in his diary a few weeks later. When he went on a holiday with Mayrhofer during the summer Schubert wrote to him: "Schwind has come down

131

in the world as far as Nettel [Netty] is concerned. Vogl has been married!!"

The months as they passed were a torture to Schwind. Netty Hönig was temperamental, and a yet greater plague was the lack of money. True, Schwind had painted a Turk and a Turkish woman as signboards to Bogner's coffee-house in order to clear his debt for food and drink at the café, but, as Schubert and Bauernfeld informed him, he could not keep a wife by painting Turks on signboards. Not, at any rate, a Netty Hönig.

After a protracted purgatory, an engagement was reached, and Schwind was summoned to the Hönig establishment, where a considerable gathering of Hönig aunts and uncles and Court Councillors were to receive him and load him with their congratulations. Schwind became frightened. He told Schubert and Bauernfeld that he would not go. How could he go when he had no suit to go in, and would have to wear his painter's smock! The difficulty was soon solved. Schubert and Bauernfeld rummaged in cupboards and drawers and produced an old dress-coat. They clothed Schwind in it and packed him off, Schwind declaring that he would not stay ten minutes.

It had been arranged between them that Schwind should meet Schubert and Bauernfeld at the *Gasthaus* when he left the Hönigs' party. He came at last in a great state of excitement. Netty had found her lover so passionless that evening that she had had the utmost trouble in persuading him to stay still ten o'clock. On arrival at the *Gasthaus* Schwind fell into a chair beside Schubert and broke into a storm of violent language against the whole Philistine company. Schubert sat there saying nothing, but quite unable to control his good-natured tittering, while Schwind gulped down one glass of punch after another. He was wild and frantic in his excitement. He was, he declared, completely annihilated. He had half a mind to shoot himself on the spot.[1]

There was only one thing to do with the young madman. They took him home. The Hönigs eventually prepared a plan for him. He must go away and make a desperate effort to stabilize his position. or the engagement would come to naught. They persuaded him to go to Munich. But on the night of the party Bauernfeld made a careful note in his diary: "Schwind has proposed to Netty, and that in a torn dress-coat."[2]

In Munich Schwind came under the influence of Peter Cornelius,

[1] Bauernfeld: "Alt Wien." [2] Bauernfeld: "Diaries."

and, with a future full of promise, he returned to Vienna. But during his absence Netty Hönig had become an extreme *religieuse*. Nothing that Moritz could do satisfied her. At first he was driven to despair, then to temper. After one of their scenes he turned upon her and exclaimed:

" Go and marry the Pope! "

Love affairs among the Schubertians did not prosper. First Schober, now Schwind. The gods who control these things found the Schubertian temperaments too difficult to charm. Netty went on with her playing at the *Schubertiaden,* and Schwind returned to Munich, the despised and rejected of Vienna, to sell his pictures for prices he had never dreamed of.

CHAPTER XV

The Cup of Emptiness

(1826-7)

THE total sum which Schubert made by his compositions in the entire course of his life amounted to the equivalent of £575![1] For that sum he composed considerably more than a thousand songs, symphonies, operas, dances and all forms of music. During the last year of Schubert's life, Paganini gave eight concerts in Vienna and received in a few weeks approximately the same sum as Schubert earned by all his work. Verily, the favours of music were distributed with a strange sense of justice.

As Schubert became better known by the publication of his songs, so did his receipts become smaller. A sale at almost any figure seemed to be a solace. For his first paid work—the *Prometheus* of 1816—he received £4. For the first twelve songs of the *Winterreise* cycle—composed in the last months of his life—he was paid tenpence each, ten shillings in all.

His revenue from the publishers had for some years amounted to 40 florins a work. Now (1826), with only two years of life remaining, he was averaging no more than 30 florins. The *Winterreise* cost in the music-selling trade twelve times as much as the *Erl-King*, viz., 6 florins, and Schubert was paid by Haslinger—so it is stated—scarcely one half of the usual honorarium. Although he had received as much as 300 florins for Op. 53 and 54, Sonata in " D " and Divertissement for Pianoforte Duet, yet, when in 1826 he asked Hans Nägeli of Zürich 120 florins for a Sonata which the

---

[1] This is the computation made by Professor Otto Erich Deutsch, whose many years of Schubertian study have put him in possession of all the details of Schubert's finances, and the figure can therefore be accepted without question.

MORITZ VON SCHWIND
one of the most prominent members of the
Schubert circle
(*Self-portrait in oils*)

BAUERNFELD
Schubert's great friend and author
of "Count Gleichen"

GRILLPARZER

The poet whose songs Schubert set

COUNTESS CAROLINE ESTERHAZY

a bit unappreciated portrait

publisher desired to have, and H. A. Probst of Leipsic 80 florins each for three pieces, they both declined. Schubert certainly did not expect this rebuff from Nägeli. Probably if he had not asked for the money in advance, he would not have received a refusal.

" By Mr. Carl Czerny," he wrote, " I have received the honoured commission of writing a sonata for the pianoforte for you, which it is your intention to produce in a collection of different piano compositions (entitled ' The Gate of Honour '), as you have my acquaintance through my A minor sonata. Not only your favourable criticism of this sonata, but also your most flattering request makes me willing to accede to your wish, whenever you choose.

" I must ask you to send my fee of 120 fl. in advance.

" It has been a great pleasure to me to begin a correspondence with such old and celebrated art dealers.

" I remain with esteem,

" Your devoted

" FRANZ SCHUBERT."

Schubert was obviously finding the market for his music declining in value as the brilliance of his work became more apparent. Not that the publishers were making losses over him. Diabelli, in particular, had found in Schubert one of his best sources of plunder. It can only be assumed that the publishers, aware that Schubert seldom possessed money, considered refusal of his offers the best means to purchase at a knock-out price. Probst, at any rate, would appear to have thought so, for, when in 1828 Schubert offered him the " E Flat Major " trio for 100 florins, he beat him down to 20 florins 60 kreutzers.

The reiterated requests of Schubert to the publishers for better terms usually remained unanswered. If he expected any of them to desist from driving the hardest bargain possible, he might as well have looked for the moon to fall. At one period he visited Haslinger almost daily. Beethoven and other Viennese musicians used frequently to meet at Haslinger's music shop between eleven and twelve o'clock in the morning. The shop was called the " Fox's hole." It was a vault, or rather a vaulted room, in the Paternoster Gässchen, which had formerly been inhabited by sellers of religious books, from which fact it received its name.[1] The Paternoster Gässchen was a little alley running out of the Graben.

---

[1] Anselm Hüttenbrenner: " Reminiscences."

Schubert sold his first work at the age of nineteen, therefore his earning power covered only a period of thirteen years. His average earnings during these years amounted to approximately £44 per annum. Yet he did not live in absolute destitution; it is doubtful if at any moment of his life he reached a crisis when he did not know where to find a meal. Had he lived with care, put aside the generosity which was ever present in the big heart of him, and which urged him to give to others when he had anything to give, he would have avoided those periods of acute penury that followed hard upon the receipt of any money. If Schubert had made the earnings of Handel in his years of blindness, he would certainly have spent them. He had no knowledge of money values, no knowledge of business. He lived with a convinced belief in the unfairness of mankind towards him, certain that the mischance of Fate was burying his genius.

He should have been able to live on his meagre £44 a year. The Vienna of his day fed its citizens cheaply. A portion of veal at a restaurant in 1824 cost but 28 kr., approximately $3\frac{1}{2}$d., roast beef with onions 3d., and baked calves' head $2\frac{1}{2}$d., as may be seen from a *menu* of the restaurant "Seitzerhof," on the back of which Schubert had written a poem. In 1826 a pound of beef in Vienna cost only $2\frac{1}{2}$d. In short, one can assess the value of the food and drink Schubert consumed daily at about 1 florin.[1]

Schubert therefore was not so poor as he might have been. If he had secured the music teacher's post at Laibach, as he failed to do in 1816, he would have been paid 500 fl. a year. Less money than he was destined to make as an independent composer. But now—ten years later—the desire for a settled income again became uppermost in his mind. His old teacher, Salieri, had died during the preceding year, leaving vacant the post of second Court Capell-meister, which carried with it a salary up to 800 florins. To Schubert the chance seemed like the open door of escape from continual necessity. On April 6th, 1826, he wrote to the Emperor:

" To the Emperor Francis II.
 " Your Majesty!
  " Most Glorious Emperor!

" With most submissive reverence I proffer the most humble request of Your Majesty's graciously appointing me to the vacant

[1] Professor Otto Erich Deutsch.

post of vice-conductor of the Court orchestra, and I am putting forward the following reasons in justification of this request:

"1. I am a native of Vienna, son of a schoolmaster and I am 29 years old.

"2. I enjoyed the Imperial favour of having been a Court singing boy for 5 years, pupil of the Imperial and Royal Convict.

"3. I received full instruction in composition by the late first Court conductor, Herr Anton Salieri, and am therefore able to fill the position of conductor of an orchestra.

"4. My name is well-known, not only in Vienna, but also in Germany, by the composition of songs and also instrumental music.

"5. I have finished five Masses which have been produced in several churches in Vienna, and which are composed for small or large orchestras.

"6. I have no fixed position, so have hope of attaining in this way the ambition in Art I am striving for.

"It would be my utmost endeavour to justify to the fullest extent the granting of my request.

"Your most submissive servant,
"FRANZ SCHUBERT."

The appeal fell on deaf ears. The Emperor knew nothing of Schubert. Probably he knew nothing of the application. In any case, the Masses would have made small appeal to him since his idea of religious music was something very brief, and of a nature adapted to the capacity of his musical understanding. A few months later the appointment was given to Joseph Weigl, the composer of *The Swiss Family*. Schubert retained his old philosophy and courage. "I should have been glad of the post," he declared when he heard the news, "but since it has been given to a man as worthy as Weigl, I am well content."

But not so his friends. Weigl was able, but the better man had been passed over. Whilst the appointment was under discussion, another became vacant. Krebs, the conductor at the Imperial Opera, was transferred to Hamburg, and Vogl drew the attention of the director Dupont to the qualifications of Schubert to take his place. Here at last was a position in filling which neither intrigue nor ignorance could interfere. If Schubert could prove himself a capable operatic composer the appointment would be given to him.

Excitement became intense in the Circle. Schubert had the talents. He would carry the Opera to heights it had never known. There was no other opinion than that the *Gasthaus* evenings would lose their central figure, whom the Opera had claimed.

The test was quickly arranged. The theatre-secretary Hofmann compiled a *libretto* of five or six numbers. The whole was to be preceded by an overture. A solo soprano and a chorus divided the action.[1] Schubert quickly set it to music, and the administration was so attracted by the score that it resolved to give it a public evening performance.

The solo part was given to Fräulein Schechner, who sang Schubert's songs continually. The stars seemed set in their courses for Schubert.

But trouble began at rehearsals. The singer wanted several intervals removed, and with ill grace Schubert conceded the request. She then demanded that certain high notes should be taken out of the music, and Schubert refused. With the accompaniment of a piano, the rehearsals were continued until Fräulein Schechner declared that she would break down in the great Aria with chorus if the alterations which she desired in respect to the high notes were not made. There was no response from Schubert. He became sullen. He expressed no anger and no opinions. The management intervened, but in vain. The stubbornness which had on occasion refused even to Vogl changes in songs yielded no concession. Even the members of the orchestra freely expressed the opinion that such a massed combination of instruments had never been known before.

Still Schubert was silent.

The day of the final rehearsal arrived, and the *impasse* between singer and composer remained. Three Capellmeisters, all of whom had gained high honours in opera, were present. Schubert had invited also his patrons, his special friends. The rehearsal was begun and everything went well until the Aria opened. Fräulein Schechner struggled bravely with it in continuous battle with the orchestra, especially the wind instruments (brass), until her powerful voice was overwhelmed. Then she sank down exhausted into a chair at the side of the proscenium.

Deep silence fell over the house. Schubert was in defeat. On every face was tense excitement. Schubert, they said, had wilfully ruined his singer, and thrown his opportunity to the winds. Dupont

---

[1] A. Schindler: "Reminiscences of Franz Schubert." From the *Niederrheinische Musik-Zeitung*, Cologne, March 7th, 1857.

moved from one to another of the groups that had collected on the stage. He spoke in low tones to the singer and the Capellmeisters. But Schubert sat in his chair, staring with a fixed look at the opera score in front of him.

Dupont at last approached the orchestra. He hesitated, then he said:

"Herr Schubert, we will postpone the performance for a few days, and I beg of you that you will make the necessary alterations at least in the Aria, and so make it easier for Fräulein Schechner." Several members of the orchestra also endeavoured to bring Schubert to see reason. "And I," says Schindler,[1] "sitting by his side tried to do the same."

Schubert listened to all the arguments against him. He said nothing; his face was a mask. Then, with gradually rising anger, he shouted out in a loud voice: "I will alter nothing!" He shut the score with a bang and walked out of the theatre.

In later years Schindler, when recalling the incident, compared it with a similar episode in the case of Beethoven and the Ninth Symphony, but the older master at least modified the Recitative in the Fourth Movement to suit Leipel's low compass. But Schindler would have been as much surprised as the rest of his contemporaries if he had found that the high soprano parts and the famous double-bass passages in the same Symphony, which at that time were declared to be impossible, are no obstacle to our modern singers and players. Probably the same would be the case with this work of Schubert's, if it were to be performed now. Schubert, perhaps, felt that. At all events, the episode destroyed for ever any chance he had of an operatic conductorship. With his bohemian habits, his total disregard for the hours of the clock, he might not have retained the post had he secured it.[2]

Schubert, so accustomed to disappointments, was little disturbed. Whatever opinion he may have expressed to the Schubertians who had prophesied his acquisition of the post, he left no written comment. The pattern of his life did not change. He returned with new fervour to his songs. His drinking song from *Antony and Cleopatra, To Sylvia, Hark! Hark! the Lark!, Hippolit's Song* from Johanna Schoppenhauer's *Gabriele*, all came from his pen in one month. He had made himself a little book consisting of eight pages

[1] Anton Schindler: "Reminiscences of Franz Schubert."

[2] Another account of the affair states that Fräulein Schechner was already in failing voice, and that the conflict was directly caused by theatrical intrigue.

of paper which he ruled with pencil, and on these pages he is said to have written these four songs.[1] Possibly he carried the book about with him, for the evidence is tolerably clear that he composed *Hark! Hark! the Lark!* at the Moonshine house. Moreover, the drinking song is supposed to have been composed in the garden of an inn, the " Biersack," after he had been for a walk with Schwind. Legend has given Doppler—Schubert's early confidant in the wine room when he left the Convict—the credit of having ruled the lines on the back of a *menu* card when Schubert, picking up a book, saw the words which brought the inspiration and exclaimed: " A beautiful melody has come into my mind." There amid the clatter of falling ninepins, and the chatter and laughter of the beer-house, he is supposed to have composed the drinking song. If a *menu* card was ruled and scored with Schubert's notes it has long since been lost, and Doppler, the tottering figure, with the black skull-cap, whom Grove and Sullivan met when, in the later sixties, they went to Vienna to discover the lost *Rosamunde* music, has been forgotten. But the Viennese love their legends. As late as 1885 the " Social Union of the Savages of Währing " affixed a tablet to the hostel, now called the " Beer House to the Schubert Garden," recording the fact that Schubert had composed the drinking song there. Legend can live longer than fact. Handel had passed to dust in Westminster Abbey before someone discovered his exercises for a Princess who had been his pupil, named them *The Harmonious Blacksmith,* and invented the story of the thunder-storm and the blacksmith's forge.

At the end of March (1826) Bauernfeld and Mayrhofer departed to Carinthia after a vain effort to persuade Schubert to accompany them. Mayrhofer had been ordered on a surveying expedition by the Government. He was to be paid ample expenses, and he wanted a companion. Bauernfeld, the more practical dreamer, joined him with alacrity. He had no money, but as the Government was sponsoring his companion all would be well. " The gods will take care of the future," Bauernfeld wrote in his diary. They believed that Schubert would join them at one of their halting-places. Bauernfeld was then writing *The Count of Gleichen,* a *libretto* intended for Schubert, so there seemed some certainty of their meeting. The two voyagers set out, followed by a caravan of vehicles of various kinds containing surveying officers, their wives and orderlies. They passed through woods fresh with the new

[1] Dahms: " Schubert."

140

green of Spring, then in a couple of days the caravan dropped away and Bauernfeld and Mayrhofer went on alone. Mayrhofer proceeded to the main farms; Bauernfeld remained in the hostel in the valley working at *The Count of Gleichen.*

He wrote to Schubert acqainting him with the progress of the *libretto,* step by step.

" That was clever of you, having written the opera," Schubert replied. " I only wish I had it before me. I have been asked for my opera *libretti* in order to see what could be done with them. If yours were finished I would suggest it, and if it were considered worthy—which I do not doubt—they would start with it or send it to Milder in Berlin.

" Schechner has appeared in the *Swiss Family* and met with considerable success. As she is very much like Milder, she will do for us. Do not stay away too long; it is very sad and lonely here. From Schober and Schwind[1] we hear nothing but lamentations which are more heart-rending than those to which we are accustomed on Good Friday. I have only been to Grinzing once since you left. From all this you can gather how very happy I am. . . . The poetry of yours which appeared in the fashion paper is very beautiful, but I consider the poem you sent still better. The sublime merriment and humorous devotion, and especially the delicate note of pain . . . is simply grand, and can take its place as a model of this form of poetry.

" I am not working at all. The weather is truly abominable. Our Lord seems to be forgetting us, as the sun is never shining. We are in the month of May, and yet we never sit in the garden. Dreadful! Awful ! ! Frightful ! ! ! For me, it is the worst that can happen. Schwind and I intend going to Linz in the month of June, accompanied by Spaun. We could meet you there, or at Gmunden—only please let us have a fixed rendezvous—as soon as possible. Not after two months ! "

Schubert had financed his holiday with Vogl, and he had every reason to expect that he could pay his way on a journey with Schwind. He had faith in the annual pilgrimage from Vienna as a defence against the constantly recurring attacks of ill-health. He was not unconscious of the menace of Viennese night-life. The wondrous country around Vienna, its woods, its rich pastures, were free to his feet, and he sought these places regularly, often alone,

[1] Then in Munich.

141

sometimes with Schwind. But he came back to the same place, the nightly *Gasthaus,* the moonlit mornings, and the heaviness of night driven into day.

He did not go to Linz as he had planned. Money failed him.

Songs were being published rapidly, but his earnings remained small. Twelve pounds in April for his Sonata in " D " (Op. 53) and the *Divertissement à la Hongroise.* Songs composed in 1814, 1815, 1816, 1820, 1822 and 1823 followed each other into print at short intervals. His Mass in " C," his *Salve Regina* and innumerable other works appeared, many of them taken from the seldom-opened drawers, and brought him a certain amount of money, very little money, but, by the grace of his publishers, a pittance.

He was feeding the publishers, who were tearing him to pieces like vultures upon carrion, and he was aware of it. He made frantic efforts to break away, to discover new outlets and just dealing. He wrote to Breitkopf and Härtel in Leipzig : " I am politely making an inquiry as to whether you would feel inclined to take some of my compositions on moderate terms." He wrote again to Probst in the same city offering him a full range of his works, and received in return a sharp reminder that, although Probst would do his utmost to widen Schubert's reputation, he " must candidly confess that your efforts so often full of genius, but also somewhat eccentric, are not as yet sufficiently understood by our public. In the selection, therefore, and delivery of your manuscript works, please be good enough to take the greatest care."

Probst's caution to Schubert had been that of other publishers. The curse of the age was the mediocre amateur for whom much of Schubert's music was too difficult. The Rossini invasion of Vienna had created the vogue of amateur Italian singing which, instead of passing with the change of fashion, blundered through the work of other contemporary composers, Schubert among them. When Hiller, disgusted with the Rossini singing craze, expressed his feelings to Beethoven, the master replied: " The popular cry is ' Vox populi, vox Dei,' but I have never believed it to be true." The musicians in Vienna, Beethoven among them, complained about the interference of the amateurs. They formed a profession, deprived the musicians of their living, gave lessons, big concerts, etc., and were most arrogant in their judgment, whilst forbidding all criticism directed against themselves; and, in this case, sheltered under the privilege of being amateurs.[1]

[1] Ferdinand Hiller : " Künstlerleben."

Schubert had now begun to attend the Fröhlichs' house again. If the friendship had been under a cloud for a while, it was now stronger than ever. He returned once more to most of their musical evenings. He sang, he played. During the afternoon he would call in as if a thought had struck him whilst walking up the street. Kathi's reproach to him was forgotten. She was more charming than ever. Grillparzer was sunning himself in the warmth of a great love, pedantic, petulant, but very sure that Kathi's love was as necessary to him as his daily bread. Berg had just arrived in Vienna—the Swede, who was ultimately to become Director of the Conservatoire at Stockholm and the trainer of Jenny Lind. It was at the Fröhlichs' house that Schubert met him, and was filled with admiration. The Swedish songs he had composed, his knowledge of music, his playing—certainly here was a kindred soul from out of the north! If the Fröhlichs asked Schubert to spend the evening with them the reply was always the same: " If Berg is coming, well, then I shall certainly come too." (*Kommt der Berg, nun, dann komme ich auch ganz gewiss.*) " Then," said Anna Fröhlich,[1] " Schubert would sit down on a chair by the door in the second room, opposite the piano, and listen to Berg with the greatest delight. One of his songs pleased Schubert so much that he used the theme of it for one of his quartets."[2]

By the summer Schubert was practically destitute of money. Bauernfeld on his rambles had finished the *libretto* of *The Count of Gleichen* in eight days, and now urged Schubert to join him at Gmunden.

" It is impossible for me to go to Gmunden or any other place," Schubert replied, " as I have no money whatever. Altogether I am in a very bad way, but I do not mind and am merry. Do come to Vienna as soon as possible. Dupont wishes to have an opera of mine. As the *libretti* I have put together do not find favour with him, it would be delightful if he found yours suitable. Then we should have some money, and possibly achieve honour."

So Bauernfeld returned. Before the end of July he had reached Vienna.

" When we landed at Nussdorf in the evening," he wrote,[3]

---

[1] From MS. " Grillparzer's House," by Frau Gerhard von Breuning.

[2] This disposes of Pohl's assertion that the melody in question was that of the Andante of the Trio in " E Flat," Op. 100, apart from the fact that the Andante is thoroughly Schubertian without any traces of Swedish origin.

[3] Bauernfeld: " Diaries."

" Schwind and Schubert came running towards me from the coffee house. Great jubilation!

" ' Where is the Opera? ' asked Schubert.

" ' Here! ' Solemnly I handed over to him *The Count of Glei-chen!* "

Then a new difficulty presented itself. In October the *libretto* was submitted to the Censor, who promptly prohibited its presentation at any theatre in Vienna. The fortunes of Schubert were as luckless as ever. The edict aroused the stubborn spirit of him. He would defy the Censor, and set the opera. He was hurling himself blindly and fearlessly at a wall. But if Vienna was inhabited by fools, Vienna was not the world, he reasoned. The courage of his desperation was a little pitiful.

So Schwind deemed it.

" The more I become aware of what he is, the more I know what he suffers," he wrote.

CHAPTER XVI

Beethoven – and a Journey to Graz

(1827)

FOR years Beethoven and Schubert had lived within a mile of each other, and yet they had scarcely met. Schubert had frequently complained to Spaun that Beethoven was unapproachable. But was this Beethoven's fault? When Schubert's music was first brought to his notice, Franz was a young man of considerable promise. Beethoven had no leisure to follow young men of considerable promise, who invariably disappeared as failures.

Moreover, he lived in a world of his own, drawn into himself by the tragedy of his deafness. How he had sought to spare his ears, to save the failing sense of hearing that remained! When the French were bombarding Vienna he had lain in a cellar, cushions over his ears to kill the sound of the bursting shells that were dropping around his apartments. Now that hearing had gone, the outer world was a place he had left, a place upon which he had no more tangible hold than by the medium of a correspondence book. He grew into his isolation, clung more firmly to his own particular friends, and forgot the others. His circle thinned; he appeared less frequently in the *salons* where he had always been welcomed as the master. Since only certain sections of Vienna had come to understand the better work of Schubert, how then should Beethoven, shut away in his kingdom of solitude, grow to know these things? Even in the Vienna of 1827 news, reputations, moved at a snail's pace. Beethoven had moved in the highest circles of Viennese society, the ramparts of which Schubert had never sought to storm.

At no time did Schubert seek to attract the attention of Beethoven. They had mutual friends—the Hüttenbrenners, Teltscher, Vogl, Schindler. But in his shyness Schubert was undoubtedly

145

afraid of Beethoven. He was hypersensitive in this respect. He believed that he had still to do his best work, and he underestimated his qualities when he thought about Beethoven. He was afraid of him with the terror of a young man for one who, rugged and ageing, had conquered the world of his desires. That the twain were not more closely linked in the friendship of their art was entirely the fault of Schubert. The last interview Schubert had with the dying master leaves this fact clearly proven.

They both dined at Bogner's; frequently they were at near-by tables. When Rochlitz, the poet, was in Vienna, Schubert offered to take him to one of Beethoven's haunts, so that he might catch the master unawares and listen to his talk. They went together, found Beethoven and listened to him. He was talking in his raucous voice—the qualities of the English, the abominations of the French. Schubert went out of the coffee-house without making himself known to the man who sat like a storm-god upon his mountain.

And now, in February, 1827, Schubert was composing the first twelve songs of his *Winterreise* cycle, while Beethoven lay dying. His admirers were sending special dainties to Beethoven. The doctor, as if to pander to the plaint of a dying man, was providing him with bottles of his favourite Gumpoldskircher, while Schubert was setting Müller's verses—he set six of the *Winterreise* songs in a single morning.

Of all the contemporary poets of Schubert's setting, Müller was undoubtedly one of the best, from the composer's point of view. Müller had none of the mediocrity of Mayrhofer. And yet Schubert and Müller never met. Müller, who was born and lived at Dessau, and died there before Schubert had set the last of his *Winterreise* songs, probably never even knew that Schubert had set his verses. A musician could set any song without the courtesy of asking permission, or paying a fee. He could go into print, and, if his music were good, it added only honour to the poet. Müller was brillant in the tone painting of his words. He had a rare sense of humanity. He set down with the most natural ease the atmosphere of a life. " I can neither play nor sing," he wrote. " But when I compose my poems I sing all the same and play as well. If I could express the tunes that come to me, my songs would please better than they do now. But, patience. There may be found a sympathetically tuned soul, which will discover the tunes in the words, and give them back to me."[1]

[1] Müller: Diary.

Unknowingly he found that soul in Schubert. The last twelve songs in the *Winterreise* cycle show the gloom gathering about him, the infinite sadness which, with the end of all endeavour approaching, had taken its hold on Schubert at the time he composed them. Müller died in September, 1827; Schubert was to set his last songs and pass out little more than a year later. The last *Winterreise* songs are an epic in sadness, the blending of two moods of beauty—both in verse and in music—overshadowed by death.

Early in March the news of Beethoven's condition spread through Vienna. The dying man was engaged in writing short letters of thanks for the gifts of food and wine to those intimate friends who had given these things to assuage the fierce desires of a dying body. Schotts[1] sent him a dozen bottles of Rüdesheimer Berg, eleven years old in the vintage, and hurried forward some bottles mixed with healing herbs. The great life that lay in jeopardy surely called for effort, every effort that would stay the departure of its soul for a single hour. Anselm Hüttenbrenner took to the stricken giant some of Schubert's songs—*The Young Nun, The Miller Songs, Omnipotence* and several others. Beethoven fingered the pages carefully. It was a gift that brought pleasure to a few of the last days of the dying master. Hüttenbrenner had discovered the real Schubert for him.

" Truly in Schubert lives the divine fire! " Beethoven exclaimed.

In those last days Schubert is said to have visited Beethoven twice. When on one occasion Hüttenbrenner announced him, and asked who should come into the room first, Beethoven replied: " Let Schubert come first." And then when they were together beside the bed he said: " You, Hüttenbrenner, have my heart; Schubert has my soul."

The veteran was dying inch by inch. They had tapped him thrice. And he craved eternally for wine, special growths of wine. He, who had never been particular about the cup, provided the cup was good, now had the judgment of nothing less than a connoisseur. He wanted the best things. He lay without speaking, sweat beading his forehead. He made signs with his hands. The death rattle sounded for hours in his throat till, during a blast of thunder that shook the window frames, his body died.

Schubert was one of the thirty-eight torch-bearers who saw Beethoven to the Währing cemetery. Amidst his crêpe he wore

[1] The famous music-publishers in Mayence.

white lilies and roses. Eight Capellmeisters held the pall as the procession passed to the music of the dead man's funeral march from his Sonata, Op. 26.

On the way home, Schubert, Randhartinger and Lachner stopped at the Mehlgrube *Gasthaus* and drank wine. Schubert raised his glass and exclaimed: " To him we have just buried! " Then he refilled his glass, and, raising it again, said: " To him who will be the next! "

Unknowingly he had drunk to himself.

Two months before the death of Beethoven, Schubert reached his thirtieth birthday. His spirits were high; for the illness within him had remained in a state of inactivity for a considerable period. The only inconvenience from which he now suffered came from his purse.

To some extent this shortage was caused by his own wilfulness. The gentleness, which amounted almost to tenderness, in Schubert's treatment of certain people was one extreme in a complex character, his stubbornness the other. Anselm Hüttenbrenner declared that Schubert's stubbornness kept him poor; that he would let any opportunity pass if it did not conform to his opinion. He had thrown aside his chances of being Capellmeister with a bang of his book. Certain publishers asked for simpler music; he sent them music more difficult. He seemed to prefer a flat purse to being a slave to dictation. At the *Schubertiaden,* which were now frequently held at the house of the amateur Pinterics, or at that of Frau von Lacsny-Buchwieser, the operatic singer, he rightly acknowledged no superior in music.

Schindler states[1] that when they remonstrated with him about the length of certain movements he would pass off the criticism in silence if it was expressed in a general manner. " If we allowed ourselves, however, to point out this or that passage as recurring too often, or as being not sufficiently new and interesting, Schubert boiled over at once, and his moodiness would not pass away for the rest of the evening. Vogl and Pinterics took little notice of his moodiness, but at the next meeting the criticism would be heard again. Schubert expected it and was ready for it. ' Well,' he would say as he seated himself at the piano, ' to-day you'll be going on at me again. Go on, abuse me as much as you like.' "

[1] Schindler: " Reminiscences of Schubert."

Schubert could not enter into argument or refute criticism. He had not the gift of words. The retorts that often flamed across his mind were seldom spoken. He became tongue-tied, secretive in mood. When irritated he spoke in short sentences, or took refuge in the Viennese expression, "Wurz!" (Nonsense). Or he would utter a brief and cutting sarcasm in Viennese dialect. He seemed indifferent to praise; Schindler says [1] that he never saw his expression change when praise was given.

But he felt the kindliness of friends deeply. He did not want praise, but he appreciated understanding above all else. One evening Pinterics gave a party, to which Schubert and Bauernfeld were invited. Franz Stohl, an amateur with a good voice, was present and met Schubert for the first time. " I was introduced to Schubert by Pinterics as an excellent singer of his *Der Zwerg*," says Stohl. [2] " Against this I protested, but this did not prevent Schubert from immediately preparing to accompany me in his *Zwerg*. I sang with real enthusiasm; Schubert's accompaniment fired me. When the song was ended and rewarded with the praise of those present, Schubert took my hand, and, pressing it, he said : ' You are another of those who understand me.' "

Vogl was now a regular figure at the *Schubertiaden*. He would sing the Schubert songs, and Franz had to accompany him until his short thick fingers almost refused to obey any longer, says Bauernfeld. [3] " At the house balls in those simple days he fared still worse, but charming women and girls were by no means wanting. On such occasions our ' Bertel '—a pet name we gave him occasionally—had to play his latest waltzes, and play them again and again, and wind up with an endless cotillion, so that the corpulent little man, dripping with perspiration, only found ease again at the modest supper. No wonder then that he sometimes absconded, and many a *Schubertiade* had to take place without him if it so happened that he was not in a sociable mood, or that one or other of the guests was not to his liking. Sometimes he kept invited guests waiting in vain, for he had comfortably settled himself behind a bottle of wine in some obscure tavern in the company of some half a dozen assistant-schoolmasters, his former colleagues. Then when we upbraided him on the following day, he would answer with a genial titter : ' I did not feel disposed! ' "

[1] Schindler: " Reminiscences of Schubert."
[2] Franz Stohl: "Gedenkblätter"
[3] Bauernfeld: " Alt Wien."

In addition to the first twelve *Winterreise* songs already referred to, Schubert also composed in the month of February Klopstock's *Battle Song*, some variations to an air from Hérold's operetta *Marie*, and two songs by Schober. His energy was tireless, his versatility never more pronounced. His mind appeared to be able at any moment to forget a theme that had been safely committed to paper in order to pass on to the creation of some new masterpiece of beauty. In April he composed his beautiful *Nachtgesang im Walde*, his *Spring Song* and his *Das Lied im Grünen*. A month later he produced in a few hours his beautiful *Serenade*, Op. 134.

Anna Fröhlich was responsible for the *Serenade*, and happily she has left the story of its making.[1] She had asked Grillparzer to write a poem to celebrate the birthday of one of her pupils, Fräulein Gosmar, who afterwards married Leopold Sonnleithner. She was the daughter of the owner of a sugar factory in Vienna, and a girl of considerable musical ability. Grillparzer at first was thoughtful. Then he told Anna that he would write a poem for the occasion if he got an idea. " Well," Anna replied, " see to it that you do get an idea! "

In a few days Grillparzer produced the words of the *Serenade*. " Only Schubert must set it; only he could find notes for such a poem." When Schubert came to the house a few days later, Anna placed the Grillparzer manuscript in his hand and asked for a setting. He leaned over the piano and read the poem. It moved him deeply. For awhile he looked vacantly across the room as if lost in thought. " How beautiful it is! " he said presently. And then again: " How beautiful it is! "

Three days later Schubert returned to the Fröhlichs' house with the *Serenade* set for a mezzo-soprano and four male voices.

" No, Schubert," said Anna. " I cannot use it like that, since it is intended for the girl friends of Fräulein Gosmar. You must write me a chorus for female voices."

" I remember quite well when I told him this," said Anna Fröhlich. " He was sitting there in the right-hand niche by the window in the entrance room. But he soon brought me the song set for the voice of Pepi [the nickname of Josefine Fröhlich] and with the female chorus it has now. I lent that manuscript to Spaun. Had I been wise I should have had it copied, and have given him the copy. Grillparzer said: ' Lend it to him; he will take care of it.'

[1] Grillparzer Annals.

But Spaun lost it. True, he afterwards excused himself, and said that he could not remember where he had put it." The manuscript had gone for ever.

If the beauty of the *Serenade* was not apparent to Schubert until he heard it played, he had even less interest in its performance. He had written the song as a gift to a friend, and he did not bother further. Once the *Serenade* was on paper he gave it not another thought. Anna Fröhlich drove her pupils in three carriages to Unter Döbling, where Fräulein Gosmar was staying at the house of some friends. She had a piano placed secretly below the girl's window, and invited Schubert to come and play the *Serenade*. The company waited for him, but he did not arrive. Another took his place at the piano, and the *Serenade* was sung for the first time in the moonlight under the window of a girl of sixteen.

On the following day Anna Fröhlich met Schubert walking down the street and asked him why he had failed to appear. He was profuse in his apologies. " Oh," he said, " I forgot about it! "

Very shortly afterwards he forgot the *Serenade* again. It was not a pose; his mind lived always for those unborn things which to-morrow would see on paper. Anna Fröhlich decided to have the *Serenade* performed at the Unter den Tuchlauben hall, so that an audience, greater than some stragglers under a bedroom window, might hear what she considered to be one of Schubert's greatest songs. Schubert, penitent for the Döbling incident, had promised to be at the piano. On no account would he fail.

The day arrived. The hall was crowded. Again no Schubert, no message from Schubert. Anna Fröhlich stormed, then sought the only consolation of tears. Was this an insult deliberately shaped by Schubert in consequence of her reprimand? He had chosen the essence of cruelty by this method of humiliating her. Her thoughts, her imagination, leaping wildly from point to point, pictured Schubert as nothing less than a monster. In her distress, she asked Hofrat Walcher what could be done. If Walcher did not condone Schubert's bad manners, surely there was something he could do! Only two months previously Schubert had inscribed his Allegretto in " C " " In memory of my dear friend Walcher," and the friendship between them was sincere. Again and again Anna, in distracted fashion, explained to Walcher that Schubert had never heard his own piece, and apparently did not want to hear it.

[1] From a manuscript in possession of Professor Otto Erich Deutsch: " Grill-parzer's House," by Frau Gerhard von Breuning.

Walcher thought deeply. Perhaps Schubert was at Wanner's beer-house, " Zur Eiche." He knew that Schubert liked the place because the musical fraternity went there, and because the beer was good. A crowded hall, and a suggested hunt in a beer-house for the composer! Anna was horrified, more *bouleversée* than ever. Walcher departed in haste for the beer-house.

He reached the " Zur Eiche." There was Schubert with a few boon companions enjoying his beer. He had forgotten the *Serenade* entirely. He had really forgotten it. He returned to the hall with Walcher, all contrition. He went to the piano. After the performance he stood, a little plump figure, in a crowd that pressed about him. He was deeply moved and spoke only under the stress of great emotion. " I did not know that it was so beautiful! " he said. It was as if he had discovered one of his own children whom he did not recognise.

After the *Serenade* episode in July Schubert ceased work. But he had in the meantime completed his sketching out of all the music to Bauernfeld's *The Count of Gleichen,* for the manuscript is dated June 17th, 1827. He may have had his own reasons for his secrecy about his work on the opera. Even Bauernfeld's curiosity concerning Schubert's progress with the music was not appeased, indeed he appears to have known nothing about it, for exactly two months later he made a note in his diary that Schubert was composing *The Count of Gleichen.* The truth of the matter was that, having sketched out the opera, Schubert put the work aside, and did not take it up again until shortly before his death in the following year. Aware that the Censor had issued his edict against the *libretto,* he may have felt at last that the composition was mere waste of time. On the other hand, his stubbornness would not permit him to lay the work aside and bow his neck to the yoke of a Government official.

" When will the devil eventually fetch this accursed censorship? " Bauernfeld wrote of his bitterness in his diary. " We are all poor wretches. But what would have become of Goethe and Schiller had they been born in Austria? "

His spirit in revolt took comfort in the courage of Schubert, who meant to defy the Censor and his pruderies. Bauernfeld was only twenty-three, and deeply serious about his work. This censorship was equivalent to submitting his dreams to a nursemaid for criticism, to a mind unlettered that could destroy that which it did not understand.

Summer began to wane, and, tired of the heat and dust of the city, Schubert decided to accept the invitation of the Pachler family at Graz to visit them in company with Jenger. The Pachlers had striven repeatedly to bring about a visit from Schubert. Dr. Karl Pachler was an advocate of means, and a musical amateur who kept open house to all the arts. In a manner, a snob. He loved the presence of well-known people in his house. He gathered the *élite* of the countryside to the house to show them that these people were actually there. If he had not been a genuine lover of music, one could have summed up Pachler in terms more harsh.

" Although I do not know the reason why I have deserved such a friendly invitation as the one you sent in your letter to Jenger," Schubert wrote to Madame Pachler, " and I do not know how I can offer anything in return, yet I cannot refrain from accepting an invitation which will permit me to see Graz, which I have often heard praised, besides making your personal acquaintance."

By the end of August the visit to Graz was definitely arranged. Schubert was now in possession of certain funds—not funds sufficient to make Bauernfeld look up to him again as a Crœsus who was " swimming in silver "; but at least he was at the moment clear of want. The music-publishers had been more obliging than usual, not in their terms, but in the number of their publications, and even small pittances were useful. The Overtures to *Alfonso and Estrella* and *Fierrabras* had been brought out already this year, six songs, four polonaises, twelve waltzes, a Fantasia in " G." Every one of these works as it emerged rather obscurely from the press was a missioner for Schubert. None of them swelled his purse appreciably. Each of them only carried his name further, brought him a little more esteem—unprofitable esteem in a financial sense; the publishers saw to that.

He left Vienna with Jenger on September 2nd, travelled by the express coach, and arrived at Graz two nights and a day later. He was in Graz exactly three weeks—three weeks of convivial evenings and day-time expeditions. He was gay, and his host and hostess were kind. He had gone for a holiday, but his restlessness produced from him twelve waltzes whilst away, prompted possibly by the festivities of the evenings. These Haslinger published later as Op. 91. Moreover, he had taken the ill-fated *Alfonso and Estrella* with him, hoping that Graz, with its musical society more alive than that of Vienna to the musical brilliance of the day, would perform it and shame the capital. He put it into the hands of Capellmeister

153

Kinsky, who admired the work. Kinsky was warm and diplomatic in his praises. But *Alfonso* was no work for the Graz amateurs. It was too difficult for their chorus and orchestra. If it could be altered—— then perhaps something could be done.

The demon of stubbornness stalked abroad in Schubert again. He would alter nothing. *Alfonso* might go unperformed, but he would alter nothing Nor did he. When he departed from Graz he left the *Alfonso* manuscript in the keeping of the Pachlers, and there it remained for nearly twenty years unperformed.

His hostess, Marie Pachler, was a woman of charm and ability and three years his senior. As a pianist she was superb. Beethoven had told her that he had found no one who played his compositions as well as she did, not excepting even the famous professional pianists of the day. And Beethoven did not waste his compliments. She took pride in the visits of people of high artistic degree to her house, and had more genuine reverence for their Art than her husband. The coming of Schubert was an event of magnitude. The Graz musical life twittered with excitement. Schubert may have enjoyed these things, but it was the country, the absence from the noisy routine of the city that brought to him the real happiness. The glorious solitude of the farm at Wildbach, where the widowed Frau Massegg—his host's aunt—ruled as an ageing queen in a state of loneliness, appealed to him. Someone put his portrait over the stable door in remembrance of his visit, and there for many years it remained as if to mark the fact that once the farm had housed a person of more than ordinary interest. A genius had passed by and left his portrait—in the stable!

A round of visits was arranged. Schubert was made the guest of honour by kind friends at the little Hallerschlössl. The peace and simplicity of the place! Vienna and its worries, the sameness of Vienna—how distant these things! At the Hallerschlössl another visitor was introduced to him. The two men faced each other and the host introduced them: " Franz Schubert—Franz Schubert! " The other man had been given the same name at his christening. That night they sat together at a family concert, when the Schweig-hofer family and the other Schubert sang and played many of the compositions of the Schubert of Vienna. The composer turned at last to the bearer of his own name.

" Cease playing my compositions," he said. " I hear enough of them in Vienna. Play something Styrian." And a Fräulein Graveneck broke into a series of Styrian songs.

At the end of September Schubert and Jenger set out for Vienna again. Promises to return to Graz the following year were made never to be kept. Another promise to write a piece specially for little Faust Pachler, aged eight, *was* kept. On reaching the capital Schubert wrote to Madame Pachler:

" Only now I am beginning to realize how well I was at Graz. I am not ready for Vienna yet. True, it is a rather large place, but quite devoid of congeniality, honesty and fine thoughts, sensible words, and especially good deeds. One can never quite discover here whether one is sane or stupid. There is so much talking, and one seldom arrives at real happiness. Perhaps I have myself to blame for this, owing to my slowness in warming up. At Graz I soon discovered the simple and open way of being part of one another. If I had stayed there longer I should have felt quite at home.

" I shall never forget my pleasant quarters with my dear hostess, the strong Pachleros and the little Faust. Not for a long time past have I spent such happy days. Trusting to be able to express my gratitude in a more worthy manner one day,

"I remain with high esteem,

"Your honour's most devoted

" FRANZ SCHUBERT."

Scarcely had Schubert settled down anew to his accustomed life in Vienna than he was attacked by illness. The old headaches and congestion of blood that brought moments of vertigo returned, and blinded his eyes to the paper as he worked. The rest at Graz from which he had expected so much had produced no real benefit. He must have become aware that any belief in an ultimate and permanent cure was based on false hopes.

" On account of serious illness Schubert regrets not being able to assist at a party, as he is quite unfit for Society," he wrote, in refusal of an invitation on October 15th. A few days later he sent to Madame Pachler the duet he had promised her boy, and in doing so complained of the return of the headaches.

" I am enclosing the piano duet for little Faust. I am rather afraid that it will not meet with his approval, as such compositions are not much in my line," he modestly wrote. " I trust your honour is in a better state of health than I am, as my usual headache is troubling me again. Kindly give my best wishes to Dr. Karl on the

155

occasion of his birthday, and tell him, please, that I cannot get the *libretto* of my opera, as it was sent to Mr. Gottdank and the lazy monster has had it for months already."

The attack was sharp and brief. In a few days he had apparently regained his normal health. But the depression, which usually departed with each attack, clung with more than wonted tenacity. The next news his friends had of him was that he was composing the second series of the *Winterreise,* and, ere the last leaves of October had fallen from the trees in the Glacis, he had completed them.

The sadness in the last *Winterreise* songs is a reflection of Schubert's mind at this hour. But he appears to have had no surmise that death waited only a few months away, that soon the words he had set with such beauty in the first *Winterreise* cycle would be true of him:

> " *So now the last word's spoken,*
> *Myself soon out of sight,*
> *I leave this farewell token,*
> *Good night, my dear, good night.*"

He was obsessed at times by the comparative failure of his life. The diminishing fees he was receiving may have deepened the impression of failure in his mind. He became more lethargic to the attitude of his friends, who strove to urge him over the few stages remaining between himself and complete recognition. He continued to undervalue himself, to *offer* his songs at lesser prices. The belief in himself, which had kept him always working, appeared to be faltering, as if some part of him had turned rebel, and risen up in question against a world that could hand out adversity and disappointment in such superabundant measure. Of courage he had lost nothing. But sadness had now definitely etsaolished its place in his thoughts.

To his friends the long moods of Schubert's depression became an anxiety. " The choice of the *Winter Journey* proved how much more serious his condition had become," wrote Mayrhofer. " He had been very ill for a long period, he had undergone depressing experiences, all the colour had been stripped from his life. For him Winter had indeed begun."

Spaun, too, noted the gloom closing in about the mind of his friend.

" For some time Schubert had been gloomy and seemingly ill. When I asked him what was the matter he replied simply: ' You will soon know and understand.' One day he said to me: ' Come to Schober's, and I will sing you a cycle of gloomy songs. I am anxious to hear what you have to say about them. They have affected me more deeply than any songs I have composed.' He then sang through to us the whole cycle of the *Winterreise* in a voice broken by emotion. We were quite upset by the dismal character of them—the *Lindenbaum.* To this the only reply Schubert made was: 'These songs please me more than all the others, and some day they will please you too.' "

Some anthems which Schubert had composed for Professor Neumann brought him in 100 florins during October, a welcome relief, for Schubert at the time was practically without money.

"MOST HONOURED PROFESSOR"
(he replied),
"I have received the 100 florins (Viennese currency) which you sent me for the composition of the Anthems, and only hope that these same comp. will come up to your expectations.
"Your most devoted
"FRANZ SCHUBERT."

At the beginning of November Rochlitz invited Schubert to set his poetic work *The First Sound.* He went still further, he even told Schubert what music he ought to compose! "*Fortissimo* at the beginning," he said, "and then a long sustained passage for clarinet or horn with pauses. Then opening calmly and slowly, music that becomes more gloomy as it proceeds—a sort of chaos which by degrees develops and becomes brighter."

Schubert, who disliked any form of dictation concerning his work, who had shown a brave front to Dupont of the Opera House and others like him, surrendered to Rochlitz. Was this another sign of his willingness to accept anything within reason, suggestion and criticism alike? He could not treat Rochlitz lightly. He had founded the *Allgemeine Musikalische Zeitung,* and as editor of the journal had criticized Schubert and his *Zauberharfe.* Indeed, he had criticized everybody in music during his editorship of twenty years. He had written *libretti,* composed a Mass, a cantata, a Te Deum and other works. He was accepted and suspected. His anecdotes of Mozart, with whom he had once talked, were so specious in their apparent veracity that no one believed them.

Schubert feared no one, and had respect for few. What he had begun to fear acutely was his poverty, the receding chances of definite recognition. He probably laughed at Rochlitz and his scheme of composition, but he accepted it.

157

"I felt much honoured by your writing to me," he replied at once. "In this manner I am being associated with a celebrated man.

"I have been thinking a good deal about your proposition concerning the poetry *The First Sound,* and I believe that if it were treated in the manner you suggest the effect would be good. But if so treated it would be more like a melodrama than an oratorio or cantata, and, as the former is no longer in favour, I confess frankly that I should prefer to set some poetry which could be treated as an oratorio.

"To begin with, an elocutionist like Anschütz is not always to be had for the asking, and, moreover, it is a great desire of mine to set to music a piece of poetry without additions apart from the sublime idea. That I consider you a worthy writer of such poetry, and that I should do my utmost to compose music worthy of such poetry, I think I need scarcely tell you. As *The First Sound* is such a glorious piece of poetry, I should like to try to set it to music if you would like me to do so. If you agree with me I propose to begin the singing with the words 'Then he was told.'

"With distinguished esteem,

"Your most devoted

"FRANZ SCHUBERT."

What Rochlitz had offered to Schubert was a poem which Beethoven had refused, and which, set by Weber, had never found success. Whether Schubert was aware of this imposition cannot be said. But he changed his mind about Rochlitz, forgot him, and never set a word of his poem.

The New Year came—the last New Year Schubert was to know—and found him planning a new symphony and an oratorio. He seemed to throw aside the pestilential doubts that had filled his mind—doubts of everybody, doubts of himself. His imagination burned with new fires. So rapidly did it compel him to write down the notes that his manuscript now often became difficult to decipher.

"The Austrian character sometimes manifested itself too tempestuously. At other times the demon of sadness and melancholy spread its sable wings about him. In the dark hallowed hours he often created the most sadly-beautiful songs," Bauernfeld wrote.[1]

And then, as if to call down a curse upon the "System" that withheld honour from his friend: "Schubert has the misfortune to be an Austrian, and the Austrian 'System' reserves its honours

[1] Bauernfeld: "Alt Wien."

158

and preferments for golden mediocrity, and looks upon anyone possessing even a little talent as its enemy."

Possibly the Censor's recent mauling of his own *The Count of Gleichen* had put an added venom into Bauernfeld's tirade. He suffered as Schubert had suffered from the throttling grip of official-dom. It was breaking his spirit, forcing him into those depths of despondency which Schubert had known so well.

" If only I could pray! " he cried. " If only I could pray! God will not take it amiss that I do not force myself to it."[1]

[1] Bauernfeld: " Diary."

CHAPTER XVII

Last Works and Poverties

(1828)

DURING the later months of 1827 Schubert went to
live with Schober on the second floor of the "Blue
Hedgehog," (*Zum Blauen Igel*), a tavern of some repute in the
Tuchlauben. Kenner gave it as his opinion that Schubert in his
closing years discovered the shallows in Schober's character. He
may have done so, but it did not change his attachment to him. To
Schubert there was no man like Schober. Never in his life would
he find such a friend again. He deplored any absence of Schober
from Vienna; a *Gasthaus* night without Schober was never the
same. And yet, of all the Schubertians, who resembled him less
than Schober?

If the attachment became closer, the influence of Schober over
Schubert was dying. Indeed it was already dead. To Schubert the
high lights of Life which Schober knew so well were becoming
dimmed. Life—his life—was now ordained to remain a sombre
thing, and suppression to be the meed of the world's estimate of his
worth. Innumerable works of unknown people, of mediocre people
—mostly French importations—appeared in Vienna and were
staged. The majority of them came and disappeared, and were of
trifling consequence. But some of them made money, and were an
attraction to the town, whilst Schubert was ignored.

He seemed to become fatalistic in his outlook on the future. The
close association with Schober provoked contrasts which must have
been apparent to him. " Some men," he wrote, " are destined never
to live in the shadow." Was he thinking of Schober who, even
during the ill-fated adventure in northern Europe, his failure as
Mr. Torupson upon a luckless stage, had found Life still amiable

160

and kind? Sometimes Schubert's failure to reach a definite position appalled him, and his life seemed ruled by a Fate brooding with malevolence. Although he believed so deeply in his *Lieder* they had yielded him little. He would now compose opera, symphony. He had finished with songs! He told Schober so. He told everybody.

Whilst he was considering the possibilities of entirely changing the manner of his composing, he set two of Leitner's songs in the first days of 1828—*Die Sterne* and *Der Winterabend*. His thirty-first birthday was passed in a Vienna swept with snow. March came. At the beginning of the month he composed his cantata *The Song of Miriam*, which Anna Fröhlich claimed as having been written for herself and her sisters. The words of *Miriam* were Grillparzer's; the influence Handel's. Throughout the work are the unmistakable traces of Handel.

Schubert left no expression of his own opinion concerning *Miriam*. Often when he felt that a new work was good he proclaimed the fact gladly in his letters. But he wrote no letters about *Miriam*, and he made no notes. His friends record no conversation in which this work is mentioned.

Why did he suddenly resolve to compose oratorio? His *Lazarus* had approached the manner of oratorio, but he had not pursued it. Religious music had always stirred him deeply. He was impressed by the religious motives of Michael Haydn. A Mass by Haydn or Beethoven captured his admiration and held it. He was a man who accepted religious principles and strict dogmas. In spite of the pitiless beat of the world upon him which might have suggested to others a God that slept and cared not, his faith remained unshaken and was adorned by some of his richest composition.

A few weeks before *Miriam* was written an episode took place which offers some suggestion as to its origin. One afternoon he had appeared at the Fröhlichs' house, very excited and voluble.

"I had to come this afternoon," he said to Kathi Fröhlich, "because a most joyful thing has happened. I have had Handel's works given to me.[1] Now for the first time I see what I still lack, and realize what a lot I have to learn."[2]

He talked in this manner for an hour, full of ardent delight in the books that had come into his possession. He was never to enter the house of the Fröhlich sisters again, nor to take part in any of

[1] This is said to have been the identical set of Handel's works that had belonged to Beethoven.
[2] From MS. "Grillparzer's House," by Frau von Breuning.

their musical evenings. Death, that would have seemed so very far away that afternoon, was but a few months distant.

Did a close perusal of these volumes—and he who loved Handel so much would have studied them very closely—provoke in him a desire for a form of music in which Handel ruled as master? Was this gift of books responsible for the birth of *Miriam?* Or was *Miriam* an experiment, an attempt to prove to himself, to his friends, that he could produce such work as easily as his *Lieder?* He was never to hear the work performed, never to know the impression it left upon the public. Not until he had been dead two months was it publicly sung. And then—the triumph of irony!—it was given at two concerts arranged by Anna Fröhlich to raise funds for the purchase of a headstone to adorn the tomb of the man who had composed it.

He seemed to work now with redoubled vigour. The vast quantity of compositions he had poured out only left a brain with energies and creative power unspent, untired. He sat deeper into the night and met his friends in the morning with no shadow of fatigue on his face. His majestic Symphony in " C," the crowning work of a brilliant life, was composed during the same month as *Miriam.* It is dated " März, 1828," so that it is probable that it was completed before the month closed. More than two hundred pages of manuscript were composed with such speed that in places it is difficult and almost impossible to decipher the score. Never had his inspiration glowed more brightly.

When the Symphony was finished he took it to the " Musik-verein " in Vienna, and it was decided to perform it immediately. The parts were copied out, the Symphony put into rehearsal. Then it was discovered that the work was too difficult for some of the players. Others declared it to be too long. Schubert thereupon withdrew it, and substituted his Sixth Symphony in "C" of 1817-18. This action robbed him of the opportunity of ever hearing his finest Symphony performed. It was not given until twenty years after his death, when Schumann secured the manuscript from Franz's brother Ferdinand, and Mendelssohn performed it at Leipzig.

An important cantata and his greatest symphony in a month! Also a song for voice and horn, *Auf dem Strom,* as if to prove that the old craft of *Lieder* was alive in him still! He sought no seclusion during this month. His friends had access to him at all times, and he was at Bogner's daily. Moreover, the old sickness had ceased to trouble him for a while. He was elated by the reception of the first *Winterreise* cycle, which Haslinger had published in January, and in his elation probably forgot the tenpence apiece which Haslinger had paid him for the songs.

It was undoubtedly Bauernfeld who suggested the only concert ever given by Schubert—a concert held in Vienna at the end of March. Whilst engaged in the composition of his Symphony he was actually making arrangements for it. During the previous summer he had taken a long walk with Bauernfeld, who, as they walked, dilated upon the rosy character of his own prospects. He was making headway in the district Court, and believed that before long he would gain admittance to " the hallowed boards of the Burg theatre." He described joyously to Schubert all his hopes and plans.

" With you, things are progressing," Schubert replied.[1] " I see you already as *Hofrath* (Court-Councillor) and famous writer of comedies! But I! What will become of me, the poor musician? When age comes on I may be compelled, like Goethe's harper, to ' steal to the doors and beg my bread.' "

Bauernfeld looked at him in surprise.

" You are a genius certainly," he said. " And likewise a fool. You doubt yourself? Are you crazy? He who has your talent, who stands where you stand, has received the main gift. All minor things will follow. What will become of the rest of us I do not know. But you are what you are, and if Moritz [Schwind] will follow in your footsteps and approach you, I shall be very pleased. They have lately refused you the post of Kapellmeister, and chosen an amateur in place of you. But what of that? Seen in the right light, you are suitable, and much too good for such servitude.

" Do you want my advice? " Bauernfeld continued. " Your name is in everybody's mouth, and every new song of yours is an event. You have also composed the most wonderful string quartets and trios, not to mention the symphonies. Your friends are charmed with them, but no publisher will buy them, and the public has as yet no idea of the beauty and grace that slumbers in these works.

" Therefore make a start. Overcome your laziness. Give a concert during the coming winter—performing only your own works, of course. Vogl will be pleased to help you. Bocklet, Böhm and Linke would consider it an honour to serve a maestro like you with their virtuosity. The public will fight for the tickets, and, if you do not become a Crœsus on the spot, one evening will suffice to provide for the whole year. Such an evening may be repeated

[1] Bauernfeld: " Alt Wien."

163

every year. If your novelties create a furore—which I do not doubt in the least—you can screw up your Diabellis, Artarias and Haslingers with their shabby fees to pay you immeasurable sums! Therefore a concert! Follow my advice. A concert!"

"Perhaps you are right," replied Schubert thoughtfully. "If only I were not obliged to ask those fellows!"

But he did ask them, and the Concert took place on March 26th, the day on which Beethoven had died just a year previously. Bauernfeld's estimate was correct. Schubert received £32, and proved to his satisfaction that there was a public sufficient to make such concerts profitable to him. He gave his *Serenade,* some of his settings of the songs by Leitner, Pyrker, Rellstab, and the new trio in "E Flat Major," first performed early in January at Schuppanzigh's house by the latter, Bocklet (pianoforte) and Linke (violoncello). At the concert Böhm took Schuppanzigh's place. The programme Schubert selected for the occasion was representative of the versatility of his genius.

The concert was supposed to be private; but the little hall *Zum Roten Igel* (The Red Hedgehog), where the "Musikverein" gave their performances, was crowded to the point of discomfort. Schubert was then living next door to the hall, at the *Blauen Igel* with Schober. Such was the enthusiasm which the concert aroused that a demand was made for a second performance, but it was never given. What was Schubert's motive in refusing to yield to a popular request it is impossible to say. That he was pleased is obvious from his subsequent letters to the music publishers abroad. It was probably obstinacy, shyness, the peculiar devil in him which so often refused to let him go the way he should have gone.

He was now making efforts to get his music published abroad, since the negotiations with his Vienna publishers had drifted from bad to worse. Some correspondence was opened with Schotts of Mayence, who at first seemed inclined to purchase. At the end of February Schubert wrote:

"I feel much honoured by your letter of February 8th, and am prepared to enter with pleasure into negotiations with such renowned Art dealers who are able to make my compositions known outside Austria. I can put the following pieces at your disposal:

" (A) Trio for pianoforte, violin and violoncello, which has been performed with much approval.

" (B) Two string quartets (G Major and D Minor).

" (C) Four impromptus for pianoforte alone, which could be published singly, or all four together.

" (D) Fantasia, pianoforte duet, dedicated to Countess Caroline Esterhazy.

" (E) Fantasia for pianoforte and violin.

" (F) Songs for voice with pianoforte accompaniment, words by Schiller, Goethe, Klopstock, etc., etc., and Seidl, Schober, Leitner, Schultze, etc.

" (G) Four-part choral songs for male voices, also such for female voices, with piano accompaniment, two of these with a solo part; words by Grillparzer and Seidl.

" (H) Chorus for five men's voices, words by Schober.

" (I) Battle-song by Klopstock, double chorus for eight male voices.

" (K) Humorous Terzet, the Wedding Feast, by Schober, for soprano, tenor and bass, which has been performed with great approval.

" This is the list of my compositions, apart from 3 operas, one Mass and one Symphony. I only mention the latter composition in order that you may see that I am aiming at the highest in Art.

" Should you desire to have any of the above-mentioned for publication by your house, I would send them to you, with pleasure, on moderate terms.

" With esteem,

" FRANZ SCHUBERT.

" My address:

" Unter den Tuchlauben,

" At the Blue Hedgehog, 2nd Floor."

To this letter Schotts replied ordering the greater part of the works on Schubert's list. It was, they said, their intention to publish them by degrees, provided that terms could be arranged. But Schubert, busy with his symphony and the arrangements for his concert, neglected to reply till April 10th, when he wrote:

" The arrangements for and the performance of my concert have prevented me from replying to your letter. All the musical pieces which were performed were my own compositions. Meanwhile I have had copies made of the Trio you requested, of the impromptus, and of the chorus for five male voices. The Trio was performed before a closely-packed hall, at a concert which met with such approval that I was requested to repeat it. If you are willing to pay 100 fl. and 60 fl. for the two other compositions I will forward them immediately. I only beg you to publish them soon.

" With esteem,
" FRZ. SCHUBERT."

At first nothing came of the offer. Meanwhile he had written to Probst of Leipzig in April:

" SIRS,
—You have honoured me with a letter which remained unanswered up till now, as I had to arrange my concert. Perhaps it would interest you to hear that this concert of mine consisted entirely of my own compositions, and they met with great approval. One in particular, a trio for pianoforte, violin and violoncello found especial favour, and I was asked to give a second concert, that is to say, to repeat my first one. I will let you have the compositions of mine with pleasure if you are willing to pay me the modest fee of 60 fl. for a good work. I shall only send you compositions which I consider a success. I need not remind you that it is to my own interests to send good compositions of mine abroad."[1]

The hundred florins for the Trio which he had asked of Schotts, was reduced to sixty florins in his offer to Probst. The letters of both publishers became more suave in their praise of Schubert's genius, but the writers beat down his price many florins with each letter they wrote. Probst eventually bought the Trio from Schubert for 17s. 6d.!

Such was Schubert's need of money at this period—and only six months of his life now remained to him—that he was practically compelled to accept just what a publisher would give. Probst could have obtained the Trio for 7s. 6d., if he had chosen to waste time and money on costly postage. He was well aware of the fact or he would never have driven a bargain as merciless as that of any highwayman on his Saxon roads. The moral effect upon Schubert of seeing the value of his work diminish with each succeeding year must have been devastating in the extreme.

Towards the end of May he wrote to Schotts again:

" I am enclosing the two compositions you requested, each at the price of 60 fl. I beg of you to publish them as soon as possible. I trust you will do good business with them, as both pieces met with

[1] Professor O. E. Deutsch.

great approval here. In expectation of the promised honorarium, I remain, with esteem,

" FRZ. SCHUBERT."

To this letter the publisher, who had with such a magnanimous gesture asked Schubert to suggest his own terms, replied on October 30th, saying that he would pay no more than 30 florins for the Quintet for male voices (Op. 102), and he sent back the " Impromptus " because they were too difficult and would find no market in France! Again had Schubert's hopes come to naught.

The urgency of his need at this time did not hinder his work, nor spoil the beauty of the themes that were waiting for his pen to set them down. In May he composed his *Hymn to the Holy Ghost* for eight male voices. At the beginning of June he went to Baden, where he composed his Fugue in " E Minor," and during the rest of the month worked at his Mass in " E Flat."

The sadness of the *Winterreise,* the sombre beauty of his com-posing in 1828, may have been indicative of more serious thoughts passing across his mind, but outwardly the man was the same. He had become perhaps a little quicker to anger at the senseless behaviour of some of his friends, and was more easily wounded. The growth of bad amateurism in music during the last few years made him agressively critical. He disliked any person who lowered the standard of music even in the most minute degree.

When the Mass was completed at the end of June he put his work aside. There was no immediate prospect of its being performed. He had no objective before him and no idea of gain when he composed it. But the Mass had moved him very deeply. " Schubert lives with his Mass," said Hüttenbrenner.

The obstinacy of Schubert has proved the good fortune of posterity. He was one of the few great composers who had the courage to compose just what they wanted to compose. He con-formed to no fashion. He had no restrictions to any particular theme like those which forced opera after opera out of Handel to save a commercial enterprise.

He now gave himself up to leisure. He walked with his friends, and made excursions to Grinzing. He loved Grinzing, the little township lying on the outskirts of Vienna. He loved its woods, its nightingales, its taverns, its " New Wine " festival which brought together those people of the vineyards. The old romance of Grinzing seemed to cling about its fields and the few buildings which the French had left after they descended upon the place in Schubert's youth. They had ravaged and plundered and destroyed. Even the old Trummelhof—an ancient mansion dating from 1114—now showed but a few heaps of tumbled-down and weather-worn stones as memories left in the wake of a destroyer. Schubert frequently walked in Grinzing with Schwind and Bauernfeld. " Straight to ' Grinzing Sievering ' with many boon companions, and zigzag would many a one walk home," wrote Bauernfeld. Often had Lachner discussed musical projects with Schubert as they walked together through these woods. And the moods of Nature reflected so truthfully in Schubert's songs were often those of Grinzing.

At Grinzing he yielded to the weakness within him. He drank wildly. Life had offered him so little in reward for what he had done. He had always worked, fearlessly worked. If he had strolled through life like Schober. . . . One can understand the mood that delivered him over to weakness. Franz Hartmann, who was a member of the party, left a note of the happenings of one day.[1]

" With Enk and Louis, after we had got hold of Schubert, to Grinzing. All four tipsy, more or less. Especially Schubert. Went home at 12 o'clock." And again another entry: " There was some drunkenness, especially Enk, who started in the street on a non-stop run."

It was a brief orgy. Schubert's orgies were always brief. He came back to his work. In July he set the 92nd Psalm for the Viennese synagogue—set it in Hebrew. Then, in spite of his emphatic declaration that he would never compose any more *Lieder*, he wrote thirteen in August! It was typical of the lack of plan in a mind led hither and thither by the music that arose in it. He would make any arrangement with the utmost sincerity. He would break it with the greater sincerity he owed to his music.

The thirteen songs composed in August were part of the cycle of fourteen known as the *Schwanengesang* (Swan-song). The title of the series was never Schubert's. His publisher, Haslinger, gave the songs this title when he issued them in May, 1829, six months after their composer's death. The songs originated in Schindler's discovery of a number of poems by Rellstab among the effects of the dead Beethoven. The master had carefully marked those which he intended to set, and had put them away to await the day when freedom from other work would allow him to embark upon their composition. It is said that on Beethoven's death they were returned

[1] Franz Hartmann: Diary. Professor O. E. Deutsch: " Documents," etc.

to Rellstab, who in turn sent them to Schubert. The other story—and that more probable—is that Schindler gave the poems to Schubert, who took them away in order to study them more closely. When he gave them back on the day following he had already set two of them.

Schubert set seven of the Rellstab poems, then he set six of Heine's. Why Schubert suddenly left the poems of Rellstab for those of Heine, when composing his cycle, has been regarded as mysterious. But on January 12th and 19th previously there had been a reading at Schober's house, and the book read was the first volume of the *Reisebilder* by Heine, the book in which these poems were to be found. We have this on the evidence of Hartmann, who was present at the reading, and who declares that the poems impressed Schubert deeply at the time.[1]

Schubert therefore had at hand two sets of poems—thirteen in all—which were quickly set during August. The final song in the series—the *Taubenpost* by Seidl—was not composed until October, and is dated for that month. It is the only song in the cycle that bears a date. Moreover, it was the last song Schubert wrote, and its notes are supposed to be the last he ever put to paper. With the *Taubenpost* he put down his pen, all unknowing that the companion that had travelled so far with him would never be taken up again. He had completed his Swan-Song. He had written his last pages of manuscript.

Early in the year Schubert had intended to go to Gmunden with Jenger during the summer. A visit to Traweger's had been arranged. Traweger had written to Schubert stating that he would like to have his company at his house, but since Schubert preferred to pay for his keep he would charge him " for the room which you had before, and three meals per diem, fifty kreutzers a day, and drinks extra." The arrangements for the trip had been begun by Jenger in January. In July he wrote that the excursion would probably take place in September.

It would appear from the letters that passed between Jenger and Madame Pachler during the year that it was also their intention to spend at least a portion of the holiday with the Pachlers at Graz. Irene Kiesewetter, one of the foremost pianists of Vienna, had been advised by her doctor to go to Steyr to recuperate after a serious

---

[1] Baron Schönstein told Kreissle that Schubert had given him at the *Blauen Igel* the volume of poems with the pages turned down marking those he had set. But the noble baron was less sure of his fact in his communication for Reissmann's " Life of Schubert " (1873).

illness. " If this is done," Jenger wrote to Madame Pachler, " then Schwammerl [Schubert] and I will be taken along as ' Marshals of the journey ' [couriers], and so we might see you in the course of a few months. A second matter concerning friend Schu. is that you, dear Madam, will give your permission for the inscription to be engraved on a little book of songs which Schubert has dedicated to you, so that the manuscript may not have to be sent to Graz. I have already spoken to Miss Irene about it, and she will be pleased to undertake this office.[1] This, however, should be done soon, and I beg you to send the permission very soon! "

Writing a few weeks later, Jenger told her: " The little book of songs by friend Schubert, which he has dedicated to you—and in which Miss Irene Kiesewetter (your proxy) has adopted your name—has been handed over to the engraver. It contains the following songs: (1) *Heimliches Lieben* (Secret Love), (2) *Das Weinen* (Weeping), (3) *Vor meiner Wiege* (By my Cradle), the latter two by Leitner; (4) *Altschottische Ballade* (Old Scottish Ballad).[2] The first and last composed at your house. By the time Schubert and I visit you—probably at the end of August—we shall bring you a few copies."

At the beginning of July, Jenger wrote to Madame Pachler:

" The absence of two officials from my bureau who have gone to the baths at Baden, also the none-too-brilliant financial circumstances of friend Schubert—who begs to be kindly remembered to you and friend Dr. Karl, little Faust and all acquaintances—are the obstacles which prevent us both at present from taking advantage of your kind invitation to come to Graz. Schubert had in any case planned to spend part of the summer in Gmunden and its environs, whence he has already received several invitations, but from accepting which he has been prevented by the above-mentioned financial embarrassment. He is still here at present working hard on a new Mass, and only awaits the necessary money—wherever it may come from—to fly at once to Upper Austria. Under these circumstances our trip to Graz would take place, as last year, at the beginning of September."

The summer hurried by without any improvement in Schubert's

---

[1] That is, to act as proxy for Madame Pachler in signing the latter's name to the authorization for the dedication, which, lacking it, could not have been engraved.

[2] The fourth song in the book, which appeared in June with the dedication to Mme. Pachler, is *An Sylvia* (To Sylvia), and not the ballad " Edward," which is meant by the above " Old Scottish Ballad," translated from the Percy Reliques by Herder in his " Stimmen der Völker." This was included in another set.

finances. The outlook was as black as ever. But with the arrival of September there seemed a likelihood of better conditions, and it then became more than probable that Schubert would arrive at the Pachlers' during the month. On the 6th, Jenger wrote again to Mme. Pachler:

" Friend Schubert and I moved into new quarters on the 1st inst. . . . I found Schubert no longer in his old, and also never in his new quarters on the Wieden. Last night I spoke to him at length at the Burg theatre, and now, dear madam, I can tell you that friend Schwammerl expects shortly an improvement in his finances, and counts upon it confidently. As soon as this happens he will immediately follow your kind invitation, and will arrive at your house at Graz with a new operetta. In any case you will receive definite advice either from him or from me a week before his arrival at Graz. He wished, of course, that I should make the journey with him, but as I said in my last letter, I cannot get away at the present time. If Schubert remains with you till the end of October it might be possible for me to come to Graz for at least a week, to see all my dear ones again, and fetch friend Schwammerl."

Whatever expectations Schubert had, they did not materialize. He knew at last that all chance of a holiday had gone, and wrote to Jenger on September 25th:

" I have handed over the second part of the *Winterreise* to Haslinger. I cannot go to Graz this year as financial affairs and the weather are most unfavourable. I accept Dr. Menz's invitation with pleasure, as I enjoy hearing Baron Schönstein sing. You might meet me at Bogner's coffee house, Singerstrasse, between 4 and 5 o'clock on Saturday.

" Your friend,

" SCHUBERT."

So grievous was his financial state that he wrote to Probst about the Trio,[1] offering at the same time other compositions in the hope of their being accepted.

" I am writing to inquire when the Trio is going to be published. In case you do not known the number of the Opus, it is 100. I am looking forward to publication with great longing. I have also composed three sonatas for the pianoforte which I propose dedicating to Hummel. Moreover, I have set to music several songs of Heine from Hamburg which met with great approval here. And, finally,

[1] Professor O. E. Deutsch: Undated letter.

FRANZ SCHUBERT

I have composed a quintet for two violins, 1 viola and two violoncellos. I have played the sonata at several places and always with success. The quintet is going to be performed before long. If you would like to have any of these compositions please let me know.

" With esteem,
" Yours,
" FRZ. SCHUBERT."

The battle was ending, the struggle nearly finished. This letter was his last effort to sell his works. And even as he wrote it he was condoling with Bauernfeld on the failure of his play.

" After the honourable failure of what was not my first, but the first-performed of all my comedies, *The Match-Maker,* my friend [Schubert] found an occasion to console me, as I had consoled him before," wrote Bauernfeld.[1]

" I had arranged a meeting with Grillparzer, Schubert, Schwind, Schober and other friends at our usual tavern, but felt unequal to keeping the appointment. I would rather have hidden in the bowels of the earth. I ran about the dark streets. About midnight I came across Grillparzer, who endeavoured to give me courage in the most friendly manner. Next morning came Schwind and Schubert. They could not understand my melancholy at all. ' The play pleased me exceedingly,' Schubert assured me repeatedly, ' in fact, all of us! And, after all, we are not asses.' "

Who could have understood Bauernfeld's grief better than one who had lived with disappointment all his life!

[1] Bauernfeld: "Alt Wien."

CHAPTER XVIII

The Dimmed Lamp

(1828)

ON September 1st, Schubert left Schober and the " Blue Hedgehog " (*Blauen Igel*). The motive for this change was that he wished to be an encumbrance upon his friend no longer. He went to live with his brother Ferdinand who had moved into a house in the Neue Wieden suburb—No. 694 Firmiansgasse—which the builders had but recently vacated. Schober was certain that he would come back. He kept Schubert's rooms vacant for him, believing that one day he would enter it and find Franz returned, like a pigeon to its loft.

The Neue Wieden was then a rural suburb of Vienna, far removed from the disturbance of the city life and its commerce. Here Franz could rusticate, take his walks abroad in the fields. Here the fresh winds of the Danube and the country air would restore his health. Dr. Ernst Rinna, a young and brilliant physician no more than a few years older than Schubert, had advised the step, and so it was taken.

With the passage of more than a century, the widening arms of Vienna have folded about the Neue Wieden. Its fields have disappeared, the river, which in summer time lay glittering like glass in the sun, is hidden behind endless rows of buildings and crossing streets. Ferdinand's house was a building of two storeys under a rust-coloured roof, a wide arch in the centre—an arch with double doors through which one passed to a little sanctuary of coolness and shadow at the back. The front windows were long and narrow, mullioned, many of them, as became a building of some pretensions, which it unquestionably was when Ferdinand Schubert moved into it.

173

How far Rinna was sound in his advice to Franz Schubert is an open question. The building was damp; its walls reeked with damp. But this disadvantage was to some extent discounted by the fact that Ferdinand now had his brother in his immediate care. He showed no sympathy for the *Gasthaus* nights, which of late had been more frequent than prudent. He compelled Franz to take exercise. Franz had not been in his brother's house a month before they set off on a three days' walking tour. They went to Eisenstadt and visited the grave of Josef Haydn. Franz ate and drank but little. Sometimes he complained of feeling tired, but as he had not taken such strenuous exercise for years there was nothing remarkable in that. When he returned to Vienna he was in high spirits, and his health betrayed no sign of any disturbing influence at work. He composed a new Benedictus to his Mass in " C " immediately he reached the Neue Wieden rooms again.

October passed. On the last day of the month he had supper with Ferdinand and some friends at a tavern near his birthplace in Lichtenthal, known as *Zum Roten Kreuz*. He ordered a plate of fish, but hardly had he begun to eat before he threw down his knife and fork and declared that he was poisoned. He returned home supperless, but apparently none the worse. Three days later he walked to Hernals to hear Ferdinand's new Requiem, and then tramped for three hours afterwards. He again said that he was tired. Again little notice was taken of the complaint. But his languor was that of a man who had no strength, whose vitality had been slowly draining away for more than four years.

During one of these last days he met Anschütz in the street, and the actor made a note of their conversation—a conversation which almost suggests that Schubert was full of subconscious foreboding.

" Schubert often came to my house in these latter days," said Anschütz.[1] " He was a downright, honest, simple-hearted being whom one could not help loving. His eyes, which ordinarily appeared dull through his short-sightedness, flashed up when he talked about music. This he loved to do, his regular theme being to grumble about the bad taste of the public and the wretched Italian music.

" That was precisely the theme of his last conversation with me. I met him shortly before his death in an avenue off the Burg-glacis. A short time previously the magnificent enterprise of Barbaja at

[1] Johann Anschütz: Reminiscences from his notes and verbal communications.

the Court Opera had come to an end, and Count Gallenberg had taken over the management.

" 'Thank God,' said Schubert, 'that we have got rid of that Turkish music!'

" 'I will not contest the view of an authority, but I am indebted to the enterprise of Barbaja for many enjoyable hours,' I replied. 'Think of Lablache, Rubini, Tamburini, Donzelli and the Fodor!'

" 'Well, yes, it's all very well,' Schubert made answer, 'but leave me out with the music. It sometimes appears to me as if I belonged no more to this world.' "

And yet he was laying plans for the future. He had no premonitions beyond those in his chance words to Anschütz which might have been those of a passing mood of gloom. Who could foresee the shadows so swiftly on-coming? He determined to take lessons in counterpoint and fugue from Sechter, and Sechter was the greatest authority in Vienna on the subject. The day after his three-hour walk with Ferdinand he decided to trudge in on foot to Vienna, see Sechter and arrange the lessons.

He was eating nothing, drinking nothing. He was a starved man, for no food had passed his lips since that evening at the *Roten Kreuz*. So certain was he that the sickness within him was no more than a phase that he undertook what must have been a wearying journey to a man in his condition.

He met a pianoforte player named Josef Lanz in Vienna, and together they saw Sechter and arranged the lessons. Sechter actually gave Schubert one lesson, for he wrote afterwards:[1] 'We only had a single lesson. When Herr Lanz came the next time he appeared alone."

During the next few days Schubert's condition became threatening. He was still without food, but he walked about. He refused to keep to his room or to take to his bed. Even when the rising fever weakened him the more, he shuffled round the house as if his body was making some final protest against the inevitable call. He was not alarmed about his condition, but was driven to despair by his weakness. He talked of his plans for the future with the certainty of one who sees them clearly attainable. The fever burned on, and drew his vitality more surely away as each day passed. Schubert was sinking slowly into that physical inertia which invites

---

[1] Simon Sechter: Letter to Luib. Kreissle, Grove and other biographers have declared that no lessons were given to Schubert by Sechter. But they were unaware of this letter which sets all doubt upon the point at rest.

death. His body was dying, but in his brain life, the power of thought, of invention, refused with fierce obstinacy to pass.

On the 12th he wrote to Schober:

"DEAR SCHOBER,

"I am ill. For eleven days I have neither eaten nor drunk anything. I am tottering from the chair to the bed, and vice versa. Rinna is attending me. Whenever I eat anything I promptly bring it up again. Do be kind and help me in this desperate condition by sending me some books. I have read Cooper's *The Last of the Mohicans, The Spy, The Pilot,* and *The Settler.* In case you have any other books by this author, I beg you to leave them for me at the coffee house with Bogner's wife. My brother, who is conscientiousness itself, will certainly bring them to me. Or anything else you have.

"Your friend,

"SCHUBERT."

On Friday, the 14th, he took to his bed. His friends came. Spaun brought a copy of the *Serenade* which he had made for Schubert to correct. He found Franz being nursed by Josepha, his small stepsister of thirteen. "There is nothing really the matter with me," Schubert said, "but I am so weak that I feel I shall fall through the bed."[1] When Spaun had gone, he sat up in his bed and corrected the proofs of the second cycle of the *Winterreise* songs which he had just received from Haslinger. It was the last work he was to do.

Two days later Dr. Rinna is stated to have fallen ill, and, for this reason, to have handed Schubert over to Dr. Wisgrill and Dr. Josef von Vering.[2] But was illness the cause of Rinna's retirement? Or was it that his medicines and his treatment had failed, and his patient was more than ever in the grip of a disease for which a specialist was required? Vering was the specialist—he was *a specialist in venereal disease.*

Wisgrill and Vering threw away Rinna's medicine and substituted their own. But for what malady were they treating Schu-

[1] Spaun: "Memoirs."
[2] Kreissle and other biographers are at fault in giving von Vering's name as Behring. Von Vering's father had attended Beethoven for his deafness, and the son, Josef, became one of the most important writers of medical books—especially on the subject of venereal disease—after Schubert's death. Kreissle also confuses father and son.

bert? A tragedy of the utmost importance in the musical history of the world may, or may not, have been enacted at this stage. Vering had been a school comrade of Schubert at the Convict. Even so, he would not have remained in attendance on Schubert if Wisgrill and himself had not suspected venereal disease as the primary cause of the illness. It is permissible to inquire if their treatment was not for venereal disease alone at this stage, whilst typhus was gaining the mastery over Schubert more insidiously, hour by hour, day by day. It was not until Thursday the 14th that these two doctors appear to have been united in the diagnosis of typhus.

They engaged a female nurse in place of the young sister. A few hours later they also engaged a male nurse. It was by then quite obvious to the doctors that Schubert had contracted a dangerous form of typhus. Desperate as his condition had become, there still seemed some chance of saving his life. He was quite clear in his mind, and there had been as yet no signs of delirium. But the fever remained unabating, and pieces of lemon were held to his lips to assuage the terrible thirst.

On Monday the 17th Bauernfeld came to see him. So certain was Schubert of his ultimate recovery that he not only discussed the music he was going to compose for Bauernfeld's opera *The Count of Gleichen*, the whole of which he had sketched out, but he asked his friend for a new *libretto* to follow it. Lachner called, only to listen to the same remarks from the patient about the opera.

"When I visited Schubert for the last time—it was on November 17th—he was lying on his bed very ill," says Bauernfeld.[1] "He complained of weakness and heat in the head, but he was still quite lucid and without any signs of delirium. Nevertheless the depressed spirits of my friend filled me with grave forebodings. His brother came with the doctors. By the time evening arrived the patient was wildly delirious. The most virulent form of typhus had manifested itself."

The following day Schubert remained in a state of delirium. But at times his mind would clear; memory in a fantastic form would move aimlessly across his brain. He would struggle violently to get out of bed, fall back, then struggle again. Ferdinand held him in his arms and endeavoured to calm the spirit in torment.

"What are they doing with me?" Schubert exclaimed when, in a short-lived moment of sanity, he was conscious of those about him. "What are they doing with me?"

[1] Bauernfeld: "Alt Wien."

Ferdinand bent over him the closer. " Trying to make you well," he whispered. " You must not try to get out of bed."

Useless counsel, for the mind of the sufferer had left the world again in its wild wandering.

He seemed to sleep. Hours passed. Presently consciousness returned once more, and Schubert's eyes opened. More struggle, the desperate struggle of a fear-driven creature. In his imagination they were burying him alive!

" Put me in my own room," Schubert cried. " Don't leave me in this corner under the earth. Do I not deserve a place above the ground? "

" You are in your own room," Ferdinand assured him, " and lying on your own bed."

" It is not true! " came the swift denial. " No, Beethoven is not lying *here!* "

One can only surmise what was passing over his deranged mind. They were burying him, and Beethoven who was dead was not here. Mysterious confusions and terror drove him to fresh struggle.

Wednesday the 19th arrived. St. Elizabeth's Day. It was obvious now to the doctor, to Ferdinand, that Schubert's life was slipping away. His brief periods of freedom from delirium became fewer. When he spoke the words were usually so detached as to convey little or no meaning to those who heard them. About midday he had a violent fit of struggling, the same frantic desire to get out of bed. Again Ferdinand vainly tried to calm him. The doctor then bent over his pillow and urged him to be still.

Schubert lay in quiet, looking vacantly at the ceiling. He was now fully conscious. To those who watched, it might have seemed that he had made a rally. But suddenly he put out his hand. His fingers clutched at the wall. Probably only now he realized that death waited beside the bed, that the opera would never be com- posed, that his work was finished.

" Here, here is my end! " He spoke slowly and fully conscious of what he said.

Then he closed his eyes and lay in the quietude of stupor or sleep. The day crept on until, at three in the afternoon, somebody observed that he had ceased to breathe. . . .

The following day Schoolmaster Schubert issued an obituary notice of his son from the school in the Rossau. " My beloved son, Franz Schubert, artist and composer," he wrote. It further stated that he had received Extreme Unction, and would be buried the following day in the Church of St. Josef in Margarethen. But Ferdinand intervened. His brother's words about the absence of Beethoven—almost his last words—had deeply impressed his mind. He declared that Franz must be buried beside Beethoven in the Währing cemetery. It cost the Schoolmaster and Ferdinand 70 florins, a sum they could ill afford, but they did what they believed Franz would have wished them to do.

Moreover there were the expenses of Franz's illness to discharge, for he had left nothing of material value at the time. All his clothing and effects, including his manuscript music, realized only £2 10s. The music alone—and it comprised over 500 works—was valued at 8s. 6d. ![1] The bill for the expenses of his illness was prepared by Ferdinand for his father, and is as follows:—[2]

FRANZ'S ACCOUNT.

Vienna, December, 1828.

			Fl.	Kr.
12th November, 1828		Medicine	1	5
		2 lemons		14
		1 ounce (lot) Dutch Tea[3]		24
13th	,,	Medicine	1	15
		1 lemon		7
14th	,,	Phlebotomy	2	
		Lemon, etc.		19
15th	,,	Medicine	2	5
16th	,,	Ointment and vesicatory plaster		24
		To the barber		30
		Medicine	1	23
		½ lb. sugar		36
17th	,,	Medicine		58
		Mustard Powder		12
		Medicine		57
		1 lemon		7

[1] The tragedy of Schubert's low value in his own time is demonstrated by the fact that in 1927 £149 10s.—or more than a quarter of the sum Schubert earned in his whole life—was paid for the original manuscript of one of his songs (6½ pages of manuscript) composed a few months before his death. This was one of more than 500 of his manuscripts, valued on his death at 8s. 6d.

[2] This document is in the possession of Fräulein Marie Schubert, of Vienna. Apart from its general interest, it also reveals the fact that two nurses were called in to attend to Schubert.

[3] This was China tea, which came via Holland.

	The 16th for the carriage for Herr v. Gagstatter	2	
18th ,,	Wine, 15 kr., tea, 9 kr., lemon, 7 kr.		31
	Ointment and meat	1	8
	For three days for each meal, 1 s. wine		36
	Powder		18
19th ,,	Medicine		40
	On the 18th to the Verger	1	

		Fl.	Kr.
19th November, 1828	A Gattie	2	
20th ,,	Herr Dr. Wisgrill for consultation	5	
	The Totenbeschauer (Inspector of the Dead)	1	40
21st ,,	The Male Nurse	8	20
	The Female Nurse	10	30
	Quartiergeld (rent) pro November	12	30
	Heating	5	
	Laundry	5	
	The Male Nurse, 3 days' board and wine	2	30
	The Female Nurse, 6 days' board and wine	3	
	For the carriage to fetch the Male Nurse (H. v. Ponfikl)	5	

Ferdinand rendered later an additional account to his father:
For my Herr Father, Franz Schubert.
June, 1829.   Jan. 21, 1829, Dr. v. Rinna   25 fl. 20 kr.
From these accounts it would appear that Dr. von Vering did not make any charge.

The day following Schubert's death he lay in state in his coffin. They had dressed him in the garb of a hermit and placed a wreath of laurels about his forehead. A vast procession of people filed through the room to see in death the man who had given so much, and yet had received so little. They brought wreaths and bunches of flowers, so that soon the room was piled with flowers, its atmosphere sickly and stifling with their perfume.

The family selected Schober as chief mourner—the friend who had been so close to Schubert, but who in his last illness did not come near him. What was the mystery of Schober's neglect in those last days? Were the three miles from Vienna to Neue Wieden too long for him, or was the gallant afraid of the contagion of typhus which was destroying Schubert as it had destroyed his mother? Or did he attribute the illness of Schubert to another phase of the malady that lived in his blood—a phase that would soon pass? The absence of Schober from the death-chamber provoked no ill-feeling in the family or he would not have been given the place of chief mourner. If neglect there were, it was a matter for Schober and his conscience.

On Friday afternoon at 2.30 the funeral procession set out for the Church of St. Josef in Margarethen, and close behind the coffin followed a number of young men dressed in red cloaks, and carrying sheaves of flowers. It was raining, and the streets were desolate save for the groups who braved the wet to see another musical genius pass, all unaware of the true heritage he had left to them.

At the Church, Schubert's *Pax Vobiscum* was sung to some words which Schober had written for the occasion. The first memorial service was held at St. Ulrich, when a mass for the dead was celebrated, and a music society of the parish performed Mozart's *Requiem*. The " Miserere " and "Libera " and a German funeral song were sung at the second blessing of the corpse (*Einsegnung*) at the Währing parish church of St. Lorenz and St. Gertrud.[1] Schubert was then committed to the earth so close to Beethoven that the two giants lay with only three graves between them—closer in death than they had ever been in life.

Schober designed the headstone, and Grillparzer wrote the epitaph which aroused a storm of controversy; as it was justly said that Schubert had reached the highest mastery, and left such a rich legacy of musical treasures as few before him. Grillparzer's words appeared to imply that he had not yet reached the height of his powers.

Music has here buried a rich treasure,
But much fairer hopes,
Franz Schubert lies here.
Born January 31, 1797.
Died November 19, 1828.
31 years old.

[1] Dahms, p. 295.

Here the two masters lay until they were both disinterred in 1863, when, with the grizzly curiosity of the scientific mind which respects nothing and has no reverence, the skeletons were laid out and measured bone by bone, the skulls compared, and photographed. All this in order to discover that Beethoven was four and a half inches taller than Schubert!

The skeletons were then reburied, and, in 1872, a new monument was erected to Schubert by the Friends of Music in Vienna, at a cost of 42,000 florins, from which monument the words by Grillparzer were omitted. Even then the two great composers were not to rest in peace. In 1888 they were disinterred again and brought to the Central Cemetery in Vienna, where they take their final rest near together, with other masters of the art of music about them, in one of the most beautiful gardens of simplicity ever made for the great dead who honour it.

On the afternoon of Schubert's funeral, Wilhelm von Chézy, whose mother had written for Schubert the *libretto* of *Rosamunde*, was walking down the Singerstrasse. It suddenly occurred to him that he had not seen Schubert for a considerable time, nor heard anything about him. He could not have explained why Schubert should have entered his thoughts just then.

He walked into Bogner's coffee house, and took his place at the table usually occupied by Schubert and his friends between five and seven in the evening. There was no Schubert, nor any of his friends. The waiter came up to the table.

" Is your honour already back from the funeral? " he asked.

" Whose funeral? " Chézy inquired.

" Schubert died two days ago. They buried him this afternoon," the waiter said.

No other friends came to Bogner's that day. Mayrhofer, after the ceremony, went to the rooms in the Wipplingerstrasse where he and Schubert had lived together, and there he sat down and wrote his poem " Secret Remembrance," to the memory of Schubert, recalling his own failure and the brilliance of his friend. Very truly he wrote:

" . . . *a struggler's serious wrestling*
You take for freely welling life."

Bauernfeld returned to his diary: " The most honest soul, the finest friend! I wish I were lying there instead of him," he wrote

THE GREEN ANCHOR,
a favourite haunt of Schubert's. For a number
of years he could be found here daily

BOGNER'S COFFEE HOUSE
Beethoven and Schubert were always at Bogner's. In his last two
years Schubert was there practically every evening

SCHUBERT'S GRAVE IN THE
CENTRAL CEMETERY,

THE HOUSE IN WHICH
FRANZ SCHUBERT DIED,

in his grief. And a day later: " Schwind and I have lost all courage. What a life this is! "

Full of sincere emotion, despair and words, he then composed a poem of twenty-nine verses to the man upon whom the Währing gravediggers were shovelling down the earth.

CHAPTER XIX

The End of the Circle

S CHUBERT is dead, and with him all the brightest and most beautiful we had (in life)."

So wrote Schwind to Schober on Christmas Eve, 1828. The Circle was devastated, the life seemed to have departed from it with Schubert. Not until now did the Schubertians fully realize what he had meant to them. The atmosphere of Bogner's changed, even the punch-bowl appeared to lose its old flavour. " I now view life as some dreary path which I must walk alone," said Lachner.

Now that the magic figure had gone the Circle began to weaken. With the passage of time one member after the other retired more closely into himself; one after another they departed on the individual missions of their lives. The meetings became fewer. Old friendships remained, but the old intimacies had gone for ever. Letters, which in absence had been so frequent, now became desultory. It was the slow drifting apart of those who had been welded into one by a personality that had passed.

It may be of interest to follow some of the Schubertians on their several ways, and watch them grow old. It is significant that the devotion to Schubert did not perish in one of them. Schwind endeavoured to establish a Schubert-saal to his memory. Liszt, possibly at Schober's request, had *Alfonso and Estrella* performed for the first time in Weimar, on June 24th, 1854, when Schubert had been dead almost thirty years. Vogl, too aged and infirm to stand, used to sing Schubert's songs sitting in his chair.

Schober was the first to leave the Circle. A few months after the death of Schubert he left Vienna with the intention of never returning. He went as a tutor to Count Leo Festetics at Tolna in Hungary, and the only one of the Schubertians with whom he kept up any correspondence was Schwind. At Tolna he met Theresa

Brunswick, who was called " Beethoven's Immortal Beloved." At that time she was engaged in the foundation of schools for small children, and Schober gave her considerable assistance with the work.

Schober's fortunes were about to rise. He had an uncle named Derffel who possessed a small estate at Chorherrn in Nether Austria. Derffel was an unattractive miser, who quarrelled continuously with all the officials and servants on the estate. Once Schober had taken Uncle Derffel to a night at Bogner's when Schubert was present, and it is deplorable that the nephew did not keep some record of what Derffel thought of the gathering of irresponsible youths. He who viewed life through spectacles of grey, who was quite sure in his own mind that everyone had been born into the world with the express purpose of swindling him, must have endured an evening of unspeakable boredom and suspicion.

Before Schober had been tutoring at Tolna very long, Uncle Derffel, disgusted with his servants, offered him the estate at a moderate price. Schober bought it. He threw up his post, went to Chorherrn, and set about putting the place in order. His intention was to re-arrange the estate on a sound basis and then sell it at a profit. The work prospered, and as it prospered Uncle Derffel became more antagonistic. There was some value in the estate after all, and he had not noticed it! Again he had been swindled! He went to his lawyers to wrest the estate from Schober's hands, brought an action and lost it. Soon afterwards Schober sold the estate at a large profit, and, with the money he had inherited from his mother, he now had enough to enable him to give his life to Art and idleness. Uncle Derffel and his storming were forgotten. Schober went to Weimar.

He soon began to figure at the Court. His personality, his cleverness, and the artistry of his reciting and reading to the Court audiences, carried him into favour with the Grand Duke. He became, in a manner, a Poet Laureate. Poems were demanded from him for state occasions, and were as readily produced. Birthday poems, prologues for the theatre flowed from a pen as graceful as it was agile. He became indispensable and received the title of Councillor of Legation.

He met Liszt, and for some time acted as secretary to him. Liszt wanted a work for the Weimar festival and consulted Schober. It was too opportune an occasion for Schober to overlook. He had written *Alfonso and Estrella*, Schubert had composed it, and it had

185

never been produced. It should now be produced and their names would shine together. The opera was put on at the Court Theatre in June, 1854, and was a dismal failure.

For some reason or other he was suddenly pensioned off from the Legation, although well below the age which demanded retirement. The mystery was never explained. Some talked of a scandal, but if such scandal there was, Schober was too clever to let the truth be known. His poems had been published, and many of those unset by Schubert were set by Goethe's son, Walter.

What was there left for him to do? There still remained the adventure of marriage. In 1856, at the age of 60, he married a woman of fine appearance named Thekla von Gumpert, whom he had met at Posen in 1841. She had literary abilities. Was this the lure she had for Schober when prettier women had one and all failed through the years to take him in the marriage net? But literature, which for him was an art, became in her more commonplace. She wrote annuals for girls!

After four years of marriage, Schober left her. She had taken too great a chance of his fidelity. He went from place to place, amorous still, and seeking only the pleasure of bright eyes. Four years later he was divorced. Still he wandered, until perhaps the wearisomeness of life began to creep through his ageing limbs and he settled down at Dresden. He became half-deaf and almost a recluse. He, who had known everybody, now shunned everybody. Only the family of the violinist Schubert and Frau Babette Wolf amused him. And in the quietude of seclusion, which he had never known before in all the wild fever of his life, he died.[1]

Mayrhofer, whose poetry Schubert had set so freely, lived but eight years after the composer was buried at Währing. Eight years of unhappiness and mental torment, of gloom and ceaseless fear. He had never been *en rapport* with Schober, whose gaiety and easy treatment of life he did not understand. To Mayrhofer, life seemed a serious burden laid upon any man, a worthless gift which might be thrown away with advantage. And now as his years drew towards their close, his melancholy destroyed the spirit of brightness he had borrowed from Schubert. He would walk about the streets, the country lanes where he had walked with Schubert, a figure of gloom.

[1] His Art collection, etc., was sold in 1885 at Leipzig, but his papers, including approximately one thousand letters from famous people of various countries, were acquired for the city of Vienna by Professor Otto Erich Deutsch, in 1914, from Frau Babette Wolf, shortly before her death.

The dread of cholera became so intense that it appeared at times to take possession of all his mental faculties. His office work—his literary work would cease. He would sit at his window looking out on the street with half-closed eyes, always smoking, always brooding, until his melancholy became an actual pain too terrible to bear. Then he would leave his rooms, seek a kindred soul, and sit for hours in his apartment without speaking, or play a game of cards, or dilate upon the bestiality of Fate which made man no better than a fly in the web of some gigantic spider.

One of these episodes occurred in March, 1836. In a mood of deep depression he went to the house of a friend. They played a game of Taroc. As they were playing a young doctor came in and said that cholera had broken out again. Mayrhofer ceased to play. He did not speak. The doctor stayed to supper and began to drink beer, and Mayrhofer declared that he would follow his example but for the fact that most certainly his glass would be charged with cholera germs.

Mayrhofer was then Censor in Vienna, and next morning he appeared at his office as usual. He was calm, and apparently had forgotten all about the cholera rumour of the previous night. Presently one of the officials entered in a great state of distress and told him that the nurse of his child had died of cholera.

Mayrhofer got up from his chair.

" So! " he exclaimed. He passed slowly out of the room, went up the stairs to the third storey and flung himself out of the window. He was found in the street with terrible injuries, but still living and conscious. On the way to the hospital they gave him the last sacrament, but when they reached the door of the hospital his soul had departed.

Only two of the Schubertians met violent deaths. Mayrhofer was one, Teltscher, the water-colour and miniature painter, the other. Nine years after Schubert's death Teltscher perished by drowning at Athens in trying to save the life of an official of the Austrian Embassy.

Of the two brothers Hüttenbrenner, Anselm was unquestionably the more interesting to Schubert, while Josef was the kindlier, the more devoted friend. In the worst hours that Schubert knew, Josef was running the round of the publishers peddling Schubert's wares, writing letters towards the same end, striving to discover a few florins for the man he adored. His service was votive offering, his watchfulness at the bed in those last days of typhus a self-imposed

187

suffering to bring some comfort to Schubert. He was sincere with a sincerity unknown to Anselm. It is part of the irony of Life that the man who gives less than another should earn the greater favour. Schubert had called Anselm Hüttenbrenner his " musical support." He saw in Anselm a man who thought as he thought, who dreamed as he dreamed. Josef was just a lovable companion, but it was Anselm who shared with him those lonely heights of music where two minds met and understood one another.

At the time of Schubert's death Anselm Hüttenbrenner had just composed his Requiem for Beethoven. A few months later he was to produce it again for Schubert. He gave by composition what he felt was the best expression of which he was capable. Schubert's death had affected him deeply, and, in so far as his cold nature could be affected, he was one of the few who truly understood what the world had lost.

He was the man of cleverness who had somehow missed brilliance. After Schubert's death he became editor of some musical periodicals which published his compositions, and he held various honorary offices in musical circles in order to preserve his prestige. In 1835 he composed an opera—Leonore—and was amazed at its failure. He could not remember that Schubert had striven in opera and failed, that all his fanfares had not reduced the walls of an unconquerable Jericho.

In 1835 Anselm sold the two estates he owned and went to Graz with a large family trailing after him—a family that did not understand the soured monster in eternal complaint, complaints about his soup, the cooking and the hardness of his bed. Once settled in Graz, he composed a third act to an opera which was never performed. He composed a new Requiem for the Duke of Reich-stadt, which was given a solitary performance in Graz in 1840. He gathered up the honours of minor societies, including one from the Society of Musical Science, of which Spohr was president. Then, in one of those wild moods that were the outcome of ambition unachieved, he burnt his diary, which held so much about the Schubert friendship.

In 1835 he began to give music lessons again—how many years since he had given music lessons!

> " And now when of that day I mind me,
> Id fain look back along the road,
> Retrace the weary steps behind me. . . ."

How richly Schubert had set those words in his Rückblick!

The years in their passing changed Anselm Hüttenbrenner—
changed him very gradually into a person with an eternal grievance.
He challenged his old friendships in the secrecy of his thoughts
when sitting alone, discounted them, wondering if he had been wise
in honouring this friend, that friend, with the intimacy of his secret
opinions. He had, he once observed, given the key of his heart into
hands unworthy of it. Anselm had aimed high, and now, carping
and obscure, he was bitter in his loneliness. His wife died, his nine
children left the Hüttenbrenner hearth one by one to escape the
ceaseless whine of complaint. Anselm was gradually becoming a
decrepit figure, wrinkle-faced, sardonic in expression rather than
sad—a figure that had shed all vestiges of human sympathy.
Warped, mentally warped, by disappointment.

He became the prey of rheumatism, and was prisoned in a chair
at Graz. He doted upon any little word of praise that came to him,
lived on that word as if it were bodily food. Relegated to semi-
obscurity, he became prouder than ever of his friendship with
Schubert, and, in order that this friendship should be the more
widely known, he wrote his " Fragments from the life of Schubert
the Song-maker." He sent a copy to Liszt, which Liszt did not even
trouble to acknowledge.[1]

The slight, the apparent slight, wounded Hüttenbrenner. He
sank the deeper into his chair by the fire. His peevishness increased
with his rheumatism. It had now become almost impossible for him
to raise his arms, and he made a daily practice of doing so, believing
that he could beat the malady which, day by day, was beating *him*.
The pangs of gout made him shut those thin lips the tighter. Gout
—was this a memory of Schubertian days, a reminder of tavern
nights as departed and forgotten as last year's leaves?

Anselm went down to Marburg on the Drave to enjoy, or, more
possibly, to endure, the patronage of Baron Rast. Here, at all events,
he was accepted at his proper value. The Baron wrote execrable
verse under the *nom-de-plume* of " Hilarius," and Anselm, reduced
to nothing better, had to set his freak words to music.

Anselm retained his old prides, which were more powerful than
his poverties. Rast's *libretti* drove him at length to desperation. He
left the Baron without warning. He wandered round the homes of
his various children, and descended in unobtrusive fashion upon his

[1] Several years later he sold a copy of these Fragments to a publisher Mühl-
feit at Graz, and, as a result, a few excerpts from them appeared serially in a
Graz *daily paper*.

friends. Then the children decided that something must be done to put him in a place whence he could launch his bolts at Vienna without disturbing the lives of those he had brought into the world. They bought him a little estate, " Strasshof " in the neighbourhood of Ober-Andritz, and fashioned for him a luxurious bedroom that faced the western sun. They may have thought of him as a westering sun—a sun slow in departure.

For a time he lived in melancholy happiness at " Strasshof." Then he discovered suddenly—or thought he discovered—that he was an unwanted person. Rebellion came to him, the swift desire to re-establish himself. He got up one day and walked out of the house and ordered his coach. Where was he going? He did not know, but he would leave " Strasshof." They were trying to poison him there; he *knew* they were trying to poison him. He went out of " Strasshof " like an old dotard who had been disturbed from his secret retreat by some mad mood. He would go to Vienna, drive through its streets, be recognized, possibly acclaimed afresh. Yes, he would go to Vienna.

He started out; then a new decision, born of nothing, changed his plans. He turned the coach. He drove to the house of his youngest daughter Angelika, and he stumbled in, a tottering old man asking for any sanctuary. His persistence had sped its course. He was tired, terribly tired.

He stayed there until one day, without any threatening symptoms, he dropped down upon his bed with typhus. His bitterness had gone, and now his memories were departing one by one. Only one memory remained standing out in the darkness of his mind like a solitary star in a night sky. Schubert. He talked of him in rambling fashion. But there was something more necessary to him in this hour even than his memory of Schubert. He cried for a lemon!

And he died even as they pressed a cut lemon to his lips. . . .

The romance of Grillparzer and the Fröhlich sisters went on until it was terminated by death. Anna continued to teach at the School of Music until 1854. Josefine, after her retirement from the stage, seldom sang in public again, except on those occasions when she appeared with her sisters. Only on Christmas Night their rich expressive voices would fill the lofty aisles of St. Michael's Church. Barbara, after her marriage to Ferdinand Bogner the flute-player. departed from the family circle. For many years she was a drawing-mistress at the Institute for Officers' Daughters at Hernals. Her husband found his success in musical circles alone, for he rose to no height in his post under the Government. He was far happier as honorary professor at the Conservatoire than in the unromantic ways of his official employment. When he died and was followed to the grave by his son, Wilhelm, Barbara's less amiable qualities became more and more pronounced, and she died, estranged from the family, an eccentric original.

" I must love you all! " Grillparzer had written to the sisters from Jamnitz. "Leave me to my delight! " he would exclaim. ' This is the only house where I can give full vent to my complaints, where I can grumble to my heart's content. Let me be disagreeable! "

The more he grumbled the greater became the devotion of the sisters. " This person will kill me yet with her apathy! " he declared of Anna. " Take her away! She murders me, and she sings terribly out of tune! "[1] That was the Grillparzer they knew and understood, a man in love with all of them in his own passionless fashion. In 1848 he made his will and appointed Kathi his sole heiress, only to change it again a few years later and substitute all three sisters. Even this did not satisfy him. He made his will again, and this time Kathi was put back to her original place.

The three sisters nursed him throughout his last illness, and it was Kathi who closed his eyes in death in 1872. In spite of all his carping and bickering, Grillparzer was only known to have had one quarrel with the sisters, and that with Kathi when he broke off their engagement. A strange friendship of complete devotion, and that it endured is the more remarkable in view of his eccentricities. But, as the Countess Wickenburg said of the sisters a little later: " The care of the poet was the vocation of their lives, and his memory remained with them like a pious creed throughout their remaining years." He belonged to these women, and they belonged to him.

Schubert's death brought to Bauernfeld not only grief but isolation. Schwind was now living almost continuously in Munich, and, with the departure of Schober early in 1829, only Bauernfeld remained of the four intimates who, for the past few years, had lived in such close association. He was employed in the Diplomatic service, and his income had reached such a figure that he had no longer to beg his dinner at the tavern on credit. If he was not " swimming in silver," as he had said of Schubert, he was no longer

[1] Grillparzer: Annals.

in want. He rose rapidly in the Diplomatic service, in which he remained for twenty years, and wrote his books, his plays. But with the passing of Schubert something was taken from him which his later success failed to replace, a fact he made so clear in his writings.

Bauernfeld's life was fulfilled as he had planned it. Its romance had departed with Schubert. He sought no adventure; he was too balanced and careful. He became humdrum and interested only in what he wrote. It was Schwind who carried romance through his life. Could a man who had slept so often on the floor of Schubert's room wrapped in a leather coat, who had painted Turks on two signboards to pay his debts at Bogner's, who had made an offer of marriage in a torn dress-suit, be expected to cast away romance?

Ten years after Schubert's death Schwind returned to Vienna to paint some frescoes at Döbling, then he went to Karlsruhe. Sixteen years after the adventure with Netty Hönig in the torn dress-suit, he married a daughter of the grand-ducal Major Sachs of Karlsruhe, and started on a honeymoon to introduce his bride to his brothers and sisters. Then he was offered the Professorship at the Academy at Munich and a salary of 1,150 florins per annum, and at the beginning of 1847 he settled down. He had times when money was plentiful, others when he had not enough to pay his debts. When he had no money he went on painting. Possibly he remembered Schubert's ceaseless output during the worst days of poverty. That the work might never be sold did not trouble Schwind at all. "An artist who is always waiting till he gets an order before he starts painting," he said, " is like a cab-driver who stands about waiting for hire." And a little later he wrote: " I can prove to you that my expenditure on gilders, colours, canvasses and models during the six years that I have been in Munich amounts to more than I have received for pictures. Under the circumstances I prefer to pinch and economize and work for myself and my friends."

In 1853 he began to travel Europe. He visited Prague, Dresden, Leipzig, and then at Weimar he met Schober. It was a meeting of veterans. Schober had reached the height of his Court *réclame*. The old friendship for Schwind, with whom he had ceased to correspond for years, was awakened as fresh and strong as if it had never been forgotten. Schober interested the Grand Duke in a scheme for a set of historical cartoons for the Wartburg, and Schwind was to paint them. " I shall have an income of 5,000 thalers for three years," Schwind wrote. " I feel very rich." When the cartoons were complete a musical celebration was held at the Wart-burg, and Schwind played the violin in the orchestra.

Schwind then built himself a little house at Nieder-Pöcking, on the shore of the Starnberg lake, and in June, 1856, gave it to his wife as a birthday present. He called the place "Tanneck" (Pinewood Corner) and carved the date into the panelling. He wanted to settle down quietly at "Tanneck," to be left undisturbed to carry out the themes which were ever present in his imagination. He had tired of cities. Tired of the hack-work of making money, when the works he regarded as the finest from his brush lay dusty in their corners. Possibly he would not have left "Tanneck" again, but in 1857 the King sent him to the great Exhibition at Manchester.

Schwind had never seen the sea. He knew ships only from pictures. When he reached Dover he was amazed at the sight of the iron hull of a ship in course of construction. "I remember measuring St. Peter's (Rome) and the Square of St. Mark's with 260 full steps," he wrote, "and that is the length of this ship."[1]

The National Gallery in London surprised him. He had always heard it spoken of "with a certain amount of indulgence." He found the collection unique, with only two pictures—a *Noli me tangere* by Caracci, and a head by Lawrence—to which he took exception. Westminster Abbey drew from him the opinion that its monuments should be looked upon as curiosities, rather than works of Art. "But nothing is mean, and all—even in its bad taste—is still bold and rich."

He returned to Munich in August, sold his house there, and settled down at "Tanneck," where he completed the cycle of "The Seven Ravens and the Faithful Sister." For thirteen years this cycle had been in his mind, and now that it had been given expression the work was proclaimed at once to be a classic. Cornelius, the old master, wrote to him from Berlin: "Combined with Truth, Nature and Life, everything breathes grace and soul. This shows itself in the smallest detail, in every lock of hair, in every pleat of drapery."

In the Autumn of 1858 Schwind began his coloured cartoons for the windows of Glasgow Cathedral, and at the same time painted three windows for the church of Sonnberg. A year later he painted on a ground of gold a triptych for the church of Our Lady at Munich. But his heart was still in Vienna. He had heard that the

[1] Führich: "Schwind."

193

city was growing rapidly. The Vienna of his youth was a dear place to him still, and, accompanied by his daughter, he returned to it for a brief visit at Easter, 1861. He found a Vienna changing. Some of the taverns of the Schubert days had gone, but Bogner's and the *Grüne Anker* remained. The thoroughfares which he had trodden with Schubert—little dismal, lamp-lit lanes as he remembered them—were passing into prouder, wider streets, their houses new and widespread, and often ugly.

Schwind remained in Vienna only a few days, then he went to Traunkirchen and met Josef von Spaun—the Spaun he had not seen for thirty-three years.

"The first evening was magnificent," he said, " and the marvellous scenery made a deep impression on me like a glass that is full of Youth. I am tempted to swear that Traunkirchen is the most wonderful place in the world."

It was the last he was to see of Spaun, who, now seventy-four years of age, was still clear in his memories, and Schubert had always been to him the greatest memory of all. Schwind proceeded to Ischl and visited Kenner—Kenner still cutting out figures and views in paper with a pair of scissors as he had always done. He met Hartmann again. Then he returned to Munich and the travel pictures which he had painted as a diary from the days of his youth.

For nearly a quarter of a century Schwind continued his efforts to establish in Vienna a *Schubert-saal* in which only Schubert's music was to be performed. He intended to paint the walls of the chamber with scenes from the songs of his friend. One was to be a Mayrhofer wall, with pictures from the Mayrhofer *libretti;* another a Goethe wall. But nothing came of the idea, and, although he continued to write letters to the Schubertians about the scheme, he did not see his dream memorial become a reality, although numerous sketches for it still exist.

When age began to afflict him and his eyesight to fail, he still worked ceaselessly. A storm of controversy had shaken the world of Art, but the veteran had weathered it. No longer had he to wait like the cabman for hire; he was piled high with commissions. The more they overworked him the greater was his joy of living, but a commission he received from Glasgow in the early sixties worried him more than any work had done for years. He had to paint ten figures six feet high " in a sentry-box scarcely six feet wide."

In 1868 the trouble in his eyes became acute. He was warned to rest, but he refused rest. He was then working on the cycle of the

" Fair Melusine." By the end of January the first nine feet had already been drawn to ascertain if the size was correct. " It is to be feared that it will succumb to the model-drawing," he said. "With the spectacles I cannot see the model; without the spectacles I cannot see the drawing."

His nerves began to break up. He was eager for a winter in Rome, but he refused to leave his work for Rome. Days, weeks passed now when he could do nothing, only in this spasmodic fashion did he yield to the weariness of a body that was tired out, worn out. Then he would discover some new vitality and return to his work with a vigour that sought to defy the measure of his years.

The Franco-Prussian War of 1870 descended like a blight on Europe. Seventeen of Schwind's near relatives were in the Army; two nephews fell on a single day. He could think of nothing but the War. The September battles and their mad slaughter haunted him with the dread fears of the casualty lists. His eyes had now almost ceased to see, and in October he had a bad attack of suffocation, but he refused to take to his bed. By the end of January, 1871, he was definitely bedridden. His work was done. He had laid aside his brush for ever, and he spoke of the fact with emotion and resignation.

On the morning of February 8th, he decided that he would get up. He asked his daughter to help him from his bed to his chair. She propped him in his armchair and arranged his pillows.

" How do you feel? " she asked him.

" Excellent! " he said.

In a minute he was dead, even as the word was spoken.

The Schubertians may have forgotten each other in the later years. Wanderings broke them apart. The Circle—the wonderful Circle—became to most of them a memory of a cherished chapter of Youth. But none of those who had known its intimacies ever forgot the man who had formed it.

A year before his death Vogl, tottering from chair to chair, peevish, pain-racked with his gout so that beads of sweat appeared on his forehead when he endeavoured to hobble about, gave a party. That night he sang the full cycle of the *Winterreise*. His voice was weak, but there was a lingering sweetness in it still, an expression so vibrant with life that they declared the best tenor of the day could not sing those songs as Vogl sang them. Men and women sitting in the room, some of whom remembered the old *Schubertia-*

den, found tears upon their cheeks and were not ashamed. They called it his Swan-song.

A little later Holzapfel, Schubert's comrade of the Convict, was pounding round his room on crutches. He was paralysed and slipping slowly into death. But he would go up and down stairs on his crutches with the agility of a man in full possession of his legs, and flounder round the room whilst talking, carefully avoiding furniture and the legs of visitors with the cleverness of an expert on wooden feet. He desired nothing better than to get his friends together, and talk to them about the Schubert he had known. And he always began his story in the same way:

" He was a very little man, but he was a giant. . . ."

Holzapfel loved his epigram, because it was the truth.

APPENDIX

IT has only been possible in this book to deal with the main figures and prominent friends of Schubert's life.

But Schubert was a man with a vast number of acquaintances. In the following pages an attempt has been made to give details in brief of many of those with whom he came in contact, or people who had some bearing, direct or indirect, upon his work.

The men and women who figure prominently in the story of Schubert's life have not been included in the Appendix. Most of them are fully dealt with in the text, and to include them here would only entail repetition.

AUTHOR.

Barth (Josef), b. Grossliffen, December 29th, 1781; d. May 19th, 1865. He had an excellent tenor voice, and was a close friend of Schubert. With him the brothers Czerny and Gross, Linke, Giuliani (who was a remarkable guitarist), Binder and Rauscher, Barth used to meet at the house of Frau von André for musical evenings.

Barth, with Umlauff, Götz, Nejebse and several others, took part in the first performances of Schubert's vocal quartets.

Barth was the son of the manager of an estate in Grossliffen, who, as the father of seven children, had little money to spare for the education of his son as a musician. The son secured an engagement as a violinist on the *Heiligen Berg*, near Pribram, where he began to study classics. He graduated at Prague. In 1807 he went to Vienna and attempted to get an engagement with the ruling Prince Joseph of Schwarzenberg, and this estimable person appointed him to the Princely Court Book-keeping Department, where he served for over half a century. After 1819 he was a member of the Imperial Vocal Chapel. Schubert dedicated to him the vocal quartets *Das Dörfchen, Die Nachtigall,* and *Geist der Liebe.*

Blahetka (Leopoldine), b. Guntramsdorf, November 15th, 1811; d. Boulogne, January 17th, 1887. Famous pianist and composer. She had been a pupil of Czerny and Sechter. Doppler, in a letter, asks Schubert to compose a Rondo brilliant for L. Blahetka. Her father wrote Schubert's necrologue in Bäuerle's *Theaterzeitung,* 1828.

Bocklet (Karl Maria von), b. Prague, 1801; d. Vienna, July 15th, 1881. Pianoforte virtuoso and friend of Schubert. Bocklet performed several of Schubert's works for the first time and was also the pianist at Schubert's only concert. The " D Major " Sonata (Op. 53) is dedicated to him.

First page of the autograph manuscript of the *Erlkönig*

198

First page of the autograph manuscript of the *Winterabend*

Bruchmann (Joh. Christian Ritter von), b. Cologne, 1768; d. Vienna, 1849, in his 81st year. Director of the Austrian National Bank. In his house, Weihburggasse 914 (now No. 21), regular readings and musical evenings took place, which were frequently attended by Schubert. The son Franz wrote poems, several of which Schubert set to music.

Claudius (Mathias), b. Reinfeld, near Lübeck, January 2nd, 1740; d. Hamburg, January 21st, 1815. Controller of and writer in the periodical *Der Wandsbecker Bote, Asmus Omnia Sua Secum Portans*. In this periodical he published his *lyrics*, many of which are popular gems of German poetry. Schubert set eleven of the songs by this writer, including " Death and the Maiden," and " At the Tomb of Anselmo " (1816), dedicated to Vogl. Kupelwieser illustrated the poem in Chinese ink.

Clody (Florian Max), b. 1740, d. in his 88th year. Owner of the castle and " Herrschaft " (a feudal estate which had to pay rent to a monastery), Ebenzweyer. The blind old gentleman and his daughter Theresa received Schubert and Vogl in 1825, during their tour through Upper Austria.

Collin (Matthäus von), b. Vienna, March 3rd, 1779; d. there, November 23rd, 1824. Poet and founder of the Austrian Annals of Literature, Professor of History and Philosophy, Vienna University. Schubert made the acqaintance of Rosel, Hammer-Purgstall, Karoline Pichler and L. Pichler at Collin's house, and he set five of Collin's poems, including " The Dwarf."

Craigher (Jacob Nikolaus), b. Lipossullo, in Friuli, December 17th, 1797, d. April 17th, 1855.
A great friend of Schubert who, in 1825, set his *Todtengräbers Heimkehr* ("The Gravedigger's Homecoming "), "The Blind Boy " and the famous " The Young Nun."

Deinhardstein (Johann Ludwig von), b. Vienna, May 21st, 1794; d. there, July 12th, 1859. Schubert composed his *Lasst im Morgenstrahl des Mai'n* (" Let in the Morning ray of May ") and the occasional poem " On the Birthday of the Emperor " (also called Folk Song) for four voices (choral) with orchestra. This was composed at the instigation of Leopold von Sonnleithner and performed on the Emperor's birthday on February 2nd, 1822.

Diabelli (Anton), b. Mattsee, near Salzburg, September 6th, 1781; d. Vienna, April 7th, 1858.
Diabelli was the first publisher of Schubert's compositions. He was a choir-boy in the Monastery of Michaelbeuren and Salzburg Cathedral. He afterwards studied for the priesthood at Munich, but continued to study music under Michael Haydn. Diabelli had already entered the monastery of Reichenhaslach when the Bavarian monasteries were secularized. He then went to Vienna, where he met Josef Haydn, who helped him. He supported himself by giving lessons on the pianoforte and guitar. In 1818 he became a partner in the music-publishing

business of Cappi, and became head of the firm (then called Diabelli & Co.) in 1824.

Dietrichstein (Moritz) Count, b. Vienna, February 19th, 1775; d. August 27th, 1864. Court-Music-Count *(Hofmusikgraf)*. Patron and admirer of Schubert. He wrote to Vogl in 1821: " . . . for since I have sounded the genius of this young, strong, and most promising composer, it is my strongest desire to work for him as much as I can." Schubert dedicated to him the *Erl-King* (Op. 1).

Dumba (Nikolaus), b. July 14th, 1830; d. Vienna, March 23rd, 1900.

Owner of the greater part of the Schubert manuscripts. He was one of the chief instigators of the great Schubert Edition, and promoter of the scheme for the erection of the Schubert statue in Vienna. He took a very active part in the Society of Friends of Music, to whom he left his priceless collection of manuscripts.

Enderes (Karl von), b. Teschen, 1787; d. Kremsmünster, 1861. Studied at Olmütz and became tutor in the family of von Pachner von Eggenstorff. Later he entered the Ministry of Finance and became a Court Councillor. In Vienna Spaun worked with him in the office of Privy Councillor Schloissnig. When Spaun went to Linz and Lemberg they remained in correspondence, and it was Enderes who informed Spaun of the opportune moment for his return to Vienna.

Enderes was one of the most popular members of the Schubert Circle and beloved of Schubert.

He fell violently in love with Fräulein Kamilla Ellmaurer, a pupil of Vogl, and when another " Schubertian," Gros, married her, he was broken-hearted. Spaun consoled him by telling him that he had escaped danger, for the lady had a violent temper. But Gros died within a year and Enderes married the widow. After some years she deserted her husband and her children.

Enderes now gave his whole time to his hobby of collecting plants, but had a fall which deprived him of the use of his feet. He finished his life among the monks at Kremsmünster.

Erl (Josef), b. Vienna, March 15th, 1811; d. Hüttelsdorf, near Vienna, January 2nd, 1874.

Between the years 1838 and 1868 Erl was a Court Opera singer. He sang Schubert's songs at his concerts. In the first performance of *Der häusliche Krieg* at the Vienna Court Opera he sang the part of Astolf.

Feuchtersleben (Ernst, Baron von), b. Vienna, April 29th, 1806; d. there, September 3rd, 1849. Poet and author, and one of the Schubert Circle. He was on intimate terms with Mayrhofer, whose posthumous works he published with a character sketch of his life.

Gahy (Josef), b. 1793; d. Vienna, March 26th, 1864. Son of a

Hungarian Court Secretary. A pianist of great repute, who played Beethoven symphonies with Schubert. He worked with Spaun in the same Government office. He was an artist of great technique, who learned much from Schubert with regard to style and expression. Gahy remained the friend and admirer of Schubert till the end. He arranged Schubert's quartets, trios and choruses for piano-duets to suit his modified technique, caused through loss of the use of two fingers, and once a week Fräulein Stoll, an excellent pianist, came to play these with him.

Goldoni (Carlo), b. Venice, February 25th, 1707; d. Paris, February 6th, 1793. Schubert set his *La Pastorella* once for a single voice and once as a quartetto.

Herder (Johann Gottfried), b. Mohrungen, August 25th, 1744; d. Weimar, December 18th, 1803.

Two poems translated from foreign languages by Herder, including the Scottish ballad " Edward " (from the Percy Reliques) were set to music by Schubert.

Hölty (Ludwig Heinrich Christoph), b. Mariensee, December 21st, 1748; d. Hanover, September 1st, 1776.

Schubert set a great many of Hölty's poems, especially in his younger years. Between the years 1813 and 1816 he set no fewer than twenty-three of Hölty's poems as songs, and eleven as compositions for several voices.

Kenner (Josef), b. 1794. At the Convict with Schubert. He was of a very artistic nature, and when he visited Spaun he used to cut out with a pair of scissors paper figures, which were so cleverly done that Spaun collected them. For many years Kenner was passionately in love with Spaun's sister, and he presented her with a set of all his poems written out in his handwriting. He eventually became a Councillor magistrate at Linz, and later rose to a high appointment under the Government.

Klopstock (Friedrich Gottlieb), b. Quedlinburg, July 2, 1724; d. Hamburg, March 14th, 1803.

Schubert set a great number of Klopstock's poems, especially between the years 1815 and 1816. He set thirteen as songs for one voice, three for several voices, and the *Stabat Mater* for solo, chorus and orchestra.

Koller (Josef von), b. February 15th, 1779; d. September 18th, 1864. A merchant in Steyr. Schubert visited him frequently, and gave him, alternately with Schellmann, the honour of being his guest when in that town. Koller was a great musical enthusiast, and his daughter Josefine (b. December 26th, 1801; d. July 8th, 1874) was an accomplished singer and player on the pianoforte, and used to sing the Schubert soprano parts. She eventually married Krakowitzer.

Körner (Theodor), b. Dresden, September 23rd, 1791, killed in battle, August 26th, 1813. Great poet. During his sojourn in Vienna he became acquainted with Schubert through Spaun, who relates the story as follows: " Körner received Schubert in the most friendly manner, and asked him to remain true to Art, which would certainly make him happy." Schubert composed twelve songs, three duets, and the operetta " The Four Years' Sentry," to Körner's words.

When the Prussian call to arms came nothing could hold him back, although the Saxon Ambassador reprimanded him severely. One day Spohr came to fetch him, and pointed out to him the agreeable prospects of Vienna, and urged him to remain. To this Körner replied: " You musicians need no fatherland, but we poets must have one."

" The evening before his departure," says Spaun, " he gave us a supper in his room. Many of his poems were sung with great enthusiasm. . . . We remained together till two o'clock that night. He kissed us many times, assuring us how he loved to be among us, and that he would come back if he should remain alive."

Körner was killed by a spent bullet near Gadesbusch.

Kosegarten (Gottlieb Konrad), b. Grevismühlen, February 1st, 1758; d. Greifswald, October 26th, 1818.

Schubert set eigtheen of his poems, one for several voices.

Kotzebue (August von), b. Weimar, May 3rd, 1761; d. Mannheim, March 23rd, 1819 (shot by Sand). Schubert composed two of his plays, *Des Teufels Lustschloss* (The Devil's Pleasure Palace), 1813, and *Der Spiegelritter* (Knight of the Mirror), 1815, only fragments of which have been preserved. In Germany they say "Kotzebue lived by ink and was shot by Sand." (The name of a young student who killed him.)

Kreutzer (Konradin), b. Messkirch, Baden, November 22nd, 1780; d. Riga, December 14th, 1849.

For many years Capellmeister at the Kärntnerthor Theatre. He was one of the applicants for the post of Vice-Court Capellmeister at the same time that Schubert made application for it.

Lachner (Franz), b. Rain (Bavaria), April 2nd, 1803; d. Munich, January 20th, 1890. Composer. Studied under Stadler and Sechter. Between 1826 and 1828 he was vice-Capellmeister, and from 1828 till 1834 first Capellmeister at the Kärntnerthor Theatre, in succession to Weigl. He was the close friend of Schubert, and one of the most popular members of the Schubert Circle. In 1852 he became general musical director at Munich. He composed two oratorios and four operas, three masses, and many symphonies, songs and various pieces. He orchestrated Schubert's "Song of Miriam." The " Lachnerrolle," depicting scenes from his life, is one of Schwind's masterpieces.

Lanner (Josef), b. Döbling, near Vienna, April 11th, 1800; d. there, April 14th, 1843.

Composer. Schubert often visited the tavern " Zum Rebhuhn " (The Partridge) in the Goldschmiedgasse, where Lanner, with four companions, played his own pieces.

203

Leitner (Karl Gottfried Ritter von), b. Gratz, November 18th, 1800; d. there, June 20th, 1890. Belonged to the Pachler Circle. Eight of his poems, including the " Crusade," were set to music by Schubert at Frau Pachler's recommendation, and several of them were dedicated to her.

Matthison (Friedrich von), b. Hohendodleben, near Magdeburg, January 23rd, 1761; d. Wörlitz, near Dessau, March 12th, 1831. Schubert composed in 1814-16 twenty-four of his poems, including " Adelaide," which had been already set by Beethoven.

Mayssen (Josef), b. Hernals, August 18th, 1700; d. there, December 17th, 1860. School- and choirmaster at Hernals. Friend of Schubert from his youth. The *Tantum Ergo,* dated August 16th, 1821, was composed in his house. He also accompanied Franz and Ferdinand Schubert on the former's last walk. Schubert used to compose in a little summer-house in the schoolhouse garden.

Milder (Anna), the great Schubertian and operatic singer. Married Hauptmann, a jeweller; b. Constantinople, December 13th, 1785; d. Berlin, May 29th, 1838. Schubert dedicated to her his Opera 31 and 129.

Mosewius (Johann Theodor), b. Königsberg, September 25th, 1788; d. Schaffhausen, September 15th, 1858. Director of Music at Breslau University. Did much toward spreading the knowledge of Schubert's work in Germany. He became personally acquainted with Schubert in later life, and afterwards remained in correspondence with him. In a letter of June 4th, 1828, he told Schubert that his compositions were becoming more and more widely known in the north of Europe.

Müller (Wilhelm), b. Dessau, October 7th, 1794; d. there, September 30th, 1827. Lyric poet. Schubert set a great number of his songs, including the *Winterreise* and *Die Schöne Müllerin* cycle of twenty songs. The latter were taken from Müller's twenty-five poems, which appeared as *Gedichte aus den hinterlassenen Papieren eines Waldhornisten* (Poems from the Posthumous Papers of a Horn Player). The songs appeared as Op. 25 and were dedicated to Karl, Baron von Schönstein in 1824. The second great cycle, the *Winterreise* from the *Reisebilder* (Travel Pictures) was composed shortly before the poet's death in 1827. Schubert also composed *Der Hirt auf dem Felsen* (The Shepherd on the Rock) from Müller's *Der Berghirt* (The Mountain Herd) for one voice, with accompaniment of clarionet and pianoforte, a mixture of song and bravura aria which he wrote for Anna Milder at her request.

Wilhelm Müller married in 1821 the daughter of the " Regierungsrath," afterwards President von Basedow, granddaughter of the famous pedagogue. She died at Dessau in 1883. According to Professor Max Müller (his son) many of Müller's songs were dedicated to her, and she is the original of the Fair Maid of the Mill.

Nestroy (Johann), b. Vienna, December 7th, 1802; d. Graz, May 25th, 1862. Actor and dramatic author. Began his career as a singer in 1822 in the *Magic Flute.* He was a friend of Schubert, and frequently took part in the performance of his work, as, for instance, in the quartet *Geist der Liebe* (Spirit of Love), with Barth, Tietze and Nejebse, at the first performance on April 15th, 1822.

Niemeyer (August Hermann), b. Halle, September 1st, 1754; d. July 7th, 1828. Professor of Theology, and author of many theological books and sacred poetry. Schubert composed his religious drama, " Lazarus, or the Feast of the Resurrection," as an oratorio in 1820. It remained unknown for many years, and was first performed by the Vienna Choral Society in March, 1863.

Palffy von Erdöd (Ferdinand) Count, b. Vienna, February 1st, 1774; d. there, February 4th, 1840. Director of the Theatre An-der-Wien 1813-25, where Schubert's *Zauberharfe* was given on August 19th, 1820. Schubert dedicated to him his Op. 30.

Pfeffel (Gottlieb Konrad), b. Colmar, June 28th, 1763; d. there, May 1st, 1809. His poem *Der Vatermörder* (The Parricide) was one of the first songs composed by Schubert (1811). He probably found it in a school reader. In the complete Schubert Edition it appears without the poet's name.

Platen-Hallermünde (August), Graf von, b. Anspach, October 24th, 1796, d. Syracuse, December 5th, 1835. Schubert composed two of his poems in 1822.

Prokesch von Osten (Irene Countess, *née* Kiesewetter), b. Vienna, March 27th, 1811; d. Graz, July 7th, 1872. Schubert composed for her the vocal quartet *Der Tanz* (The Dance), with the object of restraining her from too much dancing, a pastime to which she was passionately devoted. After her recovery from a prolonged illness Schubert wrote the Chorus *Alla nostra cara Irene.* An excellent pianist, she often accompanied Schubert when he sang, also Baron Schönstein.

Pyrker von Felsö-Eör (Ladislaus), b. Lank, in the Comitat of Stuhlweissenburg, November 2nd, 1772; d. Vienna, November 23rd, 1824. Archbishop of Erlau. Poet and patron of many artists. Schubert made his acquaintance at the house of Matthäus von Collin, and dedicated to him the fourth book of the songs, for which Pyrker sent him twelve ducats. Schubert set two of his poems.

Rellstab (Ludwig), b. Berlin, April 13th, 1799; d. there, November 27th, 1860. Prolific poet and writer on music. Schubert set ten of his poems in the last year of his life. Seven of these appear in the Swan-song. Rellstab went to Vienna in 1825 to induce Beethoven to compose one of his opera *libretti,* and at the same time he gave him a number of his poems. Several of these were afterwards set by Schubert. The song *Auf dem Strom* (On the Stream), with horn *obbligato*, Schubert composed for the horn-player J. Lewy, who produced it at a concert in the little *Redoutensaal* on April 20th, 1828, with the composer at the pianoforte and a distinguished amateur as vocalist.

Rieder (Wilhelm August), b. Döbling, September 30th, 1796; d. Vienna, September 8th, 1880.

He became Custodian of the Imperial Gallery of Paintings. The friend of Schubert, and his painter.

Rudolf (Archduke of Austria, Cardinal Archbishop of Olmütz), b. Florence, January 8th, 1788; d. Baden, near Vienna, July 23rd, 1831. Patron and friend of Beethoven.

Schubert dedicated to him his pianoforte sonata in " A Minor " (Op. 42), composed at Gastein in 1825.

Rückert (Friedrich), b. Schweinfurt, May 16th, 1788; d. Neusess, near Coburg, January 31st, 1866. Schubert set five of his poems, including the popular *Sei mir gegrüsst* and *Du bist die Ruh'* in 1821 and 1823.

Salis-Seewis (Johann Gaudenz von), b. Seewis, Graubünden, December 26th, 1762; d. Melans, January 29th, 1834.

Schubert composed sixteen of his poems in 1816 and 1817.

Schlegel (August Wilhelm von), b. Hannover, September 8th, 1767; d. Bonn, May 12th, 1845. Schubert set seven of his original poems, also his translations of two sonnets of Petrarch, a sonnet by Dante, and " Hark! Hark! the Lark," from Shakespeare's *Cymbeline*.

Schmidt (Georg Philipp), called Schmidt of Lübeck, b. January 1st, 1766; d. Ottensee, near Hamburg, November 28th, 1849. He is the author of the famous "Wanderer," which Schubert composed in 1816, and which, under the title *Der Unglückliche* (" The Unfortunate ") by Werner, had appeared in Becker's Almanack of 1808. The Reverend Horni drew Schubert's attention to the poem, which the latter at the time believed to be by Zacharias Werner.

Schönstein (Karl, Baron von), b. Ofen, June 27th, 1797; d. Aussee, July 19th, 1876. The beauty of his voice is said to have surpassed that of Vogl. His choice of the songs of Schubert was, however, different from that of Vogl. He sang the *Müller* songs, which were dedicated to him, the *Serenade, Die Zürnende Diana*, etc. Vogl usually sang the more dramatic songs.

Schubert (Anton Eduard), b. Vienna, February 3rd, 1826; d. Kaltenleutgeben, September 7th, 1892. The youngest step-brother of Franz Schubert. As capitular of the *Schotten Stift* (Scottish Monastery) was called Father Hermann. He was an eminent preacher, and delivered his thousandth sermon in 1887.

Schulze (Ernst), b. Celle, March 22nd, 1789; d. there, June 26th, 1817. Schubert composed nine of his poems for one voice, and one, *Ewige Liebe*, for four male voices. He is best known by his *Bezauberte Rose* (The Enchanted Rose).

Sechter (Simon), b. Friedberg, Bohemia, October 11th, 1788; d. Vienna, September 10th, 1867. Famous musical theorist and teacher of counterpoint. Among his pupils were Bruckner, Nottebohm, Thalberg and Vieuxtemps.

Seidl (Johann Gabriel), b. Vienna, June 21st, 1804; d. there, July 18th, 1875. Schubert set eleven of his poems as songs, and four for several voices. His *Taubenpost* (Pigeon-post) in the " Swan-song " cycle was the last song Schubert wrote.

Silbert (Johann Peter), b. Kolmar, March 29th, 1772; d. Vienna, December 27th, 1844.
In 1819 Schubert set his poems *Abendbilder* (Evening Pictures) and *Himmelsfunken* (Sparks from Heaven).

Staudigl (Josef), b. Wöllersdorf, Lower Austria, April 14th, 1807; d. Michaelbeuerngrund, near Vienna, March 18th, 1861.
Court opera singer famous for his singing of Schubert's songs.

Stolberg (Friedrich-Leopold, Count zu), b. Bremstadt in Holstein, November 7th, 1750; d. Sondermühlen, near Osnabrück, December 5th, 1819. A poet of considerable ability. Schubert composed seven of his songs, including *Auf dem Wasser zu Singen*.

Strauss (Johann) (father), b. Vienna, March 14th, 1804, d. there, September 25th, 1849. Violinist and composer. He played as a boy with Lanner at the Rebhuhn.

Tietze (Ludwig), b. 1798; d. Vienna, January 11th, 1850. Tenor singer whom Schubert frequently accompanied on the piano. The first *Offertorium* in " C Major " (Op. 46) is dedicated to him.

Uhland (Ludwig), b. Tübingen, April 26th, 1787; d. there, November 13th, 1862. The author of one of the most beautiful of Schubert's songs, *Frühlingsglaube* (" Faith in Spring ").

Umlauff (Johann Karl Ritter von), b. Schönberg in Moravia, December 23rd, 1796; d. Vienna, March 8th, 1861. Went to Vienna in 1816, where he made the acquaintance of Schubert. He had a fine voice, studied with Vogl, and was one of the small circle of friends who first introduced Schubert's part songs to the public.

Unger (Johann Karl), b. Zips in Hungary, April 12th, 1771; d. after 1836. Wrote the words of Schubert's vocal quartet " The Nightingale." It was Unger who introduced Schubert to Johann Esterhazy. He was father of the famous singer Madame Unger Sabatier.

Wilt (Marie), b. Vienna, January 1st, 1833; d. there, September 24th, 1891. Opera singer, and singer of chamber music. She sang the part of " Jemina " in the first performance of Schubert's *Lazarus* in Vienna in 1863.

BIBLIOGRAPHY

THE arrangement of the bibliography is alphabetical under authors' names, or, in the case of anonymous works, under the titles. A few entries have been made under the titles of periodicals where a number of references are grouped together, but as a rule separate entries have been made for each magazine or newspaper article.

Where it has been impossible for the compiler to examine a work, the information given has been taken from some other authority. A number of references to short or unimportant works, technical articles, newspaper criticisms of performances, etc., have been omitted, and only a few of the better known biographical dictionaries of musicians are referred to.

Information in brackets [ ] has been supplied from some source other than the work itself.

The bibliographies which are to be found in the works on Schubert, by Antcliffe, Baker, Curson, Duncan, Grove, Klatte, Költzsch, Riemann, Spanuth and Wurzbach have been particularly useful in compiling this list, which includes many references not gathered together elsewhere.

Amongst so much material, the first place must be given to the monumental work of Otto Erich Deutsch, the other larger and more important publications being those of Dahms, Duncan, Friedlaender, Gérold, Grove, Gumprecht, Heuberger, Kobald, Kreissle von Hellborn, Niggli, Reissmann and Wurzbach.

Aktenmässige Darstellung der Ausgrabung und Wiederbeisetzung der irdischen Reste von Beethoven und Schubert. Veranlasst durch die Direction der Gesellschaft der Musikfreunde des österreichischen Kaiserstaates im Oktober, 1863. Pp. 16. Vienna, 1863.

AMBROS, AUGUST WILHELM:
"Bunte Blätter," etc. *Neue Folge.* Leipsic, 1874. Pp. 174-191, Schubertiana.
Second Edition. Edited by Dr. Emil Vogel. Leipsic, 1896.

ANTCLIFFE, HERBERT:
Schubert. (Bell's Miniature Series of Musicians.) Pp. 72. London, 1910.

ARONSON, M.:
"Franz Schubert." *Music,* Chicago. 1897. Vol. 11 P. 420; Vol. 13. P. 799.

AUDLEY, AGATHE:
Franz Schubert, sa vie et ses œuvres. Pp. 352. Paris, 1871.

" Aus Schubert's Leben." *Blätter aus Krain,* Laibach. 1864. No. 4.

AUSTIN, G. L.:
The Life of Franz Schubert. Boston, 1873.

BACH, ALBERT B.:
The Art Ballad. Loewe and Schubert, with musical illustrations.
Pp. 215. Edinburgh, 1890.

BARBEDETTE, H.:
Franz Schubert, sa vie, ses oeuvres. Paris, 1866.

BARNETT, JOHN FRANCIS:
Musical Reminiscences and Impressions. Pp. XVI, 341. London,
1906. Pp. 312-322, " The Sketch Symphony " (Schubert's).
" Schubert's Sketch Symphony in E." *Proceedings of the Musical
Association,* London. 1890-91. Pp. 177-190.
" Schubert's Unfinished Symphony in E, No. 7." *The Musical
Review,* London. May 5th, 1883. Pp. 289-291.

BARTSCH, RUDOLF HANS:
Schwammerl. Ein Schubert-Roman. Pp. 308. Leipsic, 1912.

BATES, RALPH:
Franz Schubert. Pp. 171. London, 1934.

BATKA, RICHARD:
" Streiflichter auf Schubert's Lieder." *Neue Musikzeitung,* Stuttgart, 1905. Heft 18.

BAUER, MORITZ:
" Franz Schubert." *Jahrbuch des freien deutschen Hochsstifts zu
Frankfurt a. M.* 1909. Pp. 67-126.
" Johann Mayrhofer." *Zeitschrift für Musikwissenschaft,* Leipsic.
Nov. 1922. Pp. 79-99.
Die Lieder Franz Schuberts. Pp. x, 258. Leipsic, 1915.

BAUERNFELD, EDUARD VON:
*Ein Buch von uns Wienern in Lustig-gemüthlichen Reimlein von
Rusticocampius* [i. e. Eduard von Bauernfeld]. Pp. xvi, 220.
Leipsic, 1858.
" Einiges von Franz Schubert." *Signale,* Leipsic. Nov. 15th,
22nd, 26th, 28th, 1869. Essays originally contributed to *Freie
Presse,* Vienna. April 17th, 21st, 1869. Reprinted: Bauern-
feld's *Gesammelte Schriften.* Bd. xii. Vienna, 1873. English
version: *Musical World.* Jan. 8th, 15th, Feb. 5th, 19th, 1870.
" Ueber Franz Schubert," *Wiener Zeitschrift für Kunst,* etc.
June, 1829. Nos. 69-71.
Wiener Einfälle und Ausfälle, etc. Pp. 52. Vienna, 1852.

See also Deutsch, Otto Erich: *Ein unbekanntes Schubert-Gedicht von Bauernfeld, etc.*

BEIER, FRANZ:
[Review of] *Schubert-Album. Sammlung der Lieder . . . . von Franz Schubert. Kritisch revidirt von Max Friedländer.* Peters, Leipsic, 1884, etc. *Vierteljahrsschrift für Musikwissenschaft,* Leipsic, 1886. Pp. 380-385.

BEKKER, PAUL:
Franz Schubert. Klassiker der Tonkunst. VII. Vienna.
" Franz Schuberts ' Unvollendete.' " *Allgemeine Musikzeitung,* Berlin. 1912, P. 627.

BENZ, RICHARD:
Franz Schubert, der Vollender der deutschen Musik. Pp. 48. Jena, 1928.

BETHGE, E. H.:
Franz Schubert. Ein Volksbuch für jedermann. P. 104. Leipsic, 1928.

BIE, OSCAR:
Das Deutsche Lied. Pp. 277. Berlin, 1926.
Franz Schubert. Sein Leben und sein Werk. Pp. 162, and musical examples. Berlin, 1925.
Schubert the Man. Translated from the German by J. S. Untermeyer. Pp. XVII, 215. New York, 1929.
A History of the Pianoforte and Pianoforte Players ... Translated from the German (Das Klavier und seine Meister), etc. Pp. 336. London, 1899. Pp. 224-231, Schubert.

BIRNBAUM-LUX, G.:
" Franz Schuberts Freund. Der Wiener Joseph von Spaun wendet sich an Goethe." *Signale,* Berlin. Aug. 10th, 1927. Pp. 1127, 1128.

BISCHOFF, HERMANN:
" Das deutsche Lied." Pp. 117. (*Die Musik.* Bd. 16, 17.) Berlin, [1906].

BLOM, ERIC:
Schubert. (Novello's Biographies of Great Musicians.) Pp. 14. London, [1938].

BOROWSKI, F.:
" Schubert." Character Sketch. *Etude,* Philadelphia. Vol. 44. Nov. 1926. Pp. 803, 804.

BOSCH, HANS:
Die Entwicklung des Romantischen in Schuberts Liedern. Pp. VII, 102. [With a bibliography.] Borna and Leipsic, 1930.

BOSCHOT, ADOLPHE:

Musiciens-Poètes. Bach, Beethoven, Schubert, Liszt, Chopin. Pp. 202. Paris, 1937.

BOURGAULT-DUCOUDRAY, L. A.:

Schubert. (Les Musiciens célèbres.) Pp. 128. Paris [1908].

BRACHTEL, KARL:

Franz Schuberts musikalische Eigenart. Nach den Schubert-biographien von Heuberger und La Mara zusammengestellt. Pp. 17. Friedek, 1915.

BRANDES, FRIEDRICH:

Einführung in Franz Schubert's Rosamunden-Musik, die unvoll-endete Sinfonie h moll und C dur Sinfonie. Dresden, 1896, 1897.

BRAUN, F.:

Schubert im Freundeskreis. Ein Lebensbild aus Briefen, Erinne-rungen, Tagebuchblättern, Gedichten. Pp. 80. Leipsic, 1925.

BRENDEL, ULRIK:

" Schubert in Dichtung und Malerei." *Die Musik,* Berlin. Sept. 1912. Heft 23. Schubert-Heft No. 3. Pp. 280-290.

BRENT-SMITH, ALEXANDER:

Schubert. 1. The Symphonies C major and B minor. (The Musical Pilgrim.) Pp. 48. London, 1926.

Schubert. 2. Quartet in D minor and Octet. (The Musical Pilgrim.) Pp. 55. London, 1927.

BRIAN, HAVERGAL:

" Franz Schubert." *Monthly Musical Record,* London. Vol. LIII. 1923. Pp. 205, 206.

BRIGHT, RICHARD:

Travels from Vienna through Lower Hungary; with some remarks on the state of Vienna during the Congress in the year 1814. Pp. 642, cii. Edinburgh, 1818.

BRUNOLD, FR. :

" Dichter und Componist." *Gartenlaube,* Vienna. 1866. P. 614.

BUENZOD, EMMANUEL:

Franz Schubert. Pp. 226. Paris, [1937].

BUHNE UND WELT:

" Franz Schubert-Heft." *Bühne und Welt,* Berlin. 1907. No. 18. Contains articles by Egon v. Komorczynski, Anton Lindner, O. E. Deutsch, Hans Temple.

BURKHARDT, MAX:

" Schubert und Schumann." *Rheinische Musik- und Theater-zeitung,* Cologne. 1906. P. 21.

BYRON, MAY:
A Day with Franz Schubert. Pp. 44. London [1910].

CAPELL, RICHARD:
Schubert's Songs. Pp. 294. London, 1928.

CASTELLI, I. V. F.:
Memoiren meines Lebens, etc., 4 vol. Vienna, 1861.

CHÉZY, HELMINA VON:
Unvergessenes. Denkwürdigkeiten aus dem Leben von Helmina von Chézy, etc. 2pt. Leipsic, 1858.

CHÉZY, WILHELM VON:
Erinnerungen aus meinem Leben. 4 vol. Schaffhausen, 1863-64.

Choir and Musical Record, London:
Feb. 20th to Dec. 11th, 1869, contain serial article on Coleridge's edition of Kreissle von Hellborn's " Franz Schubert."

CLÉMENT, FELIX:
Les Musiciens célèbres, etc. Pp. 680. Paris, 1868. Pp. 455-467, Schubert.
Third edition, 1878.

CLUTSAM, GEORGE H.:
Schubert. (Masterpieces of Music. Edited by E. Hatzfeld.) London [1912]. Biographical sketch. Pp. 1-30; Music. Pp. 31-63.

CROWEST, F. J.:
The Great Tone Poets, etc. Pp. 373. London, 1874. Pp. 288-314, Schubert.
New edition. London, 1926.

CURZON, HENRI DE:
Franz Schubert. (Bibliographie critique de Franz Schubert.) Pp. 7. Paris [1899].
Les Lieder de Franz Schubert. Esquisse critique, suivie du catalogue chronologique et raisonné des Lieder. Pp. 113. Paris, 1899.

DAHL, HERMANN:
"Die Stadt der Originale." (Wien zur Zeit Schuberts.) *Der Merker,* Vienna. 1911. Heft 10-11. Schubert-Bauernfeld. Doppelheft. Pp. 454-456.

DAHMS, WALTER:
" Das Schlusskapitel der neuen Schubert-Biographie." *Die Musik,* Berlin. Sept. 1912. Heft 23. Schubert-Heft No. 3. Pp. 259-279. Heft 24. Pp. 337-355.
Schubert . . . mit 230 Bildern. Pp. vii, 446. Berlin, Leipsic, 1912.
Revised and shortened editions. Stuttgart, 1922, 1923, 1928.

DECSEY, ERNST:

" Aus Josef Hüttenbrenners Schubert-Nachlass." *Die Musik,* Berlin. Sept. 1912. Heft 23. Schubert-Heft No. 3. Pp. 297-304.

" Wo Schubert gewohnt hat." *Schubert-Sonderheft der Modernen-Welt,* Vienna. Dec. 1st, 1925. P. 11.

DENT, EDWARD J.:

" The Style of Schubert." *The Dominant,* London. June, 1928. Pp. 11-17.

DEUTSCH, OTTO ERICH:

Franz Schubert. Die Dokumente seines Lebens und Schaffens. Herausgegeben von O. E. Deutsch. Leipsic, 1913.

This work is in progress. Two volumes have been published: Zweiter Band. Erste Hälfte. " Die Dokumente seines Lebens." Pp. xiii, 514. Munich and Leipsic, 1914. Dritter Band. " Sein Leben in Bildern." Zweite Auflage. Pp. 617. Appendix Pp. 43. Munich and Leipsic, 1913.

Schubert. A Documentary Biography . . . Translated by Eric Blom. Being an English version of Franz Schubert: Die Dokumente seines Lebens. Revised and augmented with a commentary by the author. Pp. XXII, 1040, 42; 40 d, line drawings. London, 1947.

" Anselm Hüttenbrenners Erinnerungen an Schubert." *Jahrbuch der Grillparzer-Gesellschaft,* Vienna, 1906. Pp. 99-163.

" Ein Aufsatz über Franz Schubert." *Grazer Tagblatt.* 1905. No. 67.

Franz Schubert's Briefe und Schriften. Mit zehn Abbildungen. Herausgegeben von Otto Erich Deutsch. Zweite Auflage. Pp. 102. Munich, 1922. First published, 1919.

Franz Schubert's Letters and other writings. Edited by Otto Erich Deutsch and translated by Venetia Savile, etc. Pp. 143. London, 1928.

" Das Grazer Schuberthaus." *Grazer Tagespost.* June 26th, 1907.

Die historischen Bildnisse Franz Schuberts in getreuen Nachbildungen, etc. Pp. 8; 7 plates. Vienna, 1922.

" Die nachweisbaren Einnahmen Franz Schuberts." *Zeitschrift für Musikwissenschaft,* Leipsic. Oct. 1926. Pp. 61, 62.

Die Originalausgaben von Schuberts Goethe-Liedern. Ein musikbibliographischer Versuch. Pp. 24. Vienna, 1926.

" Das Reifezeugnis des Schulgehilfen Franz Schuberts." *Die Zeit.* May, 1907.

" The Riddle of Schubert's Unfinished Symphony." *The Music Review,* Cambridge. Vol. I. Pp. 36-53. 1940.

Schubert-Brevier. Pp. 202. Berlin, 1905.

Articles by O. E. Deutsch in the *Schubert-Sonderheft der Modernen-Welt*, Vienna. Dec. 1st, 1925:
" Schubert als Stammgast." P. 14.
" Die 10 Ständchen." P. 17.
" Schubert am Klavier." Pp. 21-23.
" Der intime Schubert." Pp. 24-26.
" Von zwei Opern, die Schubert nicht komponiert hat." P. 27.
" Schubert im Ausland." P. 29.

" Schubert und Bauernfeld." *Grazer Tagespost*. 1905. No. 57.

" Ein Schuberthaus in Erdberg," etc. *Der Merker*, Vienna. Heft 13-14. July 15th, 1919. Pp. 478-489.

" Schuberts Aufenthalt in Graz, 1827. Neue Beiträge zur Biographie des Meisters." *Die Musik*, Berlin. 1906-1907. Heft 7. 1. Schubert-Heft. Pp. 10-35; Heft 8. 2. Schubert-Heft. Pp. 91-114.

" Schuberts Einkommen." *Frankfurter Zeitung*. Aug. 4th, 1927.

" Schuberts Krankheit. Neue Mitteilungen." *Zeitschrift für Musikwissenschaft*, Leipsic. Nov. 1921. Pp. 100-106.

" Schuberts ' Rosamunde ' mit unbekannten Briefen." *Die Musik*, Berlin, 1912. Heft 15. Pp. 152-160.

" Schuberts Totenehren. Unveröffentlichte Dokumente." *Neue Zeitschrift für Musik*, Leipsic. 1906. No. 13. Pp. 283, 284; No. 14. Pp. 307-310.

" Schuberts Vater." *Alt-Wiener Kalender für das Jahr 1924*. [Edited by Alois Trost.] Vienna. This article was reviewed by Alfred Einstein in the *Zeitschrift für Musikwissenschaft*, May 1924.

" Schuberts ' Verlorene '. Zur Aufführung der Sonaten-Sinfonie von Schubert-Joachim im Wiener Konzertverein " *Der Merker*, Vienna. Heft 8. April 15th, 1919. Pp. 281-286.

" Ein Siegesgedicht von Franz Schubert." *Der Merker*, Vienna. VII. Heft 22. Nov. 15th, 1916. Pp. 773, 774.

" Stimmen zu Schuberts Messen." *Neue Musikzeitung*, Stuttgart. 1918-19. Heft 16.

" Fünf unbekannte Ecossaisen von Schubert." *Die Musik*, Berlin. Sept. 1912. Heft 23. Schubert-Heft No. 3. Pp. 291-296.

" Ein unbekanntes Schubert-Gedicht von Bauernfeld. Mitgeteilt von O. E. Deutsch." *Der Merker*, Vienna. III. June, 1912. Pp. 458-461.

" Volker der Spielmann. Der Spitzname Franz Schuberts." *Neues Wiener Journal*. Sept. 12th, 1926.

" Eine wiedergefundene Schubert-Karikatur." *Die Musik*, Berlin. 1906-7. Heft 8. 2. Schubert-Heft. Pp. 115-117.

See also Bühne und Welt.

" Der deutsche Liederfürst." *Gartenlaube*, Leipsic. 1866. P. 388.

DICKINSON, A. E F.:
"Schubert and Beethoven: a Contrast of Methods." *Music and Letters*, London. Jan. 1928. Pp. 44-50.

DOUËL, MARTIAL:
"Le Sentiment de la Mort dans l'oeuvre de Schubert." *La Revue Musicale*, Paris. Feb. 1924. Pp. 143-159.

DUNCAN, EDMONDSTOUNE:
Schubert Illustrated. (*The Master Musicians.* Revised edition.) Pp. XI, 243. [With a bibliography.] London, 1934.

DVOŘÁK, ANTONÍN AND FINCK, H. T.:
"Franz Schubert." *Century*, New York. Vol. 48. July, 1894. Pp. 341-346.

ELSON, LOUIS C.:
Great Composers and their Work. Pp. 302. London, 1905. Pp. 128-153, Schubert. First issued, Boston, 1898.
The History of German Song, etc. (*Last Hours of Great Composers.*) Pp. 288. Boston, 1888. Pp. 157-165; 248-253, Schubert.

ENGEL, ERNST:
Franz Schubert. Ein Leben in Lied und Leid. Pp. 44. Berlin, 1928.

EULENBERG, HERBERT:
Schubert und die Frauen. Pp. 311. Hellerau, 1928.

EWEN, D. J.:
Unfinished Symphony. A story-life of Franz Schubert. Pp. 306. New York, 1931.

FAREANU, A.:
"Leopold von Sonnleithner's Erinnerungen an Franz Schubert." *Zeitschrift für Musikwissenschaft*, Leipsic. May, 1919. Pp. 466-483.

FARINELLI, ARTURO:
Beethoven e Schubert. Pp. 122. Torino, 1929.

FEIGL, RUDOLF:
Klar um Schubert. Beseitigung von Irrmeinungen, Fehlangaben usw. Pp. 83. Linz, 1936. Second edition, 1938. Pp. 94.

FELLNER, A.:
See Spaun, Jos. von. *Aufzeichnungen*, etc.

FERRIS, GEORGE T.:
Great Musical Composers ... Edited ... by Mrs. William Sharp. Pp. xvi, 335. London [1887]. Pp. 87-102, Schubert and Schumann.

FÉTIS, FRANÇOIS J.:

Biographie universelle des Musiciens. Deuxième édition, 8 vol. Paris, 1860-65. Supplement. 2 vol. Paris, 1878-80.

FIEDLER, H. G.:

" Schubert's Poets." *Music and Letters,* London. Jan. 1925. Pp. 68-77.

FINCK, HENRY T.:

" Franz Schubert." [Review of Heuberger's biography of Schubert.] *Nation,* New York. Oct. 30th, 1902.

" Schubert's Rank as a Composer." *Etude,* Philadelphia. May, 1900.

Songs and Song Writers, etc. Pp. 254. London, 1901. Pp. 40-104, Schubert.

New York edition, 1900.

FINO, M. D. GIOCONDO:

Franz Peter Schubert. Pp. 12. Trento, 1928.

FISKE, JOHN:

Famous Composers and their Works. (J. K. Paine, editor.) Boston, 1892. Pp. 349-374, Schubert.

FORBERG, ROB:

Forberg's Tonkunst-Kalender, 1928. " Franz Schubert zum Gedächtnis anlässlich des 100. Wiederkehr seines Todestages, 1928." Leipsic, 1927.

FOX STRANGWAYS, A. H.:

" The Less-known Songs of Schubert." *The Musical Quarterly,* New York. Vol. XV, No. 4. Oct. 1929. Pp. 625-638.

" Franz Peter Schubert, die Walddrossel der deutschen Musik." *Wanderer,* Vienna. 1858. No. 230.

Franz Peter Schubert, with portrait and selections from orchestral works. *Masters in Music,* Boston. Vol. 4, 1904. Pp. 97, etc.; 145, etc.

Franz Schubert. Eine Biographie. Mit Portrait. Pp. 32. Cassel, 1855.

" Franz Schubert." *Bremer Sonntagsblatt.* Redigirt von Pletzer. 1864. No. 49.

" Franz Schubert." *Deutsch-österreichische Revue,* Vienna. 1867. II.

" Franz Schubert." *Neues Familien-Journal. Extrablatt des Neuen Wiener Tagblatt.* 1868. No. 83.

" Franz Schubert." [Biography.] Pp. 27. *LV. Neujahrsgeschenk an die zürcherische Jugend von der Allgemeinen Musik-Gesellschaft in Zürich.* 1867.

Franz Schubert. Biographie (Meister der Tonkunst. No. 52.) Leipsic [1880].

217

Franz Schubert im Freundeskreis. Ein Lebensbild aus Briefen, Erinnerungen, etc. (*Österreichische Bibliothek.* No. 26.) Pp. 88. Leipsic, 1717.

" Franz Schubert in Wien." *Das Vaterland,* Vienna. 1861. Nos. 56 and 57.

" Franz Schubert und seine berühmten Zeitgenossen." *Ostdeutsche Post,* Vienna. 1864. No. 326.

Franz Schubert. 1797-1828. Eigenhändige Manuskripte, Briefe, Original- und Erst-Ausgaben, Reliquien, etc. Mit einem Vorwort von Otto Erich Deutsch. Katalog Nr. 44. V. A. Heck, Vienna. 1928.

Franz Schubert. 31. 1. 1797—19. 11. 1828. Pp. 62. Hamburg, 1928.

FRIEDLAENDER, MAX:

Beiträge zur Biographie Franz Schuberts. (*Dissertation,* 1887.) Berlin, 1889.

" Eine bisher ungedruckte Komposition Schuberts." (Deutscher mit 2 Trios für Pianoforte auf 4 Hände.) *Riemann-Festschrift,* Leipsic, 1909. P. 484. With the music.

" Fälschungen in Schuberts Liedern." *Vierteljahrsschrift für Musikwissenschaft,* Leipsic. 1893. Pp. 166-185.

" Franz Schubert. Zu seinem hundertsten Geburtstage." *Deutsche Rundschau,* Berlin. XXIII. Jahrg. Bd. LXXXX. Heft 5. Feb. 1897. Pp. 218-248.

Franz Schubert. Skizze seines Lebens und Wirkens. Pp. 43. Leipsic, 1928.

" Supplement " [to Peter's *Schubert-Album. Sammlung der Lieder*]. Leipsic, 1884, etc. The supplement contains variants, biographical and literary notes, dates etc. Particulars of the collection are given below, among editions of Schubert's works.

See also " Schubert, Franz, Zehn bisher ungedruckte Briefe," etc.

FRIMMEL THEODOR:

" Beethoven und Schubert." *Die Musik,* Berlin. 1925. Heft 6. Pp. 401-416.

FROST, H. F.:

Schubert. (*The Great Musicians,* edited by F. Hueffer.) Pp. 128. London, 1881.

GÁL, HANS:

" The Riddle of Schubert's Unfinished Symphony." *The Music Review,* Cambridge. Vol. II. Pp. 63-67. 1941.

GALLET, Mme MAURICE:

Schubert et le Lied. Pp. 300. Paris, 1907.

" George Grove and Schubert's ' Gastein Symphony '." *British Musician,* Birmingham. May, 1928. Pp. 67-70.

GERHARD, C.:
" Franz Schubert und die Frauen." *Neue Musikzeitung,* Stuttgart. 1908-9. No. 4.

GÉROLD, TH.:
Schubert. Pp. 250. Paris, 1923.

Geschichte der K. K. Gesellschaft der Musikfreunde in Wien. 1. Abteilung: 1812-1870 verfasst von Richard von Perger. 2. Abteilung: 1870-1912 verfasst von Dr. Robert Hirschfeld. (Zusatz-Band . . . Sammlungen und Statuten zusammengestellt von Dr. Eusebius Mandyczewski.) 2 vol. Vienna, 1912.
The work contains references to Schubert's association with the Society, list of Schubert autographs, pictures, etc., in possession of the Society.

GILMAN, LAWRENCE:
" Songs of a Rustic Angel." *North American Review,* New York. Vol. 213. June, 1921. Pp. 844-848.

GLEICH, FERD.:
Charakterbilder aus der neueren Geschichte der Tonkunst. 2 vol. Leipsic, 1863.

GLOSSY, CARL:
See Spaun, Jos. von. *Aus den Lebenserinnerungen,* etc.

GREW, EVA MARY:
Franz Schubert. A Sequence of Sonnets and a Prose Anthology, etc. Pp. x, 86. Birmingham, 1928.

GREW, SYDNEY:
Masters of Music. Pp. 333. London, 1924. Pp. 183-208, Schubert.

GROVE, SIR GEORGE:
" Schubert." (*Grove's " Dictionary of Music and Musicians."* Vol. 3. Pp. 319-382.) London, 1883.

Revised by Sir W. H. Hadow for the second edition of Grove. Vol. 4, 1908. Pp. 280-334. Further revised with additions by Sir W. H. Hadow and H. C. Colles for the third and fourth editions of Grove. Vol. 4, 1928, 1940. Pp. 582-637.

GUMPRECHT, OTTO:
" Franz Schubert." Eine Studie. *Unsere Zeit,* Leipsic. 1867. Jahrg. III. Heft 14. Pp. 122-142; Heft 16. Pp. 261-274.

Musikalische Charakterbilder. Pp. 341. Leipsic, 1869. Pp. 1-66, Schubert.

An expanded edition: *Neuere Meister. Musikalische Lebens-und Charakterbilder.* 2 vol. Leipsic, 1883. Vol. 1. Pp. 5-83, Schubert.

GÜNTHER, FELIX:

Mein Freund Schubert. Pp. 172. Hamburg, 1928.

Schuberts Lied. Eine ästhetische Monographie. Pp. 203. Stuttgart, 1928.

GYOMAI, IMRÉ AND MANIER, STÉPHANE:

La vie tendre et pathétique de Franz Schubert. Pp. 229. Paris, 1936.

H. G.:

" Franz Schubert. A short biography." *Strand Musical Magazine.* No. 5. New Series. Pp. 3-8. London [1899].

HADDEN, J. CUTHBERT:

Master Musicians. A book for players, singers and listeners. Pp. 254. Edinburgh, 1909. Pp. 111-128, Franz Schubert: the Master of the Lied.

HADOW, SIR WILLIAM HENRY:

" Franz Peter Schubert." *Encyclopædia Britannica.* Eleventh edition. 1911. Vol. XXIV. Pp. 379-382.

The Oxford History of Music. Vol. V. Pp. viii, 350. Oxford, 1904.

HANSLICK, EDUARD:

Geschichte des Concertwesens in Wien. (Aus dem Concertsaal.) 2 pt. Vienna, 1869-70.

HARGRAVE, MARY:

" Schubertiana." *Gentleman's Magazine,* London. Vol. 281. Dec. 1896. Pp. 620-626.

HAUSEGGER, FRIEDRICH VON:

Gedanken eines Schauenden, etc. Pp. 549. Munich, 1903. Pp. 221-228, Franz Schubert.

HAWEIS, H. R.:

" Schubert and Chopin." *Contemporary Review,* London. Vol. 2. May, 1866. Pp. 80-102.

Reprinted in *Music and Morals.* London, 1871.

HENTL, FRIEDRICH VON:

" Blick auf Schuberts Lieder." *Wiener Zeitschrift für Kunst,* etc. March 23rd, 1822.

Gedanken über Tonkunst und Tonkünstler. Vienna, 1868. Pp. 125-133, Schubert.

Second edition, Eichstätt, 1871.

HEUBERGER, RICHARD:
Franz Schubert. (*Berühmte Musiker,* XIV.) Pp. 115. Berlin, 1902.
Third edition, 1920.
" Der Stammort der Familie Schubert." *Der Merker,* Vienna. 1911. Heft 10-11. Schubert-Bauernfeld. Doppelheft. Pp. 452, 453.

HILL, RALPH:
" Mayrhofer; the hypochondriac." *The Sackbut,* London. Nov. 1927. Pp. 106-108.

HILLER, FERDINAND:
Künstlerleben. Pp. 302. Cologne, 1880. Pp. 40-62. In Wien von 52 Jahren.

HILMANN, ADOLF:
Schubert. Pp. 248. Stockholm [1921].

HÖCKER, GUST.:
Drei grosse Tondichter. Karl Maria v. Weber, Franz Schubert, Felix Mendelssohn-Bartholdy, etc. Pp. 318. Glogau [1903].

HOFFMANN VON FALLERSLEBEN, A. H.:
Mein Leben. Aufzeichnungen und Erinnerungen. 6 vol. Hanover, 1868. Vol. II. Pp. 50-52, references to Schubert.

HOLZAPFEL, ANTON:
[Two letters to Ferdinand Luib about Schubert. 1858.]
Jahrbuch der Grillparzer-Gesellschaft, Vienna. 1901. Pp. 286-299.

HÖNIG, OTTO:
" Franz Schubert." *Deutsche Sängerbundeszeitung,* Berlin. XX, 10-13. 1928.

HORNER, EMIL:
Bauernfeld. Pp. 164. Leipsic, 1900.

HUGHES, EDWIN:
" Haunts of Franz Schubert in Vienna." *Musician,* Boston. May, 1913. Pp. 297-299.

HULL, A. EAGLEFIELD:
" Schubert and his Poets." *Musical Opinion,* London. April, 1925. Pp. 713-715.

HULL, ROBERT H.:
"The Early Symphonies of Schubert." *Musical Opinion,* London. Aug., 1939. Pp. 943-944; Sept., 1939. Pp. 1029-31.

HUSCHKE, KONRAD:
" Ein Kapitel von Schubertscher Bescheidenheit." *Neue Zeitschrift für Musik,* Leipsic. 1915. No. 29-30. Pp. 251-253.

" Karl Maria v. Webers Beziehungen zu Ludwig v. Beethoven und Franz Schubert." *Deutsche Revue*, Stuttgart. May, 1919. Pp. 184-193; June, 1919. Pp. 274-283.

HUTCHINGS, ARTHUR:
Schubert. (*The Master Musicians.*) Pp. vi, 233. [With a bibliography.] London, 1945.

HÜTTENBRENNER, ANSELM:
Anselm Hüttenbrenners Erinnerungen an Schubert. See Deutsch, O. E.

JOLIZZA, W. K. VON:
Das Lied und seine Geschichte. Pp. 692. Vienna, 1910. Pp. 377-408, Franz Schubert.

KAHL, WILLI:
" Das lyrische Klavierstück Schuberts und seiner Vorgänger seit 1810." *Archiv für Musikwissenschaft*, Leipsic. 1921. Jan. Pp. 54-82; April. Pp. 99-122.
" Schubert's ' Kreuzzug,' ein Dokument der Romantik." *Der Wächter.* 1922. P. 17.
Verzeichnis des Schrifttums über Franz Schubert 1828-1928. Pp. 264. [A comprehensive bibliography.] Regensburg, 1938.

KELLER, G.:
Schubert. (*Beroemde musici. No. 5.*) Pp. 96. The Hague, 1927.

KELLER, OTTO:
" Schuberts Vater." *Deutsche Militärmusiker-Zeitung*, Berlin. 1913. P. 447.

KINSKY, GEORG:
Musikhistorisches Museum von Wilhelm Heyer in Cöln. Katalog von G. Kinsky . . . Vierter Band: Musik-Autographen. Cologne, 1916. Pp. 190-209, Schubert.

KJERULF, AXEL:
Franz Schubert. Copenhagen, 1928.

KLATTE, WILHELM:
" Franz Schubert." (*Die Musik.* Bd. 22, 23.) Pp. 113. Berlin, 1907.
Third edition. Leipsic [1925?].

KOBALD, KARL:
Alt-Wiener Musikstätten. Pp. 198. Zürich, 1919. Pp. 165-198, Schubert. Illustrated.
Franz Schubert. Aus dem Leben eines österreichischen Genies. Pp. 119. Vienna, 1922.
Franz Schubert und seine Zeit. Pp. 496. Vienna, 1927. Illustrated.

Another edition. Pp. 309. Vienna, 1935.

English edition. *Franz Schubert and his times. Translated from the German by Beatrice Marshall.* Pp. ix, 277. London, 1928.

Der Meister des deutschen Liedes Franz Schubert. Ein Wiener Volksbuch. 2. *Verbesserte und erweiterte Auflage.* Pp. 172. Vienna, 1928.

Schubert und Schwind. Ein Wiener Biedermeierbuch. Pp. 253. Zurich, 1921. Many illustrations.

KÖCHEL, LUDWIG VON:

" Nachruf an Joseph Freiherrn von Spaun." *Wiener Zeitung.* 1866. No. 72.

Privately printed, Vienna, 1866.

KOHUT, ADOLF:

" Franz Schubert in seinen Beziehungen zu den Frauen." *Neue Musikzeitung,* Stuttgart. 1905. No. 18.

" Schubert und Ungarn." *Neue Musikzeitung,* Stuttgart. 1904. No. 1.

KÖLTZSCH, HANS:

Franz Schubert in seinen Klaviersonaten. Pp. 182. Leipsic, 1927.

KOMORCZYNSKI, EGON V.:

" Schuberts Freund und Textdichter Johann Mayrhofer." *Neue Musikzeitung,* Stuttgart. 1909. Heft 21.

" Schuberts Messen." *Neue Musikzeitung,* Stuttgart. 1905. Heft 22. P. 489.

" Wienerisches bei Schubert. Schubert-Landschaften." *Neue Musikzeitung,* Stuttgart. 1905. Heft 18.

See also Bühne und Welt.

KREISSLE VON HELLBORN, HEINRICH:

Franz Schubert. Eine biografische Skizze. Pp. 165. Vienna, 1861.

Franz Schubert. Pp. 619. Vienna, 1865.

English editions:

1. *Franz Schubert. A musical biography from the German . . . by Edward Wilberforce.* Pp. 287. London, 1866.

A considerably condensed edition.

2. *The Life of Franz Schubert. Translated from the German . . . by Arthur Duke Coleridge . . . with an appendix by George Grove.* 2 vol. London, 1869.

KRETZSCHMAR, HERMANN:

" Franz Schuberts Müllerlieder." 1881. *Gesammelte Aufsätze über Musik und Anderes aus den Grenzboten,* Leipsic. 1910. Pp. 36-44.

KRISTINUS, KARL R.:

Franz Schubert. Ein Fürst im Reiche des Liedes, etc. Pp. 32. Vienna [1881].

FRANZ SCHUBERT

KROTT, RUDOLFINE:
Die Singspiele Schuberts. Dissertation. Vienna, 1921.

KRUSE, GEORG RICHARD:
Franz Schubert. Pp. 64. Bielefeld, 1924. Illustrated.

LAFITE, CARL:
Das Schubertlied und seine Sänger. Pp. 116. Vienna, 1928.

LA MARA [pseud. i. e., MARIE LIPSIUS]:
Classisches und Romantisches aus der Tonwelt. Pp. ix, 361.
  Leipsic, 1892. Contains Spaun's " Erinnerungen." See also
  Spaun, Josef von.
Musikalische Studienköpfe. 4 vol. Leipsic, 1868-80.
  Vol. I. Pp. 67-117, Schubert. Many subsequent editions of
  the collection; also separate issues of the Schubert section as
  " Franz Schubert." The catalogue of Schubert's works which
  is included in the original series also appeared as " Verzeich-
  niss der Kompositionen . . . von Karl Maria v. Weber, Frz.
  Schubert, Felix Mendelssohn," etc. Pp. 86. Leipsic [1879].
" The Sixtieth Anniversary of Franz Schubert's Death. From
  the German of La Mara. [By] Marian Milliar." *Quarterly
  Musical Review,* Manchester. Vol. IV. 1888. Pp. 108-117.

LANDORMY, PAUL:
La Vie de Schubert. Paris, 1928.

LATZKO, ERNST:
Was weisst du von Schubert? Pp. 23. Leipsic, 1931.

LEGOUVÉ, ER.:
[Article on Schubert.]
Gazette Musicale, Paris. Jan. 15th, 1837.

LEITNER, CARL GOTTFRIED VON:
Anselm Hüttenbrenner. Graz, 1868.

LINDNER, ANTON:
See Bühne und Welt.

LISZT, FRANZ:
Gesammelte Schriften. 6 vol. Leipsic, 1880-83. Vol. III. Pt. I.
  Pp. 68-78, Schubert's " Alfons und Estrella."
Other short references occur in the collection.

LUX, JOS. A.:
" Forellenquintett." *Der Merker,* Vienna. 1911. Heft 10-11.
  Schubert-Bauernfeld. Doppelheft. Pp. 446-448.
Franz Schubert. Ein Lebensbild aus deutscher Vergangenheit.
  Pp. vii, 152. Berlin, 1922.
Franz Schuberts Lebenslied. Ein Roman der Freundschaft. Pp.
  320. Leipsic, 1915.

Schubertiade. Ein literarisch-musikalisches Schubertbuch. Pp. 62. Vienna, 1921.

MAILÁTH, JOHANN, COUNT:
See Müller, Sophie.

NIECKS, FR.:
" Franz Schubert, a study." *Monthly Musical Record,* London. Vol. VII. 1877. Pp. 3-7 ; 17-21 ; 33-37 ; 52-57 ; 69-73 ; 85-88 ; 100-105 ; 115-120 ; 131-135 ; 149-151.
" Schubert Revelations." *Monthly Musical Record,* London. Vol. XV. March, 1885. Pp. 49-51.

NIGGLI, A.:
Franz Schubert's Leben und Werke. (Sammlung Musikalischer Vorträge. Herausgeber: Paul Graf Waldersee. Ser. II. No. 15.) Pp. 57-106. Leipsic, 1880.
Later editions, 1889; 1925, revised and enlarged.
" Franz Schubert, sein Leben und seine musikgeschichtliche Bedeutung." *Neue Musikzeitung,* Stuttgart. 1905. Heft 18.
Franz Schubert, grosse Symphonie in C-dur. Erläutert von A. Niggli. (Musikführer, No. 7.) Pp. 20. Frankfort on the Main, 1895.
Franz Schubert. Unvollendete Symphonie. (Hm.) Erläutert von A. Niggli. (Musikführer, No. 15.) Pp. 16. Frankfort on the Main, 1895.

NOHL, LUDWIG:
Beethovens Leben. 3 vol. Leipsic, 1864-77.

NOHL, WALTER:
Die Romantiker der deutschen Musik. Pp. 266. (I. Schubert.) Cologne, 1922.

OREL, ALFRED:
Franz Schubert. Ein Künstler seiner Heimat. Pp. 99. Altötting, 1926.
" Franz Schuberts ' Sonate ' für Klavier, Violine und Violoncell aus dem Jahre 1812." *Zeitschrift für Musikwissenschaft,* Leipsic. Jan.-Feb. 1923. Pp. 209-218.
Franz Schubert, 1797-1828. Sein Leben in Bildern. Pp. 40, ff. 20. Leipsic, 1938.
" Kleine Schubertstudien." *Archiv für Musikforschung,* Leipsic. 1937. Heft 3. Pp. 285-307.

OTTFRIED:
Schubert-Novellen. Sechs Blätter aus dem Liederkranze des unsterblichen Meistersängers. Pp. 128. Innsbruck, 1862.
American edition, *Schubert Fantaisies.* Boston [1914].

225

PANOFKA, H.:
[Article on Schubert.] *Gazette Musicale*, Paris. Oct. 14th, 1838.

PARRY, SIR CHARLES HUBERT H.:
Studies of Great Composers, etc. Pp. 376. London, 1887. Pp. 223-254, Schubert.

PAUMGARTNER, BERNHARD:
Franz Schubert. Pp. 362. Zurich, 1945.
Die Schubertianer. Ein Beitrag zur Jahrhundertfeier. Mit zahlreichen Bild- und Notenbeigaben von Bernhard Paumgartner. Vienna, 1928.

PERGER, RICHARD:
" Franz Schubert. Eine Skizze." *Die Musik,* Berlin. 1906-7. Heft 7. 1. Schubert-Heft. Pp. 3-9.

PERKONIG, JOSEF FRIEDRICH:
Schubert, Hendl und der Birnbaum. Eine Schubert-Novelle. Pp. 68. Leipsic, 1925.

PETZOLDT, RICHARD:
Franz Schubert. Leben und Werken. Pp. 80. Leipsic, 1939.

PEYSER, HERBERT F.:
" Franz Schubert." [With a catalogue of Schubert's compositions.] The *International Cyclopedia of Music and Musicians. Edited by Oscar Thompson,* New York. 1939. Pp. 1648-1677.

PEZZL, JOHANN:
Beschreibung der Haupt- und Residenzstadt Wien. 7th edition. Vienna, 1826.
Skizze von Wien. 6 Hefte. Vienna, 1786-90. And later editions.
Neue Skizze von Wien. 3 Hefte. Vienna, 1805-12.

PFORDTEN, HERMANN, FREIHERR VON DER:
Franz Schubert und das deutsche Lied. 2nd edition. Pp. 153. Leipsic, 1920. First edition, 1916.

PIRANI, E. DI:
" Secrets of the Success of Great Musicians. Schubert." *Etude,* Philadelphia. Vol. 38. March, 1920. Pp. 155-156.

PITROU, ROBERT:
Franz Schubert. Vie intime. Pp. 275. Paris, 1928.

POHL, C. F.:
Die Gesellschaft der Musikfreunde des Oesterreichischen Kaiserstaates und ihr Conservatorium, etc. Pp. 198. Vienna, 1871.

POLKO, ELISE:
Meister der Tonkunst, etc. Pp. 377. Wiesbaden, 1897. Pp. 205-245, Schubert.

PORTER, E. G.:
Schubert. New Song Translations. 3 pt. London [1944].
The Songs of Schubert. Pp. 159. London, 1937.

PRITCHARD, T. C. L.:
" Franz Schubert." *The Music Review,* Cambridge. Vol. I. 1940. Pp. 105-122.
" The Unfinished Symphony." *The Music Review,* Cambridge. Vol. III. 1942. Pp. 10-32.

PROD'HOMME, J. G.:
Schubert raconté par ceux qui l'ont vu. Souvenirs, lettres, journaux intimes, etc. Pp. xx, 300. Paris, 1928.

REBICZEK, FRANZ:
Der Wiener Volks- und Bänkelgesang in den Jahren 1800 bis 1848. Pp. 122. Vienna, 1913.

RECIO AGÜERO, PEDRO:
Schubert, su vida y sus obras. Pp. 188. Paris, 1929.

REEG, WILLI:
Franz Schubert. Vortragsbuch für Schulfeiern, Bildungs- und Gemeinschaftsabende. Pp. 111. Mülhausen i. Th., 1928.

MANDYCZEWSKI, EUSEBIUS:
Franz Schubert's Werke . . . Series 20. Lieder und Gesänge. Erster Band. (Revisionsbericht.) Leipsic, 1894-97.
Particulars of this collected edition of Schubert's works are given on page 255. The volumes mentioned here contain important text by Mandyczewski and others.

MANTUANI, JOSEF:
" Schubertiana. Ein Beitrag zur Schubertforschung." *Die Musik,* Berlin. May, 1902. Pp. 1374-91.

MARSOP, PAUL:
Musikalische Essays. Pp. viii, 287. Berlin, 1899. I. Franz Schubert, der Zukunftskomponist.

MASON, DANIEL G.:
" Franz Schubert, romanticist." *Outlook,* New York. Vol. 82. Feb. 10th, 1906. Pp. 311-315.
The Romantic Composers. Pp. 353. New York, 1906. Pp. 63-101, Schubert.

MATHEWS, W. S. B.:
" Genius of Schubert." *Music,* Chicago. Vol. 12. Sept. 1897. P. 580.

MAYRHOFER, JOHANN:
" Erinnerungen an Franz Schubert." *Neues Archiv für Geschichte Staatenkunde, Literatur und Kunst,* Vienna. Feb. 23rd, 1829. Pp. 121-123.

MELLO, ALFRED:
" Franz Schuberts Klaviersonaten." *Neue Musikzeitung,* Stuttgart. 1903. P. 258.

Der Merker:
  Österreichische Zeitschrift für Musik und Theater. Vienna,
  1911. Heft 10-11. Schubert-Bauernfeld. Doppelheft. This
  special number contains portraits, facsimiles, etc., and articles
  by Hermann Dahl, A. Fellner, Richard Heuberger, Josef A.
  Lux, Walter von Molo and Rhades.

MEYER, WILHELM:
  Charakterbilder grosser Tonmeister. Vol. II. Beethoven, Schubert, Rossini, etc. Pp. 163. Bielefeld, 1920.

" Modern Melodists. Schubert." *Catholic World,* New York. Vol.
  24. Feb. 1877. Pp. 703-712.

Die Moderne Welt:
  Schubert-Sonderheft der Modernen-Welt. Vienna. Dec. 1st,
  1925.

MOLO, WALTER VON:
  " Schubert und Wien." *Der Merker,* Vienna. 1911. Heft 10-11.
  Schubert-Bauernfeld. Doppelheft. Pp. 449-451.

MÜLLER, SOPHIE:
  Leben der Sophie Müller weiland K. K. Hofschauspielerin und
  nachgelassene Papiere. Herausgegeben von Johann Grafen
  Mailáth. Pp. 259. Vienna, 1832. Includes " Tagebücher "
  (Diary).

Music and Letters, London:
  Schubert Centenary Number. Vol. IX. No. 4. Oct. 1928.

Musical Quarterly, New York:
  Schubert Number. Vol. XIV. No. 4. 1928. Contains articles by
  Carl Engel, Guido Adler, Richard Aldrich, etc.

Musical Standard, London:
  Contains articles and references from 1866 onwards, the chief of
  which are those of Jan. 27th, Feb. 10th, 1866; June 27th,
  1874; Jan. 5th, 1895 (Polko); April 16th, 1898 (W. H.
  Hadow); May 26th, June 2nd, 9th and 16th, 1900; Jan. 7th,
  1905.

Musical Times, London:
  Contains many articles, notices and reviews of Schubert's works,
  the most important numbers of which are March, 1869; Aug.
  1874; Aug. 1893; Jan. 1897 (Joseph Bennett); Feb. 1897
  (F. G. Edwards); Sept. 1901; Oct. 1901 (F. G. Edwards);
  Dec. 1907; Feb. 1925; April, May, June, July, 1928 (R.
  Capell).

Musical World, London:
  From 1838, onwards, contains many references and reviews the
  principal numbers of which are Aug. 23rd, 1838; May 6th,
  13th, 20th, June 3rd, 1865; March 14th, April 18th, Oct. 16th,
  1868; Feb. 13th, March 20th, 1869; Jan. 8th, 15th, Feb. 5th,
  19th, 1870; Sept. 27th, 1879; Aug. 6th, 1887.

Die Musik, Berlin. [Four special Schubert numbers]:
1. Schubert-Heft. 1906-07. Heft 7. Jan. 1907.
2. Schubert-Heft. 1906-07. Heft 8. Jan. 1907.
Schubert-Heft No. 3. Sept. 1912. Heft 23.
Schubert-Heft. 1928-29. Heft 1. Oct. 1928.
Illustrated.

These numbers contain articles by Richard Perger, O. E. Deutsch, H. Wetzel, L. Scheibler, W. Dahms, U. Brendel, Ernst Decsey, Theodor Wiesengrund, Adolf Bauer, Walther Krug, Willie Kahl, T. H. Werner, etc.

NATHANSKY, A.:
Bauernfeld und Schubert. Programm. Pp. 28. Vienna, 1906.

NAUMANN, EMIL:
Illustrirte Musikgeschichte, etc. 2 vol. Stuttgart, 1880-85.
The History of Music . . . Edited by the Rev. Sir F. A. Gore Ouseley, etc. 2 vol. London [1882-86].
Several later editions.

NEUMANN, WILHELM:
Die Componisten der neuern Zeit in Biographien geschildert. XLV. Franz Schubert. Leipsic [1855?].

NICHOLS, EDITH STERLING:
"Franz Peter Schubert and the German Song Forms." *Musician,* London. Aug. 1906. Pp. 287-288.

REEVE, HENRY:
Journal of a Residence at Vienna and Berlin, in the eventful Winter 1805-6, etc. Pp. xi, 215. London, 1877.

REISSMANN, AUGUST:
Allgemeine Geschichte der Musik. 3 vol. Munich, 1863-64. Vol. III. Pp. 228-238, Schubert.
Das deutsche Lied in seiner historischen Entwicklung, etc. Pp. 290; 41. Cassel, 1861.
Franz Schubert. Sein Leben und seine Werke . . . . Mit Portrait . . . . Notenbeilagen und einem Facsimile. Pp. 349; 19. Berlin, 1873.
Geschichte des deutschen Liedes, etc. Pp. 284; 48. Berlin, 1874.

REUTHER, HERMANN:
Katalog der Schubert-Zentenar-Ausstellung der Stadt Wien 1928 im Messepalast. Pp. viii, 158. Vienna, 1928.

La Revue Musicale, Paris:
Schubert number. Dec. 1928.

RHADES:
" Die Werke und Wir. Wilhelm Müller und Franz Schubert.'

Der Merker, Vienna. 1911. Heft 10-11. Schubert-Bauernfeld. Doppelheft. Pp. 436-445.

RIEMANN, HUGO:
Geschichte der Musik seit Beethoven, 1800-1900. Pp. vii, 816. Berlin, 1901. Pp. 121-140, Schubert.
Handbuch der Musikgeschichte. 2 vol. Leipsic, 1904-13. Second edition, 1919-22.

Musik-Lexikon, etc. Pp. 1036. Leipsic, 1882. *Dictionary of Music.* Translated by J. S. Shedlock. Pp. 895. London [1893-97]. Many subsequent editions. 10th and 11th German editions, edited by Alfred Einstein, 1922, 1927.

RISSE, JOSEPH:
Franz Schubert und seine Lieder. Studien . . . I. Müllerlieder. II. Goethe-Lieder. 2 nos. Hanover, 1872, 1873.

RITTER, HERMANN:
Franz Schubert. Gedenkschrift zur 100. Geburtstagsfeier. Pp. 47. Bamberg, 1896.

ROCHLITZ, FRIEDRICH:
Für Freunde der Tonkunst. 4 vol. Leipsic, 1824-32. Vol. IV. Pp. 317-363, Musik und Musiker in Wien. Zwei Briefe vom Jahre 1822.

ROGGERI, EDOARDO:
Schubert. La vita, le opere. Pp. 246. Torino, 1928.

ROWBOTHAM, FRANCIS J.:
Story Lives of Great Musicians. Pp. 369. London, 1907. Pp. 269-311, Schubert.

ROWBOTHAM, JOHN F.:
The Private Life of the Great Composers. Pp. 340. London, 1892. Pp. 192-210, Schubert.

RÜHLE, OTTO:
" Schubert." *Monatsblätter für deutsche Literatur,* Leipsic, 1901. Pp. 38-44.

RUNCIMAN, JOHN F.:
Old Scores and New Readings. Discussions on Musical Subjects. Pp. 279. London, 1899. Pp. 119-128, Schubert.
Second edition, 1901.

RUSTIOCAMPIUS:
See Bauernfeld, Eduard von.
S., C. P.:
" Schubert's Opera ' Der häusliche Krieg ' in Leipzig." *Monthly Musical Record,* London. Vol. VII. 1877. P. 8.

S., J. S. [i. e. J. S. SHEDLOCK]:
  " Franz Schubert." *Monthly Musical Record*, London. Vol.
  XXVII. Feb. 1897. Pp. 25-27.

SALZER, FELIX VON:
  " Die Sonatenform bei Franz Schubert." *Studien zur Musikwissenschaft, Bd. xv.* Pp. 86-125. Vienna, 1928.

SANDBERGER, ADOLF:
  Johann Rudolph Zumsteeg und Franz Schubert. (*Ausgewählte
  Aufsätze zur Musikgeschichte.*) Pp. 288-299. Munich, 1921.

  The article originally appeared as a supplement to the *Allgemeine
  Zeitung*, Munich. Dec. 15th, 1906.

SANN, HANS VON DER:
  " Anselm Hüttenbrenner und Franz Schubert." *Tagespost*, Graz.
  1894. Nos. 304, 306 and 307.

SCHEIBLER, LUDWIG:
  " Franz Schuberts einstimmige Lieder, Gesänge und Balladen mit
  Texten von Fr. Schiller." *Die Rheinlande*, Düsseldorf. April-
  Sept. 1905.
  " Franz Schuberts einstimmige Lieder im Volkston." *Neue Zeit-
  schrift für Musik*, Leipsic. 1905. No. 51. Pp. 1051-1055;
  No. 52. Pp. 1091-1094.
  " Franz Schuberts einstimmige Lieder nach österreichischen Dich-
  tern." *Musikbuch aus Österreich . . . Redigiert von Dr. Hugo
  Botstiber*, Vienna. 1908. Pp. 3-35.
  [Review of M. Bauer's " Franz Schubert."] *Zeitschrift der Inter-
  nationalen Musik-Gesellschaft*, Leipsic. 1909-10. Pp. 297,
  298.
  [Review of T. Müller-Reuter's " Lexikon der deutschen Konzert-
  literatur." Vol. I. P. 64. Franz Schubert. 1909.] *Zeitschrift
  der Internationalen Musik-Gesellschaft*, Leipsic. 1909-10.
  Pp. 194, 195.
  " Die Textdichter von Schuberts einstimmigen Liedern." *Die
  Musik*, Berlin. 1906-7. Heft 8. 2. Schubert-Heft. Pp. 75-90.
  " Zur Datierung von Schuberts Klaviersonate in A." Op. 120.
  Zeitschrift der Internationalen Musik-Gesellschaft, Leipsic.
  1906-7. Pp. 485-487.
  " Zur Datierung von Franz Schuberts ' Letzten Walzern,' Op.
  127, für Klavier." *Zeitschrift der Internationalen Musik-
  Gesellschaft*, Leipsic. 1906-7. P. 487.

SCHELLENBERG, E. L.:
  " Schubert als Melodiker." *Der Türmer*, Stuttgart. Jahrg. 22.
  [1919-20.] Vol. II. P. 426.

SCHINDLER, ANTON:
  " Erinnerungen an Franz Schubert. Aufgezeichnet von Anton

Schindler." *Niederrheinische Musik-Zeitung für Kunstfreunde und Künstler,* Cologne. 1857. No. 10. Pp. 73-78; No. 11. Pp. 81-85.

1. " Geistliche Lieder von Franz Schubert nebst einem Beiwort über dessen musikalischen Nachlass."
2. " Gedanken über die ' Fantasie ' für Piano-Forte zu 4 Hände von Franz Schubert. Op. 103."
3. " Noch etwas Schubert betreffend."

These three articles appear in Supplements 1 and 3 to Adolf Bäuerle's *Allgemeine Theaterzeitung und Originalblatt,* Vienna. March 1st, May 3rd, 1831. The last article of the three records the incidents of Beethoven making acquaintance with Schubert's songs on his deathbed.

SCHMID, HEINRICH KASPAR:

" Franz Schuberts neuentdecktes Quartett," etc. *Zeitschrift für Musikwissenschaft,* Leipsic. Dec. 1918. Pp. 183-188.

SCHMID, RICHARD:

Franz Schubert als Gitarrist. Eine musik-historische Skizze. [With ten Schubert Songs arranged for the Guitar.] Leipsic, 1918.

SCHNAPPER, EDITH:

Die Gesänge des jungen Schubert vor dem Durchbruch des romantischen Liedprinzipes. Pp. 168. Berne and Leipsic, 1937.

SCHNERICH, A.:

Messe und Requiem seit Haydn und Mozart. Pp. vii, viii, 178. Vienna, 1909.

SCHOLL, FERDINAND:

Reden zur Erinnerung an zwei Heroen im deutschen Liede, Franz Schubert und Ludwig Uhland . . . . Ausgegeben als Beiträge für das Schubert-Denkmal in Wien. Pp. 23. Stuttgart, 1865.

SCHUBERT, FERDINAND:

" Aus Franz Schuberts Leben." *Neue Zeitschrift für Musik,* Leipsic. Vol. 10. Nos. 33-36. April 23rd-May 3rd, 1839.

SCHUBERT, FRANZ:

Franz Schubert's Briefe und Schriften. See Deutsch, Otto Erich.

Franz Schubert's Letters and other writings. See Deutsch, Otto Erich.

" Zehn bisher ungedruckte Briefe von Franz Schubert. Herausgegeben von Max Friedlaender." *Jahrbuch der Musikbibliothek Peters für 1894,* Leipsic. 1895. Pp. 92-115.

" Reliquien von Franz Schubert." [Four letters, two poems and a dream, published by Robert Schumann in his] *Neue Zeitschrift für Musik,* Leipsic. Vol. 10. Nos. 10, 11. Feb. 1st, 5th, 1839.

" Schubert." *Klagenfurter Zeitung.* 1864. No. 34.

Schubert. (*Thumb-nail sketches of great Composers.*) Pp. 14. London [1926].

" Schubert and Mayrhofer." *Orchestra,* London. Sept. 14th, 1867. P. 391.

Schubert-Ausstellung der K. K. Reichshaupt- und Residenzstadt Wien verbunden mit einer Ausstellung von Werken der Maler Moriz v. Schwind, Josef Danhauser und Leopold Kupelwieser. Pp. 229. Vienna, 1897. A catalogue.

" Schubert, Chopin, Liszt." *Edinburgh Review.* Vol. 158. Oct. 1883. Pp. 475-509. A review of contemporary biographies, including the Schubert article in Grove's *Dictionary of Music and Musicians.*

Schubert-Museum der Stadt Wien in Franz Schuberts Geburtshause. Führer durch das Museum. Vienna, 1912.

" Das Schubert-Wirtshaus." *Neue Freie Presse,* Vienna. Feb. 12th, 1911.

SCHUMANN, ROBERT ALEXANDER:

Gesammelte Schriften über Musik und Musiker. 4 vol. Leipsic, 1854.

English edition, *Music and Musicians,* 1877-80.

Many subsequent editions.

" Die 7te Symphonie von Franz Schubert." *Neue Zeitschrift für Musik,* Leipsic. No. 21. March 10th, 1840.

SCHÜTZ, KARL AND ZIEGLER, JOHANN:

Sammlung von Aussichten der Residenzstadt Wien von ihren Vorstädten und einigen umliegenden Oertern, gezeichnet und gestochen von Karl Schütz . . . und von Johann Ziegler, etc. Vienna [1779-90].

SCHWEISHEIMER, WALDEMAR:

" Der kranke Schubert." *Zeitschrift für Musikwissenschaft,* Leipsic. June and July, 1921. Pp. 552-561.

" Schwind and Schubert." *Bayerische Zeitung,* Munich. 1863. No. 45.

SEELIGER, HERMANN:

" Franz Schubert. Ein Gedenkblatt." *Westermanns Monatshefte,* Brunswick. July, 1915. Pp. 628-633.

SELINCOURT, BASIL DE:

" Schubert's Songs." *English Review,* London. Vol. 8. April, 1911. Pp. 46-59.

An abbreviated edition appeared in *The Musician,* Boston. Oct. 1911.

SHARP, R. FARQUHARSON:

Makers of Music, etc. Pp. 237. London [1898]. Pp. 127-140, Schubert. Fourth edition, 1913.

SIEBERT, DANIEL:
Franz Schubert. Pp. 15. Vienna [1901].

SILVESTRELLI, ANITA:
Franz Schubert. Das wahre Gesicht seines Lebens. Mit vierund-zwanzig Bildtafeln. Pp. 340. Salzburg, Leipsic, 1939.

SITTENBERGER, HANS:
Schubert. Pp. 122. Zurich, 1928.

SIX, DOLF:
Knoch's Album. Schubert and Vienna. Der Liederfürst Franz Schubert und Wien, 1828-1928. Pl. 80; Pp. 64. Vienna, 1928.

SKALLA, FERD.:
Franz Schubert. Pp. 16. Prague [1897].

SMEKAL, RICHARD:
" Grillparzer und die Gesellschaft der Musikfreunde in Wien." *Der Merker,* Vienna. 1915. P. 447.

SONNLEITHNER, LEOPOLD VON:
" Biographie des Franz Schubert." *Monatsbericht der Gesell-schaft der Musikfreunde des Kaiserstaates Österreich.* 1829.
Leopold von Sonnleithners Erinnerungen an Franz Schubert. Von A. Fareanu. See Fareanu, A.

SOUCHAY, MARC-ANDRÉ:
" Zu Schuberts 'Winterreise'." *Zeitschrift für Musikwissen-schaft,* Leipsic. Feb. 1931. Pp. 266-285.

SPANUTH, AUGUST:
" Franz Schubert." [Sketch and Bibliography prefixed to *Selected Piano Compositions. Franz Schubert.* Edited by A. Spanuth. The Musicians' Library.] Pp. vii-xi. Boston, 1912.

SPAUN, JOS. VON:
" Aufzeichnungen des Josef Freih. von Spaun über Franz Schu-bert. Mitgeteilt von A. Fellner." *Der Merker,* Vienna. 1911. Heft 10-11. Schubert-Bauernfeld. Doppelheft. Pp. 421-435.

" Aus den Lebenserinnerungen des Joseph Freiherrn von Spaun. Mitgetheilt von Carl Glossy." *Jahrbuch der Grillparzer Ge-sellschaft,* Vienna. 1898. Pp. 287-290.

Erinnerungen. See La Mara. *Classisches und Romantisches aus der Tonwelt,* etc. 1892.

" Schubertiana." [Extract from Von Spaun's Reminiscences.] *Musical World,* London. Aug. 6th, 1887. Pp. 609, 610.

Erinnerungen an Schubert. Josef von Spauns erste Lebens-beschreibung. [Edited by Georg Schunemann.] Pp. 125. Berlin and Zurich, 1936. [Second impression.] 1938.

Neues um Franz Schubert, etc. (Einige Bemerkungen über die Biografie Schuberts von Herrn Ritter v. Kreissle-Hellborn.) Pp. 14. Vienna, 1934.

SPECHT, RICHARD:

Franz Schubert. [Programme Book of Centenary Festival of the " Gesellschaft der Musikfreunde."] Vienna, 1912.

SPIRO, FRIEDRICH:

Franz Schubert. Kleine Konzertführer durch seine Werke. Messe (Es). Messe (As). 2 Nos. Leipsic, 1909.

SPITTA, PHILIPP:

[Review of M. Friedlaender's] " Beiträge zur Biographie Franz Schuberts." *Vierteljahrsschrift für Mussikwissenschaft,* Leipsic. 1889. Pp. 347-350.

" Franz Schubert." *Baltische Monatsschrift,* Riga. Bd. 13. Heft 6. June, 1866. Pp. 447-473.

SPITTELER, CARL:

Lachende Wahrheiten. Gesammelte Essays. Pp. viii, 340. Florence and Leipsic, 1898. Pp. 135-140, Schuberts Klaviersonaten. English edition, 1927, *Laughing Truths.*

STARK, L.:

" Franz Schubert." *Deutsche Vierteljahrsschrift,* Stuttgart. 1869. No. 127. Pp. 318-327.

STATHAM, H. HEATHCOTE:

My Thoughts on Music and Musicians. Pp. xiii, 475. London, 1892. Pp. 314-329, Schubert.

STEFAN, PAUL:

" Auftakt zum Schubert-Jahr." *Musikblätter des Anbruch,* Vienna. Dec. 1927. Pp. 407-410.

Franz Schubert. Pp. 251. Berlin, 1928. Illustrated.

STEGER, FRIEDRICH:

Ergänzungsblätter, etc. VII. Leipsic, 1852. Pp. 503-511, Franz Schubert.

STERNBERG, CONSTANTIN VON:

" Franz Peter Schubert. A child of genius." *The Musician,* Boston. Vol. 16. Sept. 1911. Pp. 577-579; 630.

STREATFEILD, R. A.:

Modern Music and Musicians. Pp. 355. London, 1906. Pp. 197-214, Schubert. Second edition, 1907.

STREATFEILD, R. A. AND OTHERS:

Life Stories of Great Composers, etc. Pp. xvii, 585. Philadelphia, 1910. Pp. 239-259, Franz Schubert.

SURETTE, THOMAS WHITNEY:

" Schubert and his Music." *The Chautauquan,* Chautauqua, N. Y. Vol. 41. March, 1905. Pp. 41-47.

SWAYNE, E.:
" Schubert as a Song Writer." *Music,* Chicago. Vol. 19. Feb. 1901. Pp. 388-392.

TEMPLE, HANS:
See Bühne und Welt.

THAYER, ALEXANDER W.:
The Life of Ludwig von Beethoven. Edited, revised and amended . . . by H. E. Krehbiel. 3 vol. New York, 1921.

TIBALDI CHIESA, MARY:
Schubert. La Vita. L'Opera. Con 26 illustrazioni. Pp. viii, 330. [With a bibliography.] Milan, Rome, 1932.

TIETZE, HANS:
Alt-Wien in Wort und Bild, etc. Pp. 64; pl. 143. Vienna, 1924.

Das vormärzliche Wien in Wort und Bild. Pp. 116; pl. 132. Vienna, 1925.

TILFORD, W. R.:
" Schubert's Life in Anecdote." *Etude,* Philadelphia. Vol. 44. Nov. 1926. Pp. 813, 814.

TOVEY, DONALD FRANCIS:
" Franz Schubert." *The Heritage of Music. Essays . . . Collected and edited by Hubert J. Foss.* Pp. 82-122. London, 1927.

TROLLOPE, FRANCES:
Vienna and the Austrians, etc. 2 vol. London, 1838.

TROST, ALOIS:
" Franz Schubert's Bildnisse," etc. *Berichte und Mittheilungen des Alterthums-Vereines zu Wien.* XXXIII. 1898. Pp. 85-95. Illustrated.

VANCSA, MAX:
Schubert und seine Verleger. Vortrag, gehalten in der 11. Schubertiade des Schubertbundes am 16. III. 1905. Vienna, 1905.

VETTER, WALTHER:
Franz Schubert. Pp. 160. Potsdam, 1934.

Vom Wiener Männergesangverein. Festschrift zur Enthüllung des Schubert Denkmales am 15. Mai 1872. Vienna, 1872.

WACIK, FRANZ AND KIRCHL, A.:
Franz Schubert. Künstlerbilderbuch. Bilder von F. Wacik. Text von A. Kirchl. Pp. 12. Leipsic [1915.].

WAECHTER, EBERHARD:
Musikkritische Gedanken. Erster Teil, Franz Schuberts Liederzyklus " Die Schöne Müllerin." Eine analytisch-kritische Studie. Pp. 37. Leipsic, 1919.

WEIGMANN, OTTO:
Schwinds Entwürfe für ein Schubertzimmer. Pp. 26; pl. 4. Munich, 1925.

WEIL, MATHILDE:
Schubertiaden von Mathilde Weil und 12 andere Novellen. Pp. 253. Vienna, 1917.

WEINGARTNER, FELIX:
Ratschläge für Aufführungen klassischer Symphonien. Bd. II. Schubert und Schumann. Leipsic, 1918.

Franz Schubert und sein Kreis. 68 Bilder, eingeleitet von F. Weingartner. Pp. 24, pl. 68. Zurich, Leipsic [1931].

WEISS, ANTON:
Franz Schubert. Eine Festgabe, etc. Pp. 137, iii, 24. Vienna, 1928.

Franz v. Schober. Lebensbild eines Freundes Franz Schuberts, etc. Pp. 34. Vienna, 1907.

50 Jahre Schubertbund. Chronik des Vereins vom 1.-50. Vereinsjahr, etc. Pp. 344, lxxix. Vienna, 1913. Illustrated.

WELLS-HARRISON, W.:
Schubert's Compositions for Piano and Strings. A critical study. Pp. 94. London, 1915.

WELTI, HEINRICH:
" Franz Schubert." *Allgemeine Deutsche Biographie.* Vol. 32. Pp. 614-628. Leipsic, 1891.

WEST, K.:
" Centenary of Franz Schubert." *Outlook,* New York. Vol. 55. Feb. 6th, 1897. P. 401.

WETZEL, HERMANN:
" Schuberts Werke für Klavier zu vier Händen." *Die Musik,* Berlin. 1906-7. Heft 7. 1. Schubert-Heft. Pp. 36-44.

WHITAKER-WILSON, C.:
Franz Schubert, man and composer, etc. Pp. x, 264. London, 1928.

WHITEHEAD, HENRY:
" Schubert." *Chambers' Encyclopædia.* New edition. Vol. IX. 1927. Pp. 159, 160.

WIER, ALBERT E.:
The Appleton Master-Composer Series. Edited by A. E. Wier. Vol. I. Franz Schubert at Home. Pp. 159. New York, 1928. Life story and selection of Schubert's Compositions.

WISSIG, O.:
Franz Schuberts Messen. Dissertation. Pp. 67; pl. 8. Leipsic, 1909.

WURZBACH, CONSTANT VON:

"Franz Schubert. Ein Lebensbild." *Illustrirtes Haus- und Familienbuch,* Leipsic. 1860. P. 337.

"Schubert." *Biographisches Lexikon des Kaiserthums Österreich.* Pt. XXXII. Pp. 30-110. Vienna, 1876.

WYZEWA, TEODOR DE:

Schubert. (Trois Profils de Musiciens.) Paris, 1898.

ZEDLITZ, JOS. CHR. VON:

"Nachruf an Schubert." *Wiener Zeitschrift für Kunst,* etc. Nov. 25th, 1828.

ZENGER, MAX:

"Franz Schuberts Wirken und Erdenwallen." Pp. 43. (*Musikalisches Magazin.* Heft 4.) Langensalza, 1902.

ZIESE, ELLY:

Schuberts Tod und Begräbnis in der ältesten Darstellung. Pp. 32. Grossdeuben [1933].

ZODER, FRITZ:

Franz Schubert der grosse Wiener Tondichter und Liederfürst. Ein Lebensbild. Pp. 31. Vienna, 1928.

ZODER, RAIMUND:

"Franz Schubert und die Volksmusik." *Das deutsche Volkslied,* Vienna. XI. 1909. Heft 1.

"Zur Erinnerung an Franz Schubert." *Ueber Land und Meer. Allgemeine illustrirte Zeitung,* Stuttgart. XIII. 1865. No. 18. P. 275.

LIST OF SCHUBERT'S WORKS; EDITIONS, ETC.

The standard edition of Schubert's works was pubished by Breitkopf and Härtel, Leipsic, 1884-1897, in 40 volumes (XXI Series and "Revisionsbericht") as follows:—

Franz Schubert's Werke. Kritisch durchgesehene Gesammtausgabe. Herausgegeben von Johannes Brahms, Ignaz Brüll, Anton Door, Julius Epstein, J. N. Fuchs, J. Hellmesberger, Eus. Mandyczewski.

Serie   *I. Symphonien für Orchester. Nos. 1-8.*
„   *II. Ouverturen und andere Orchesterwerke. Nos. 1-10.*
„   *III. Octette. Nos. 1-3.*
„   *IV-VI. Quintett, Quartette (Nos. 1-15) und Trio für Streichinstrumente.*
„   *VII. Pianoforte-Quintett -Quartett und -Trios. Nos. 1-5.*
„   *VIII. Für Pianoforte und ein Instrument. [Rondos, Sonates, etc.] Nos. 1-8.*

„   IX. *Für Pianoforte zu vier Händen.* [*Marches, Over-
      tures, Sonatas, Rondos, Variations, Divertisse-
      ments, Polonaises, Phantasies, etc.*) *No. 1-32.*

„   X. *Sonaten für Pianoforte. Nos. 1-15.*

„   XI. *Phantasie, Impromptus und andere Stücke für
      Pianoforte. Nos. 1-16.*

„   XII. *Tänze für Pianoforte. Nos. 1-31.*

„   XIII. *Messen. Nos. 1-7.*

„   XIV. *Kleinere Kirchenmusikwerke. Nos. 1-22.*

„   XV. *Dramatische Musik. Nos. 1-15.*

„   XVI. *Für Männerchor. Nos. 1-46.*

„   XVII. *Für gemischten Chor. Nos. 1-19.*

„   XVIII. *Für Frauenchor. Nos. 1-6.*

„   XIX. *Kleinere drei- und zweistimmige Gesangwerke.
      Nos. 1-36.*

„   XX. *Lieder und Gesänge. Nos. 1-603.*

„   XXI. *Supplement. Instrumentalmusik. Nos. 1-31. Ge-
      sangmusik. Nos. 32-44.*

Revisionsbericht. 9 Nos.

The above list is sufficient to indicate the various groups of
Schubert's compositions. More detailed information can be found
in the works of Audley, Baker, Dahms, Duncan, Frost, Grove,
Kreissle von Hellborn, La Mara, Reissmann, Riemann, Wurzbach
and the following special catalogues:—

*Bericht über den internationalen Kongress für Schubertforschung.
Wien 25-29. Nov. 1928. Pp. 242. pl. 8. Augsburg, 1929.*

*Thematisches Verzeichniss im Druck erscheinener Compositionen
von Franz Schubert.* A. Diabelli et Comp. Vienna [1852].

*Verzeichniss sämmtlicher Lieder und Gesänge von Franz Schu-
bert, Rob. Schumann, Fel. Mendelssohn und Robert Franz,
etc.* Karmrodt, Halle, 1868.

*Franz Schubert. Katalog seiner sämmtlichen Gesänge für eine
Singstimme mit Pianoforte. Neue Ausgabe revidirt von Jul.
Rietz.* Senff, Leipsic [1870?].

*Franz Schubert. Systematisch-alphabetisches Verzeichniss seiner
in Deutschland im Druck erschienenen Kompositionen. Mit
ausschliesslicher Berücksichtigung der Originale in allen den
Fällen, wo solche im Druck erschienen sind.* Fritzsch, Leipsic.
[1870?].

*Thematisches Verzeichniss der im Druck erschienenen Werke von
Franz Schubert, herausgegeben von O. Nottebohm.* F. Schrei-
ber, Vienna, 1874.

References to notices of a few of Schubert's compositions not
included in the standard edition are given in the bibliography above.

Selected collections of Schubert's works have been issued from
time to time by many of the leading music publishers. Short
particulars of some editions are indicated here:—

Immortellen. Gesänge, etc. Diabelli (Spina), Vienna [1844 etc.].

Ausgewählte Gesänge, etc. Arnold, Elberfeld [1855?]. With German and French text.

Gesänge, etc. Spina, Vienna [1855?]. With German and French text.

40 ausgewählte Gesänge, etc. Spina, Vienna [1865?].

Lieder und Gesänge, etc. Breikopf & Härtel, Leipsic [1865?].

Collections of " Lieder " and " Gesänge " [1868-73] by Arnold, Dresden ; Bauer, Brunswick ; Breitkopf & Härtel, Leipsic ; Forberg, Leipsic ; Gotthard, Vienna ; Holle, Wolfenbüttel ; Litolff, Brunswick ; Peters, Leipsic ; Schlesinger, Berlin ; Schott, Mainz ; Senff, Leipsic ; Siegel, Leipsic.

Songs . . . . Edited by E. Pauer. 3 vol. [207 Songs.] Augener, London [1874-79].

Ausgewählte Sonaten und Solostücke für das Pianoforte von Franz Schubert. Bearbeitet von Franz Liszt. Zweite revidirte Auflage. 5 vol. J. G. Cotta, Stuttgart, 1875-80.

Melodie per una voce . . . Versione italiana di A. Zanardini. 12 vol. Ricordi, Milan [1883?].

Schubert-Album. Sammlung der Lieder . . . revidirt von Max Friedlaender. 7 vol. and supplement. [443 Songs.] Peters, Leipsic [1884-87]. First six volumes appeared about 1870 in an earlier edition not edited by Friedlaender. The supplement contains variants, important biographical and literary notes, dates, etc.

Nachgelassene (bisher ungedruckte) Lieder . . . . revidirt und herausgegeben von M. Friedlaender. 2 vol. Peters, Leipsic, 1885.

The Songs of Schubert. Vol. I, containing 60 . . . . Edited by J. A. Kappey. Vol. II, containing 55 . . . . Edited by Myles B. Foster. Boosey, London, 1896. With German and English words.

Lieder und Gesänge, etc. Schlesinger, Berlin, 1898.

Sämtliche Lieder, etc. Breitkopf & Härtel, Leipsic, 1905.

Fifty Selected Songs . . . . Edited . . . by Max Heinrich. English translations by Alice Mattullath. Fischer, New York, 1912.

Schubert's Songs translated by A. H. Fox Strangways and Steuart Wilson. Oxford University Press, London, 1924. Melodies and words of 126 songs.

Franz Schubert. Eine neue Auswahl seiner Lieder besorgt und und mit Vortragsbezeichnungen versehen von Johannes Messchaett, herausgegeben von Franziska Martienssen. 2 vol. Schott, Mainz [1927].

Chor-Gesangwerke, etc. 3 vol. Peters, Leipsic [1870?].

Pianoforte Werke. (Kompositionen, etc.) Various editions [1868-79] by Breitkopf & Härtel, Leipsic; Hofmeister, Leipsic; Holle, Wolfenbüttel; Litolff, Brunswick.

The Complete Sonatas (Piano Works), edited by Ernst Pauer. 2 vol. Augener, London [1874].

Pianoforte Works. Editions have also been issued by Novello & by Augener, London.

Selected Piano Compositions. Edited by August Spanuth (Musicians' Library.) Ditson, Boston, 1912. With biographical introduction, criticism and bibliography.

Franz Schuberts sämtliche Sonaten für Klavier neubearbeitet . . . von W. Rehberg. Steingräber, Leipsic [1927].

The Appleton Master-Composer Series. Edited by A. E. Wier. Vol. I. *Franz Schubert at Home.* New York, 1928. Life story of Schubert, interspersed with vocal and instrumental works.

The Chamber Music of Haydn and Schubert. Edited . . . by A. E. Wier. Longmans, Green and Co., New York, 1945.

INDEX

A

Abendbilder (Evening Pictures), 68, app.
"Adelaide," set by Beethoven and by Schubert, app.
Advertising, new mode of, introduced in Vienna, 7
Alfonso and Estrella, Diabilli's charge for copy of, 93, 98
  Overture to, published, 153
  Overture used in *Rosamunde,* 103
  performed for first time in Weimar, 184, 185-86
  setting of completed and demanded back, 87-89
  submitted to, and returned by, Anna Milder, 115
  Weber and, 100-01
Allegretto in " C," to whom inscribed, 151
Allgemeine Musikalische Zeitung, and its editor, 157
  criticizes *Die Zwillingsbrüder* and *Die Zauberharfe,* 67, 68, 157
Altschottische Ballade (Old Scottish Ballad), 170 (and note)
Amateurism in music, growth of, criticized by Schubert, 167
Amateurs, their failure to understand Schubert's music, 142
Am See, Schubert's setting for, 35
An-der-Wien Theatre, Vienna, 65
  Die Zauberharfe produced at, 67
  management goes into bankruptcy, 67
  nature of productions at, 65
  Rosamunde produced at, 103
  stage of, the largest in Germany, 65
André, Frau von, musical evenings of, app.
Andreas, Prelate of Scottish Monastery, 42.
Anschütz, Gustav, his passion for dancing, 89
Anschütz, Johann, Christmas spent, by Schubert with, 88 *et seq.*
  his " Reminiscences " quoted, 89
  last conversation with, 174
  starts the Christmas-tree habit in Vienna, 88
An Sylvia, fourth song in book dedicated to Madame Pachler, 170 (note)

Antony and Cleopatra, drinking song from, and where written 139-40
Artaria (music publisher), 118
At the River, 89
" At the Tomb of Anselmo," to whom dedicated, app.
Auf dem Strom (On the Stream), song with horn obligato, 162, app.
Auf dem Wasser, setting of, 102, app.
Auf der Bruck, setting of, 114
Augenlied, Vogl and, 51
Ave in " C," composed for Theresa Grob, 34
Ave Maria in " E Flat Major," discovery of, 34

B

Baden, Dräxler composes poem of *Prometheus* during a walking tour at, 46
Barbaja, Domenico, 97
  commissions Schubert to write an opera, 101
  his enterprise at Court Opera, 174-75
  returns *Fierrabras,* 101
Barbel (Viennese market-woman), 5
Barth, Josef, vocalist, app.
  quartets dedicated to, app.
  sings in first performance of *Geist der Liebe,* app.
Basedow, Fräulein, marries Müller, app.
Battle Song, Klopstock's, set by Schubert, 150
  offered to Schotts, 165
Bauernfeld, Eduard von, " Alt Wien " and " Diaries " cited, 49 (note), 87, 106, 107, 116-17, 118, 125, 128, 129, 130, 131, 132, 143, 149, 158, 159, 163, 172, 177
  and Vogl's copy of a work by Epictetus, 49 (note)
  despondent cry of, 159
  enters Schubert Circle, 76, 116
  failure of play (*The Match-Maker*) by, 172
Bauernfeld, Eduard von, grief at death of Schubert, 182-83, 191-92
  induces Schubert to give a concert and perform only his own works, 163-64
  introduced to Schubert, 116, 117
  isolation after death of Schubert, 192

INDEX

and the Schubert Circle, 45

Conspirators, The, librettist and composer of, 71

Convict School, Vienna, fellow-students at, 17 *et seq.*
Schubert entered as pupil, 16
Students' Corps formed, and an organized rebellion, 21

Cornelius, Peter, and Schwind, 132
praises Schwind's finished cycle, 193

Count of Gleichen, The, librettist of, 140, 141
presentation of prohibited by Censor, 144, 152

Craigher, Jacob Nikolaus, app.

"Crusade," Leitner's, set by Schubert, app.

Cymbeline (Shakespeare's), song from, set by Schubert, 108, app.

Czerny brothers, at André musical evenings, app.

Czerny, Carl, commissions Schubert to write a sonata, 135

D

"D Major" Sonata (Op. 53), to whom dedicated, app.

Daffinger, art trainer of Barbara Fröhlich, 78

Dahms, "Schubert" by, cited, 181

Dankesreither, Court-Councillor von (Schober's uncle), 87

Das Abendroth, composed at Zelész, 58

Das Dörfchen, sung at the Sonnleithners' house, 77
to whom dedicated, app.

Das Lied im Grünen, composition of, 150

Das Mädchen (Schlegel's), set by Schubert, 68

Das Weinen (Weeping), 170

"Death and the Maiden," set by Schubert, app.

Death Fantasia, 23

Deinhardstein, Johann Ludwig von, app.

De la Garde, Count, cited, 5 (and note)

Demmer, Herr, stage manager of An-der-Wien Theatre, 67

Der Berghirt, Müller's, an aria from, set by Schubert, app.

Der blinde Knabe, set by Schubert, 114, app.

Derffel (uncle of Schober), sells his estate, 185

Der Hirt auf dem Felsen (The Shepherd on the Rock), app.

Der Jüngling auf dem Hügel, composition of, 75

Der Jüngling und der Tod, question of authorship of words of, 52

Der Kampf, sung by Vogl, 51

Der Musensohn, set by Schubert, 89

Der Schicksalslenker, sum received by Schubert for, 82

Der Spiegelritter (Knight of the Mirror), app.

Der Vatermörder (The Parricide), one of Schubert's first songs, app.
production of, 26

Der Winterabend, set by Schubert, 161

Der Zwerg, 96

Des Teufels Lustschloss, Josef Hütten-brenner and, 97
play set by Schubert, app.

Deutsch, Prof. Otto Erich, acquires Schober papers for city of Vienna, 186 (note)
and Schubert's Cantata for his father's birthday, 26 (note)
and Sonata in "C Sharp Major," 115 (note)
author's indebtedness to, 46 (note)
citations from works by and MSS. in possession of, 10, 11, 18, 33, 44, 70, 82, 84, 94, 136
confirms nature of Schubert's illness, 92 (note)
estimate of sums received by Schubert for whole of his compositions, 134 (note)

Deutsch, Prof. Otto Erich, his exhaustive Schubertian study, 134 (note) (*cf.* "citations" above)
lecture on Schober at Malmö cited, 87

Devil's Pleasure Palace, The (see *Des Teufels Lustschloss*)

Diabelli, Anton, music publisher, 118, app.
his profits on the *Wanderer,* 85.
offered copyrights, sends in an unwarrantable account, 93
preys on Schubert's poverty, 85, 135
refuses to produce *Erl-King,* 83

Die junge Nonne, setting of, 114
sung at sight by Sophie Müller, 116

Die Nachtigall, dedicated to Barth, app.

Die Rose, set by Schubert, 89

Die Sterne, setting of, 75, 161

Dietrichstein, Moritz, Court-Music-Count, app.
Erl-King (Op. 1), delicated to, 84, app.
offers Schubert post of organist at Court Chapel, 98

Die Wische (paper issued by members of Ludlam's Cave), 73

Die Zauberharfe (The Magic Harp), brief run of, 67
composition of, 64
Press criticism of, 68, 157

245

255

INDEX